OXFORD WORLD'S CLASSICS

THE OXFORD SHAKESPEARE

General Editor · Stanley Wells

The Oxford Shakespeare offers new and authoritative editions of Shakespeare's plays in which the early printings have been scrupulously re-examined and interpreted. An introductory essay provides all relevant background information together with an appraisal of critical views and of the play's effects in performance. The detailed commentaries pay particular attention to language and staging. Reprints of sources, music for songs, genealogical tables, maps, etc. are included where necessary; many of the volumes are illustrated, and all contain an index.

G. R. HIBBARD, the editor of *Love's Labour's Lost* in the Oxford Shakespeare, was Emeritus Professor of English, University of Waterloo, Ontario, Canada. He edited *Coriolanus*, *The Taming of the Shrew*, *Timon of Athens*, and *The Merry Wives of Windsor* for the New Penguin Shakespeare and *Hamlet* for the Oxford Shakespeare.

OXFORD WORLD'S CLASSICS

—

WILLIAM SHAKESPEARE

Love's Labour's Lost

—

Edited by
G. R. HIBBARD

Oxford   New York
OXFORD UNIVERSITY PRESS

Oxford University Press, Great Clarendon Street, Oxford OX2 6DP

Oxford New York

*Athens Auckland Bangkok Bogotá Buenos Aires Calcutta
Cape Town Chennai Dar es Salaam Delhi Florence Hong Kong Istanbul
Karachi Kuala Lumpur Madrid Melbourne Mexico City Mumbai
Nairobi Paris São Paulo Singapore Taipei Tokyo Toronto Warsaw*

and associated companies in Berlin Ibadan

Oxford is a registered trade mark of Oxford University Press

*British Library Cataloguing in Publication Data
Data available*

Library of Congress Cataloging in Publication Data
Shakespeare, William, 1564–1616.
Love's labour's lost / edited by G. R. Hibbard.
(Oxford World's classics)
Includes index.
I. Hibbard, G. R. (George Richard), 1915– . II. Title.
III. Series: Shakespeare, William, 1564–1616. Works. 1982.
PR2822.A2H7 1990 822.3'3—dc19 89–30056
ISBN 0–19–812947–5 (hbk.)
ISBN 0–19–283880–6 (pbk.)

1 3 5 7 9 10 8 6 4 2

Printed in Spain by Book Print S.L.

PREFACE

I AM particularly indebted to John Caldwell for contributing 'A Note on the Music', to Christine Buckley and Frances Whistler for their help in dealing with the Illustrations, and, above all, to Stanley Wells for many useful suggestions and some even more useful, not to say necessary, cautions.

G. R. HIBBARD

CONTENTS

LIST OF ILLUSTRATIONS

INTRODUCTION

IN 1598, the year in which the earliest extant text we have of *Love's Labour's Lost* appeared in print, an emphatically minor poet, Robert Tofte, published his very long and very lugubrious work entitled *Alba: The Month's Mind of a Melancholy Lover.* Bearing the discouraged and discouraging motto *Spes, Amor, & Fortuna valete* ('Farewell to hope, to love, and to fortune') on its title-page, and running to three parts, it is an unrelieved outpouring of woe. Written in the same six-line stanza form as *Venus and Adonis*, it belongs in all other respects to the tradition of the conventional Elizabethan sonnet sequence. In love with a lady who disdains his advances, the poet laments his unfortunate state. Its main interest today is an extraneous one: it contains one of the two earliest references we have to *Love's Labour's Lost.* Occurring in the Third Part of the poem, the relevant passage runs thus:

> *Love's Labour Lost*, I once did see a play,
> Yclepèd so, so callèd to my pain,
> Which I to hear to my small joy did stay,
> Giving attendance on my froward dame.
> 　My misgiving mind presaging to me ill,
> 　Yet was I drawn to see it 'gainst my will.
>
> This play no play but plague was unto me,
> For there I lost the love I likèd most;
> And what to others seemed a jest to be,
> I, that (in earnest) found unto my cost.
> 　To everyone (save me) 'twas comical,
> 　Whilst tragic-like to me it did befall.
>
> Each actor played in cunning wise his part,
> But chiefly those entrapped in Cupid's snare;
> Yet all was feignèd, 'twas not from the heart;
> They seemed to grieve, but yet they felt no care.
> 　'Twas I that grief indeed did bear in breast,
> 　The others did but make a show in jest.
>
> Yet neither feigning theirs, nor my mere truth,
> Could make her once so much as for to smile;

> Whilst she, despite of pity mild and ruth,
> Did sit as scorning of my woes the while.
> > Thus did she sit to see Love lose his love,
> > Like hardened rock that force nor power can move.
> > > (Sig. G5)

It is possible, of course, that Tofte's visit to the theatre is a piece of fiction, but this seems unlikely because there is evidence in the poem to suggest that he was something of a playgoer. He refers to Tamburlaine, echoes *The Spanish Tragedy* twice, and *Romeo and Juliet* at least once.[1] But, whether factual or fictional, this account strongly suggests that Tofte had in mind a performance at one of the public theatres, rather than one at court or at the home of a great man. Had the occasion been a distinguished one, he would almost certainly have mentioned it. As it stands, however, it all sounds decidedly familiar, an Elizabethan version, as Hugh Hunt observes,[2] of today's young man who takes his girl-friend to the cinema. The matter is of some importance, for it has often been maintained that the playwright composed this comedy with a coterie audience in view. Only those with a good education and some close acquaintance with courtly life and manners would, it has been argued, have been able to understand and enjoy the 'sets of wit' and the sustained word-play with which it is so liberally studded. Support for this idea was found in the statement on the title-page of the Quarto of 1598 to the effect that the play had been presented before the Queen 'this last Christmas', and in the fact that it was acted before Queen Anne, at the Earl of Southampton's house in the Strand, in January 1605 (Chambers, *William Shakespeare*, ii. 330–2). There is, however, nothing particularly unusual about either performance. *The Merry Wives of Windsor*, as published in 1602, proclaims on its title-page that it had been put on before the Queen; and a letter from Sir Walter Cope to Lord Cranborne says explicitly that Richard Burbage, the leading actor in Shakespeare's company, recommended *Love's Labour's Lost* as the most suitable play the King's Men could stage to entertain Queen Anne, because it was full of 'wit and mirth' (ibid.). Moreover, the title-page of the Second Quarto, published in 1631, states that the comedy had been acted by the King's Men both 'at the Blackfriars and the Globe', which implies, incidentally, that it

---

[1] Sigs. A4, E1ᵛ, G6ᵛ, E1ᵛ.   [2] Old Vic Prefaces (1954), p. 9.

still had an appeal for a popular audience in 1609 or thereafter, since it was not until 1609 that the company began to act in the Blackfriars playhouse. Indeed, it may, for all we know, have still been in the repertory of the King's Men in the 1630s.

Then, in 1642, the theatres were closed, and remained closed until after the Restoration. When they reopened, many of Shakespeare's plays were revived, but *Love's Labour's Lost*, although it was allotted to Sir Thomas Killigrew in a list of January 1669,[1] was not among them. In fact, it was not to be staged again for the best part of two hundred years. During this long eclipse an adaptation of it entitled *The Students* was published in 1762; but there is no evidence that it ever reached the stage. It did not deserve to; and its author—'Our bard, advent'ring to the comic land', as he calls himself in the Prologue—was right to remain anonymous. *The Students* is a travesty rather than an adaptation of the original. Inept, vulgar, tasteless, and foolish, it had nothing to recommend it to the theatre managers of the day, or of any other day.

Those same theatre managers also had their own reasons for not trying to put on the comedy itself as Shakespeare left it; and Doctor Johnson tells us what their main objections to it could have been. In an over-view of the play that is more perceptive and generous than anything previously written about it he has this to say:

In this play, which all the editors have concurred to censure and some [Pope among them] have rejected as unworthy of our poet, it must be confessed that there are many passages mean, childish, and vulgar; and some which ought not to have been exhibited, as we are told they were, to a maiden queen. But there are scattered through the whole many sparks of genius; nor is there any play that has more evident marks of the hand of Shakespeare.[2]

There can be little doubt as to what Johnson was thinking of when he referred to passages 'mean, childish, and vulgar'. Like his age in general and the ages before it right back to the Restoration, he had a poor opinion of puns and of Shakespeare's

---

[1] Allardyce Nicoll, *A History of English Drama 1660–1900*, 6 vols. (Cambridge, 1923), i. 354.

[2] *Dr Johnson on Shakespeare*, ed. W. K. Wimsatt (Harmondsworth, 1969), p. 108.

fondness for them. In a famous passage in his *Preface* of 1765 he writes:

A quibble is to Shakespeare what luminous vapours are to the traveller; he follows it at all adventures; it is sure to lead him out of his way and sure to engulf him in the mire. It has some malignant power over his mind, and its fascinations are irresistible ... A quibble, poor and barren as it is, gave him such delight that he was content to purchase it by the sacrifice of reason, propriety, and truth. A quibble was to him the fatal Cleopatra for which he lost the world and was content to lose it. (Ibid., p. 68)

Those words are an eloquent climax to a chorus of indictment that had been swelling for almost a century ever since Dryden in his *Essay of Dramatic Poesy* (1668) had written of Shakespeare's 'comic wit degenerating into clenches'.[1] In such a climate of opinion *Love's Labour's Lost*, in which puns are omnipresent and an essential part of the play's very being, stood little chance of a sympathetic reception. Furthermore, to an age which, from the time of Pope onwards and increasingly with the onset of Romanticism, was coming to regard the creation of highly individualized characters who grow and develop in response to experience as Shakespeare's supreme achievement, the comedy had little to offer; a couple of eccentrics in Armado and Holofernes, and, in the main plot, Biron and the Princess.

Nevertheless, two hundred years after the play's disappearance from the English stage, something spurred Madame Vestris and her husband Charles James Mathews to put *Love's Labour's Lost* on at Covent Garden in 1839. It was a lavish production, complete with gorgeous costumes and an elaborate *mise-en-scène* that was much admired;[2] but the couple made a terrible mistake. They had just taken over the theatre, and for this, their first production in it, they closed the shilling gallery. As a result there was something like a riot on the first night, with indignant theatre-goers making their protest against the move by damning the play. After this inauspicious opening the production ran for only eight more nights before it was taken off. Hitherto two obstacles had stood in the way of any proper appreciation of the play either in the theatre or in the study: the notion that it was

---

[1] *Essays of John Dryden*, ed. W. P. Ker, 2 vols. (Oxford, 1900), i. 80.
[2] See George C. D. Odell, *Shakespeare from Betterton to Irving*, 2 vols. (New York, 1920), ii. 222–3.

recalcitrantly Elizabethan in its reliance on word-play, and therefore 'not for all time'; and that it was not a play of characters. Now to these was added a third: it had not gone well on the stage. *Love's Labour's Lost* was caught, as it were, on the horns of a dilemma. Because it was thought of in this way, it was only rarely performed in the later nineteenth and early twentieth centuries, and, when it was staged, it was either by amateur actors —George Bernard Shaw saw such a production in 1886[1]—or by professionals who had no real faith in it.

One exception must, however, be made to this generalization— an essay on the play by Walter Pater, first published in 1878 and subsequently included in his *Appreciations, with an Essay on Style* of 1889.[2] Deeply interested in style—'the fancy so many of us have for an exquisite and curious skill in the use of words', as he calls it—Pater does justice to the play's 'curious foppery of language' and Shakespeare's ambivalent attitude towards it, especially as it appears in the speeches of Biron; but he says practically nothing about the comedy as a comedy. One is left wondering whether he had ever seen it, or, indeed, had any opportunity to see it.

Such were the fortunes of *Love's Labour's Lost* up to 1927. But in that year they changed radically and for the better, since it saw the publication of the most appreciative and influential piece on the comedy that had ever appeared, Harley Granville-Barker's *Preface* to it. Significantly the essay begins with an apology that shows the power the objections to the play cited above were still capable of exerting.

Here is a fashionable play; now, by three hundred years, out of fashion. Nor did it ever, one supposes, make a very wide appeal. It abounds in jokes for the elect. Were you not numbered among them you laughed, for safety, in the likeliest places. A year or two later the elect themselves might be hard put to it to remember what the joke was.[3]

Furthermore, Granville-Barker, like most scholars and critics at the time, thought of *Love's Labour's Lost* as very early Shakespeare. He writes of 'the dramatist learning his art', calls him 'a clever young man', and refers to the play as his 'earliest essay'. Yet

[1] *Shaw on Shakespeare*, ed. Edwin Wilson (Harmondsworth, 1969), pp. 33–5.
[2] Repr. 1910, pp. 161–9.
[3] *Prefaces to Shakespeare, First Series* (1927), p. 1.

despite these preconceptions he succeeds in getting to the heart of the comedy as no one before him had done, and he does so because he looks at it as a piece of theatre designed for the Elizabethan stage. He heads his first section on it 'The Producer's Problem', and moves on thence to 'The Method of the Acting', insisting on the need for the actor to let the words speak for themselves, as it were. Recognizing, as Shaw had done before him,[1] that the verse has its own authentic music, he goes on to say:

if the music is clear and fine, as Elizabethan music was, if the costumes strike their note of fantastic beauty, if, above all, the speech and movements of the actors are fine and rhythmical too, then this quaint medley of mask and play can still be made delightful. But it asks for style in the acting. The whole play, first and last, demands style. (p. 14)

His words did not go unheeded. In 1932 Tyrone Guthrie, who had read the *Prefaces* with attention,[2] put on *Love's Labour's Lost* at the Westminster, doing it in a style that led J. C. Trewin to remark: 'It was this production of the young comedy, so picked, so spruce, so peregrinate, a festival of words, that would take him one day to the Old Vic'.[3] The 'one day' was not long in coming. The Old Vic production followed in 1936. It was, to quote Trewin once more:

[an] elegant revival—two pavilions, a fountain, wrought-iron gates— with Ernest Milton's Armado to strut, a moulting peacock, across the turf, Alec Clunes in Berowne's silken terms precise, and Michael Redgrave ... as Ferdinand of Navarre. (Ibid., p. 163)

But the greatest tribute to Guthrie's achievement came from Dover Wilson who, with his characteristic generosity of spirit, wrote of the production:

it revealed [the play] as a first-rate comedy of the pattern kind—so full of fun, of *permanent* wit, of brilliant and entrancing situation, that you hardly noticed the faded jesting and allusion, as you sat spell-bound and drank it all in. It was a thrilling production, Shakespearian criticism of the best kind, because a real piece of restoration ... Mr. Guthrie not only gave me a new play, the existence of which I had never suspected, which indeed had been veiled from men's eyes for three centuries, but he set me

---

[1] *Op. cit.*, p. 135.
[2] Tyrone Guthrie, *A Life in the Theatre* (1959), p. 108.
[3] J. C. Trewin, *Shakespeare on the English Stage 1900–1964* (1964), p. 133.

at a fresh standpoint of understanding and appreciation from which the whole of Shakespearian comedy might be reviewed in a new light.[1]

Having paid this homage to Guthrie, Wilson added to it when, in 1962, he published a second and revised version of his original edition of 1923. There he says:

I had spent two years upon this edition, but Guthrie's production, which I saw in company with Alfred Pollard, convinced me that I was then beginning to understand the play for the first time, an education continued later under Peter Brook's tuition. The striking impression left in both cases was one of a ballet-like speed, tip-toe delicacy, and kaleidoscopic shifts of colour, all in the text when rightly conceived, and culminating in the grim shock of the entry of a messenger of Death, clad in black from head to foot. (pp. lxi–lxii)

The production by Peter Brook that Dover Wilson refers to followed ten years after Guthrie's. It took place at Stratford-upon-Avon in 1946, and in very different circumstances. The Second World War had just come to an end. Wittingly or unwittingly, Brook took Granville-Barker's advice. He put on the comedy in style and with style, setting it in the world of Watteau. It emerged in the theatre as a bright scintillating jewel of a play that also had its own peculiar, shifting, shadowy depths. It seemed to reflect the mood of euphoria, flecked with dark memories of the conflict now over and apprehensions about the future, that was so characteristic of Britain at the time. In a letter to J. C. Trewin, John Harrison, who played Longueville, had this to say about the first night:

Nobody outside the theatre had heard much about the production; there had been little publicity for Brook, and the audience assembled in noticeable calm. Three hours later, anyone late on the Bancroft meadow would have guessed at something uncommon. From a Stratford failure the mourners file out quietly, but any success is talked volubly through the streets, as *Love's Labour's Lost* would be all that summer.[2]

In fact, so great was the production's popularity that it was retained in the company's repertory for the following year.

One question remained unanswered: how far was the rising reputation of *Love's Labour's Lost* in the theatre to be attributed to

---

[1] *Shakespeare's Happy Comedies* (1962), p. 64.
[2] J. C. Trewin, *Peter Brook: A Biography* (1971), p. 25.

1. The Forester (Leo McKern) points out to the Princess (Angela Baddeley) a suitable location from which to shoot deer, in Hugh Hunt's 1949 production for the Old Vic company. Looking on are her lords (including Boyet, played by Walter Hudd, in embroidered gauntlets) and her ladies (Yvonne Mitchell as Katherine, Diana Churchill as Rosaline, and Jane Wenham as Maria).

the genius of Guthrie and Brook, rather than to any inherent qualities of the comedy itself? The answer was not long in coming. In the autumn of 1949 Hugh Hunt took over the direction of the Old Vic company, then acting at the New Theatre, and boldly began the season with a revival of the play. He did not, however, give it an eighteenth-century setting and costumes, as Guthrie and Brook had done. Instead, he chose to dress it in Elizabethan costumes, which worked equally well. Once again the production proved an unqualified success, with Michael Redgrave as Biron, Diana Churchill as Rosaline, Mark Dignam as Holofernes, and Miles Malleson as Sir Nathaniel. In the course of a little over twenty years *Love's Labour's Lost* had ceased to be a theatrical liability, something to be put on occasionally at Stratford more out of a sense of duty than anything else, and had become a beckoning opportunity for directors to test their interpretative insights and for actors to show off their professional skills. The part of Armado in particular has become a much coveted one.

2. The arrival of Marcadé in Hugh Hunt's production. The Princess and her ladies are still watching the impending combat between Costard (George Benson) and Armado (Baliol Holloway), while almost everyone else has noticed the presence of Marcadé (Richard Walter). Holofernes (Mark Dignam) and Nathaniel (Miles Malleson) are to left and right of the messenger.

Since 1949 *Love's Labour's Lost* has never looked back. At Stratford-upon-Avon, where it has become something of a favourite, it has been put on at least once in every decade, and as many as four times in the seventies, i.e. as often as it was played there in the entire fifty years from 1885 to 1934. Still more remarkable has been its success elsewhere. Who, for instance, even in the magical summer of 1946, would have dreamed that little more than thirty years later there would be no fewer than three separate productions of it in a single year in the western United States alone? Yet so it was. In 1980 it was staged at the Old Globe Theatre in San Diego, California, at Boulder, Colorado in a manner that Michael Mullin described as 'superb',[1] and at the Oregon Festival in Ashland, three places where it had already been produced in 1972, 1971, and 1972 respectively.

Part at least of the attraction the comedy has had for the modern director and indirectly through him for a modern

[1] *Shakespeare Quarterly*, 32 (1981), 243–5; p. 244.

audience lies in the unfinished state (see Introduction, pp. 57–65) in which the text has come down to us, a state particularly evident in the sparse and often sketchy nature of its stage directions. It not merely allows great freedom in interpreting such hints as the playwright chooses to give but it also positively demands that the director exercise his own inventiveness by supplying them where they do not exist at all. The great dramatic moment, to which all that goes before it, and especially the first seven lines, leads up, is, of course, the entrance of Marcadé a little more than two hundred lines from the end. But Shakespeare says nothing about the way in which that entrance is to be managed. The careful directions he provides, first to prepare for and then to accompany the arrival of Fortinbras at the end of *Hamlet*, are not to be found here. The director has a free hand. Peter Brook chose to herald the messenger's coming with a slow dimming of the lights and a long pause, a method that for a time became almost a tradition. At the National Theatre in 1969, however, Sir Laurence Olivier went another way to work. His Marcadé appeared suddenly 'as if from nowhere [as death so often does] in the *mêlée* of rustic actors and patrician audience'.[1] It, in turn, was an innovation that appears to have caught on. In 1973 David Jones produced the play at the Royal Shakespeare Theatre and handled this crucial moment in a fashion that led Richard David to write: 'it was not the traditional *coup de théâtre* ... [Marcadé] made his way through a scuffling crowd that had been made as undignified as possible'.[2]

A similar uncertainty lying ready and waiting to be exploited by the imaginative and enterprising director is that neither the Quarto of 1598 nor the Folio of 1623 offers any guidance as to who is to sing Spring's song and who Winter's. Most directors have preferred to hand these lyrics over to the rustics, but there have been occasions when the entire cast has joined in; and John Barton at Stratford-upon-Avon in 1978 had them 'spoken (not sung) with quiet ease, reinforced by the note of a genuine owl somewhere in the twilight'.[3] Not the least interesting and significant of the many experiments in staging that this highly experimental comedy has given rise to was Barry Kyle's casting of Josette Simon, a black actress, in the role of Rosaline at the same

[1] Robert Speaight, *Shakespeare Quarterly*, 20 (1969), 435–41; p. 440.
[2] *Shakespeare in the Theatre* (1978), p. 130.
[3] J. C. Trewin, *Shakespeare Quarterly*, 30 (1979), 151–8; p. 155.

3. The dialogue of the owl and the cuckoo at the play's close, in David Jones's Royal Shakespeare Theatre production of 1973. Sir Nathaniel (Jeffery Dench) sings Ver's song, watched by the Queen (Susan Fleetwood) and the King (Bernard Lloyd), standing centre, and Rosaline (Estelle Kohler) seated at their feet. Annette Badland, as an unnamed villager, sang Hiems' song.

theatre in 1984. Though not conforming to the letter of the text, it was wholly in keeping with the spirit of the play, which so firmly asserts the superiority in good sense and maturity of understanding, at least where matters of the heart are concerned, of young women over young men.

By the time Hugh Hunt's *Love's Labour's Lost* had run its course, it was already abundantly clear that there was nothing freakish, out of the way, or unaccountable about the change in the play's fortunes. It appealed to playgoers of the late forties— and has continued to appeal to playgoers since—because it is, in many ways, a remarkably 'modern' work of art. In a world that was exploring and enjoying the work of James Joyce its reliance on the pun had ceased to be an irritant and become a positive asset. Good puns were being recognized for what they are, a means of bringing two diverse kinds of experience into a sudden, unexpected, and illuminating juxtaposition with one another. Nor, to the reader of *Ulysses*, was there anything unduly ostentatious and jarring about the comedy's recourse to rare and learned words, some of them nonce-words. The great revival of interest in the poetry of the metaphysicals, together with its impact on the poetry of men such as T. S. Eliot, had altered our attitude to 'conceited' language in general. Most important of all, however, the pioneer work of men like William Poel and Granville-Barker in discovering and then advocating the virtues of the bare Elizabethan stage, and especially of the intimacy between players and audience to which it lent itself so well, was beginning to bear fruit in the theatre. Elaborate scenery was being discarded in revivals of plays by Shakespeare and his contemporaries in favour of a single non-representational set that would serve for the entire performance. With the disappearance of the changeable scenery went the time wasted in changing it and the consequent loss of continuity and momentum that it had entailed. The 'ballet-like speed' that so impressed Dover Wilson in 1936 would not have been possible on the nineteenth-century stage. There was, furthermore, a growing awareness on the part of producers that Elizabethan and Jacobean plays did not lend themselves readily to the 'realism' both in setting and in acting that had been so dominant in the theatre for so long. Guthrie describes what was happening:

I began to see wherein for me the real magic of the theatre lay. It was, I discovered, charming, interesting and exciting not the nearer it approached 'reality', but the further it retreated into its own sort of artifice.[1]

About no play in the Shakespeare canon is this truer than it is about *Love's Labour's Lost*. Consciously 'artificial', in the best sense of that word, from first to last, it gains immeasurably from productions that concentrate on, bring out, and even heighten its artificiality. Since 1949 the 'sparks of genius' that Doctor Johnson detected in the play have been recognized for what they really are, a brilliantly dazzling display of poetic and theatrical virtuosity.

The Play

Love's Labour's Lost is exceptional among the comedies Shakespeare wrote prior to 1602, or thereabouts, in at least three respects: death plays a direct and highly significant part in it; as its title proclaims, it neither includes, nor concludes with, a marriage or marriages; and it has little or nothing to offer in the

[1] *A Life in the Theatre*, p. 180.

way of a story. Essentially, all that happens in it is that the young King of Navarre and three of his courtiers solemnly vow to abjure all contact with women and devote themselves to a course of study that will occupy them for the next three years. In their brash and ill-considered enthusiasm they have, however, overlooked the fact that the Princess of France, accompanied by three of her ladies, is about to arrive at the court of Navarre on an embassy from her 'sick, and bedrid father'. Predictably and promptly the four men break their new-made vows by falling in love and abandoning the profits of learning for the pleasures of wooing. To further their purpose they seek to entertain and impress the four women, first with a masque and then with a pageant. Neither device works. Then, when the hilarity created by the ludicrously inept pageant is at its height, the unexpected suddenly breaks in and takes over the fragile ephemeral world of the royal park. A messenger, Monsieur Marcadé, arrives from France with the news that the father of the Princess has died. 'The scene begins to cloud.' The revelry comes to an abrupt end. Inconsiderately and unfeelingly the four men still try to persist with their wooing. But the Princess, now Queen of France, will have none of it. Uncertain about the men's sincerity, as well they might be after this gratuitous display of male single-mindedness, she and her ladies set their lovers tasks that will take a year to complete and will reveal whether the men's professions of devotion are to be trusted or not. The King and his courtiers accept these conditions, and the two parties go their separate ways, having agreed to meet again after a twelvemonth and a day. Biron, the most vocal of the men, underlines the anomaly of this conclusion and, simultaneously, the self-conscious nature of the comedy by saying: 'Our wooing doth not end like an old play:| Jack hath not Jill.'

Such complications as there are spring from those well-worn devices of the comic scene, the conversation overheard, the use of masks to conceal identities, and letters mistakenly delivered to the wrong recipients. As for the sub-plot, it is so slight, turning as it does on the efforts of the 'fantastical Spaniard' Don Adriano de Armado to win the love of the country maid Jaquenetta, that it can hardly be described as a sub-plot at all. It might better be called a parodic counterpoint to the main business of the comedy.

This slenderness of intrigue is not only one of the play's most striking and unusual features but also one of its most positive assets. No longer faced with the difficulties he had encountered when writing *The Two Gentlemen of Verona*, for instance, where he had sought to cram a long and complicated story into the brief traffic required by the stage, with a consequent loss of adequate motivation and explanation, especially in the last act, Shakespeare was now free to enjoy himself by centring his attention on other and more exciting things, including lively displays of wit, the exploration of ideas and attitudes, the development of themes, and playing games with words. He seized the opportunity with an eager and exuberant assurance. In contrast to *The Two Gentlemen of Verona*, where there is a pronounced element of huddle about the ending, *Love's Labour's Lost* is, as befits its holiday nature, remarkable for its leisurely pace and amplitude of statement. It is the longest of the comedies he wrote before 1602,[1] and also the most stylized of them.

The stylization is particularly clear in the formal groupings of the characters. There is, to misquote Thomas Sprat, 'an almost mathematical symmetry' about it. Of the King's three courtiers and fellow-students, two, Longueville and Dumaine, are the courtiers of convention. They follow the King's lead in all they say and do, and, for the reader, as distinct from the playgoer, are not easily or readily distinguishable from one another. The other, Biron, is not in the least conventional. Of an independent nature, much in love with paradox, and taking a positive delight in being different and disruptive, he can think and act for himself, criticize himself as well as others, and, above all, speak eloquently on any topic that comes his way. His is the largest role by far; he utters between a fifth and a quarter of the play's total number of lines. The three women in attendance on the Princess correspond exactly to the three courtiers. Two of them, Maria and Katherine, are fashionable beauties, that is to say blondes, fitting matches for Longueville and Dumaine. The third, Rosaline, is not a conventional beauty at all. Like the 'dark lady' of the Sonnets, she is a brunette, or, in the vivid word-picture Biron paints of her in his soliloquy at the end of 3.1:

> A whitely wanton with a velvet brow,
> With two pitch-balls stuck in her face for eyes.

[1] See *The Complete Pelican Shakespeare*, ed. Alfred Harbage (1969), p. 31.

4. The Princess of France (Emily Richard, far right) attended by her ladies, Katherine (Kate Buffery), Rosaline (Josette Simon), and Maria (Alison Rose), and by Boyet (Harold Innocent), in the 1984 Royal Shakespeare Theatre production, directed by Barry Kyle.

5. Sir Nathaniel (Timothy West) reads Biron's letter mistakenly given to Jaquenetta (Patsy Byrne). Tony Church as Holofernes looks over his shoulder, and Costard (Tim Wylton, right) shows mild interest, but the scene's verbal displays send Dull (David Waller) to sleep; from John Barton's 1965 production at the Royal Shakespeare Theatre.

The wittiest, though by no means the most sensible and judicious of the women—that role is reserved for the Princess—Rosaline is obviously the right match for Biron. It goes almost without saying that in this highly formal world the King falls in love with the Princess at first sight. One courtly figure remains, the French lord Boyet. In attendance on the Princess, and at least middle-aged if not old, he acts as an intermediary between the two groups, carrying messages, picking up bits of intelligence, and engaging in badinage with men and women alike. Much interested in match-making and gossip, he is a sort of seedy run-down Cupid, 'Cupid's grandfather', as Katherine calls him at 2.1.253.

A similar kind of grouping appears among the characters of the sub-plot. On the one side are the fantastical pretenders to fashion or learning: Armado, Holofernes, and Sir Nathaniel. All three are well-established stage types, or rather, by the time the play is over, wonderfully original variants on established stage types that go back ultimately to the Italian *commedia dell'arte*, the Braggart, the Pedant, and the *Zani*. Over against these three are set their antitheses, the genuine country folk: Costard, the clown in the sense of rustic; Dull, the village constable; and Jaquenetta the dairymaid. Having no inflated notions about themselves and their own importance, these three can see through those who have, and show no hesitation about saying what they think. And, finally, standing between these two groups is the figure of Moth, Armado's page. Precociously knowledgeable about the love-game, though as yet too young to practise it, Moth takes an impish Cupid-like delight in puncturing pretensions, and finds a natural ally in Costard, who proudly recognizes their kinship in this respect by saying to him:

O, an the heavens were so pleased that thou wert but my bastard, what a joyful father wouldst thou make me! Go to, thou hast it *ad dunghill*, at the fingers' ends, as they say. (5.1.66–9)

The formal groupings are one with and inseparable from both the conduct of the action and of the dialogue. The entire play can usefully be viewed as a country-dance, which the *OED* defines as 'A dance practised by country-people, usually in the open air ... applied to dances in which an indefinite number of couples stand up face to face in two long lines'. The dance that is the play does, indeed, take place, as stage designers have been quick to recog-

6. An aspect of the passion for elaborate and symmetrical patterning in the artificial shaping of nature—a recurrent theme in Renaissance culture—is the formal knot-garden; Armado refers to Navarre's 'curious-knotted garden' (1.1.240). This design from Thomas Hill's *The Gardener's Labyrinth* (1577) is, in fact, the horticultural equivalent of one of Armado's speeches.

nize, in the open air, somewhere just outside the gates that bar the way to the royal residence, from which the Princess and her ladies are excluded by the King's vow and edict. The first act introduces all the male characters of any consequence, apart from Holofernes and Sir Nathaniel, and one minor female figure, Jaquenetta the dairymaid, whose mere presence has proved too great a temptation to Costard and deprived him of his liberty. But as yet the King and his fellow-votaries have no partners and have solemnly sworn not to have any for the next three years. The second act, however, introduces the Princess and her ladies to line up, as it were, outside the forbidden gates. In due course the King's party appears to bid the Princess welcome, and thereupon the two lines break up into four discrete couples. The couples do not actually dance, but the metaphorical dance that is the play has obviously begun. Eventually the men return to the King's house, leaving the women and Boyet to discuss what has happened.

The two groups do not meet again until the last scene, where the women are the first to appear, busy displaying to one another the costly 'favours' they have received from the men, and also sharply criticizing the love-letters that have accompanied those 'favours'. Told by Boyet that the King and his 'book-men' are about to descend on them in order 'to parley, court, and dance' (5.2.122), the Princess devises a counter-strategy. Again the men arrive, this time disguised as Muscovites. Again the two lines become four separate couples; but these couples are wrong couples. Deceived by the fact that the women have exchanged 'favours' with one another, each man woos a lady who is not the lady he thinks she is, while the other three couples converse apart. Finally the men go, leaving the ladies to crow over their discomfiture. The men are not absent for long. Coming back undisguised to the ladies who have now removed their masks and are wearing the 'favours' that are rightly theirs, the King and his party are exposed to mockery and have to admit defeat. The men and the women then sit down to watch the Pageant of the Nine Worthies until it is interrupted by the arrival of Monsieur Marcadé. Now, for the last time, the men and the women split into four separate pairs, each of which holds the centre of the stage for a time, while the other three pairs converse apart, until the final agreement is reached to renew the dance in a year and a day.

The stylization so evident in these scenes is reinforced by yet another feature of the play: its recourse to what might not unfittingly be called the parade-ground technique of action and dialogue. There are signs of it early in the first scene when Longueville and Dumaine immediately give their assent to the King's plans and put their names to the document he presents them with. Biron, however, the subversive recruit, does not follow suit for a long time, and thus breaks the pattern. It reasserts itself soon after the opening of 2.1, when the Princess asks her followers:

> Who are the votaries, my loving lords,
> That are vow-fellows with this virtuous Duke?

Thereupon, each of her ladies in turn admits her acquaintance with one of the King's lords and gives a character sketch of him. Later in the same scene, after the King and his men have left the stage, the three lords return to it, one succeeding another, so that each can ask Boyet for the name of the lady he feels drawn to.

By this time it is clear that Shakespeare is playing with and trying out one of the oldest and most effective of comic devices, that of first raising and then satisfying certain expectations in the minds of his audience. The third scene of the fourth act is probably the most extended and hilarious exploitation of the device in the whole of his work. It begins with the entry of Biron, carrying a paper in his hand and soliloquizing on his own state. Ruefully he admits that he is in love, calls himself a fool for being so, and concludes by saying:

Well, she [Rosaline] hath one o' my sonnets already. The clown bore it, the fool sent it, and the lady hath it. Sweet clown, sweeter fool, sweetest lady! By the world, I would not care a pin if the other three were in.

In fact, as the audience knows but Biron does not, the letter has not reached Rosaline. Wrongly delivered by Costard to Jaquenetta, it is now on its way to the King. Nevertheless, at this point Biron's wish begins to be satisfied. The King enters, carrying a sonnet he has written to the Princess. Biron promptly makes himself scarce, either by climbing a tree or standing aside, in order to overlook and overhear the King, who proceeds to read out his poem. As the King finishes his reading, he sees Longueville coming, and, in his turn, stands aside. Longueville too has a sonnet, which he reads aloud, and he also steps aside as Dumaine appears on the scene to read his lyric, addressed to the 'most divine Kate'. Having read it out, he goes on to wish that the other three men were also in love. His wish is granted. The sequence of events we have witnessed so far immediately goes into reverse, as it were. Longueville comes out of hiding to chide Dumaine for falling in love. He is followed by the King who chides both of them. But the King's moment of triumph is short-lived, for Biron comes forward to gloat and crow over the three of them. He does it with such abandon and gusto that the King has already begun to suspect him of insincerity when Costard and Jaquenetta appear, bringing with them Biron's sonnet to Rosaline. Their arrival puts an end to his scoffs and taunts, forcibly converting him from seemingly tyrannical foe of love to ardent apologist for it.

When acted with the aplomb and timing it demands, the scene

is irresistibly funny, a text-book demonstration of the validity of Bergson's theory of laughter, that it is triggered by the spectacle of men behaving like machines. But, as Bottom nearly says, it does 'ask some skill in the true performing of it', in order to make the Elizabethan conventions of soliloquy and aside intelligible and acceptable to a modern audience. In the production Shaw saw in 1886 professional experience was sadly lacking, and its absence at this crucial point presented him with an easy target. He wrote:

The only absolutely impossible situation was that of Biron hiding in the tree to overlook the king, who presently hides to watch Longaville, who in turn spies on Dumain; as the result of which we had three out of the four gentlemen shouting 'asides' through the sylvan stillness, No. 1 being inaudible to 2, 3, and 4; No. 2 audible to No. 1, but not to 3 and 4; No. 3 audible to 1 and 2, but not to No. 4; and No. 4 audible to all the rest, but himself temporarily stone deaf. Shakespear has certainly succeeded in making this arrangement intelligible; but the Dramatic Students' stage manager did not succeed in making it credible.[1]

The answer to Shaw's objection that the stage manager failed to make the scene credible is, of course, that if the stage manager tried to do any such thing he was attempting the impossible, since Shakespeare had never meant it to be credible, in the sense of probable or plausible. The scene is a superb piece of artifice designed to amuse and to entertain, which is precisely what it does, because everything that happens in it, right down to the arrival of Costard and Jaquenetta, is completely predictable. From the moment Biron sees the King approaching we know substantially what is to follow, and we enjoy seeing our expectations realized. Shakespeare himself was evidently delighted with the effect, for he goes on to repeat it twice over in the last scene. We know before the masque of Muscovites begins that it is bound to fall flat on its face, just as we know that the Pageant of the Nine Worthies will be a triumph of incompetence.

What we do not know is that the sense of security we are made to feel through so much of the play's course is a false one. Shakespeare has his surprises in store for us; and surprise can be devastating when it intrudes into what has, so far, seemed a wholly predictable world and action. A hint of what is to come is given early in the long final scene. The Princess and her ladies are

---

[1] *Shaw on Shakespeare*, p. 135.

talking and jesting about the gifts they have received from the King and his men, and also about the influence of Cupid, whom Katherine describes as 'a shrewd unhappy gallows'. To this outburst Rosaline replies: 'You'll ne'er be friends with him; a killed your sister.' And Katherine then completes the little story by saying: 'He made her melancholy, sad, and heavy, | And so she died.' A momentary breath of cold air sends a ripple over the brilliant surface of witty badinage. It is almost, but not quite, forgotten by the time the Pageant of the Nine Worthies is played, which also brings its surprises with it. Exasperated beyond measure, as he has every right to be, by the outrageous abuse heaped on him by the courtiers, Holofernes turns on his tormentors to administer the rebuke their bad behaviour deserves: 'This is not generous, not gentle, not humble' (5.2.621). The foolish overbearing pedant we have seen hitherto has been transformed into a master of manners. Similarly, Armado the braggart, subjected to the same kind of insults, speaks up bravely, nobly, and humanely in defence of the dead Hector whom he is impersonating. 'The sweet war-man', he tells his unruly auditors, 'is dead and rotten. Sweet chucks, beat not the bones of the buried. When he breathed, he was a man' (5.2.651–3). Depths we had not expected are being sounded. And then, to crown these revelations, comes the great *coup de théâtre*, the unheralded entry of Monsieur Marcadé, to announce the death of the King of France. His news acts as a chilling shock, made all the more powerful by the stark simplicity of what he says: twenty-eight simple words, none of them more than a disyllable, in a blank verse that is very close to prose. Paradoxically yet rightly the most important moment in this play so concerned with words is almost wordless.

In fact—and this is yet another instance of the conscious artifice that informs the entire comedy—there is not much blank verse in *Love's Labour's Lost*. Like *A Midsummer Night's Dream*, its only rival in this respect, it prefers to rely on rhyme. About sixty-five per cent of its total lines are in verse, but of these no more than a third are in blank verse. The rest are rhymed in a wide variety of ways. Heroic couplets are common, especially in the 'sets of wit' that the courtiers and the ladies engage in. So are sonnets. There are, if one includes the first fourteen lines in which the King sets out his plans and the fifteen lines in which he describes Armado (1.1.161–75), no fewer than five of them. More-over, they are easily and invitingly detachable. *Love's Labour's Lost* was the first of Shakespeare's plays to provide material for the anthologists of the day. Biron's sonnet (4.2.104–17), Longueville's sonnet (4.3.58–71), and Dumaine's dainty lyric (4.3.99–118) all appeared in a miscellany entitled *The Passionate Pilgrim*, published by William Jaggard in 1599, and Dumaine's lyric yet again in the great collection entitled *England's Helicon*, which came out in 1600. In addition quatrains in alternate rhyme are common. It is in these measures and, of course, in blank verse that the courtly figures discourse and express themselves. The other characters, as befits their station, resort to more popular kinds of verse: ballad metre, 'fourteeners', poulter's measure, and the like, together with the shambling brokenbacked couplets, that almost cry out to be intoned in a parsonic manner, through which Sir Nathaniel voices his sense of his own superiority to Constable Dull, whose 'ignorance' he cites as the text for what amounts to a miniature sermon (4.2.24–32). In general, however, they stick to prose, of which they have almost a monopoly; and a most extraordinary prose it proves to be, at least in the mouths of Armado and Holofernes, absurd in its excesses and affectations and delightful in its absurdity.

The play opens on a confident full-throated note. The King's initial speech has a heroic ring to it. His lines sound a clarion call to endeavour, to labour. But the labour he has in mind is none of Cupid's. Like Hercules at the parting of the ways, he has, according to what he says, chosen the rough and arduous road that leads to virtue in preference to the smooth and easy road that leads to pleasure.[1] The pursuit of fame is, he asserts, the right and proper end of living, and true fame is to be sought and won through an austere course of study that will turn the court of Navarre into 'a little academe' and make it 'the wonder of the world'. Fourteen lines, that are both in structure and effect a sonnet in blank verse, suffice to set the scene firmly in the world of the Renaissance typified by the *Accademia Platonica* of Florence which Cosimo de' Medici had established in the mid fifteenth century. The King's ambition is evidently to become the philo-

---

[1] See Erwin Panofsky, *Hercules am Scheidewege* (Leipzig, 1930).

sopher-king, the ideal ruler of Plato's imagined commonwealth; and it has to be admitted that the programme he outlines represents a far better and more civilized way of earning fame than that which had so strong an appeal for most monarchs and princes of the time. This said, however, it is already plain that the King's plans, especially after more detail about them emerges, rest on an unrealistic view of human nature in general and of his own nature in particular. He is obviously indulging in wishful thinking when he addresses his fellow-students as 'brave conquerors'. They may indeed be warring against their 'affections', meaning 'passions', but they are far from having overcome them. The Archpoet of the late twelfth century could have told him better:

> *Res est arduissima*
> *vincere naturam,*
> *in aspectu virginis*
> *mentem esse puram;*
> *iuvenes non possumus*
> *legem sequi duram,*
> *leviumque corporum*
> *non habere curam.*[1]

For all its vigour and the rich resounding language in which it is couched, the King's speech is distinctly hollow; and its hollowness is underlined by the casual unthinking manner in which Longueville and Dumaine accept the conditions it lays down. Like the King himself, they seem to regard a thing well said as a thing well done.

It is all very high-minded, not to say high-falutin, and badly out of touch with the hard facts of life. The academy is a flimsy structure, carefully designed to be easily knocked down. Biron, a born wrecker, finds the temptation to begin that process irresistible. Equipped with some sense of, and some respect for, facts, he

---

[1] Quoted from Helen Waddell, *The Wandering Scholars* (Harmondsworth, 1954), pp. 252–3. Miss Waddell (p. 177) translates the lines thus:

> Hard beyond all hardness, this
> Mastering of Nature:
> Who shall say his heart is clean,
> Near so fair a creature?
> Young are we, so hard a law,
> How should we obey it?
> And our bodies, they are young,
> Shall they have no say in't?

puts the case for natural behaviour. Unlike the three previous speeches, his first contribution to the play's exposition, in which he reminds the others of precisely what they are committing themselves to—a series of 'barren tasks, too hard to keep: | Not to see ladies, study, fast, not sleep'—evolves along neat logical lines. The items in it are ticked off one by one, and the list is punctuated by the recurring refrain: 'The which I hope is not enrollèd there'.

Hitherto the dialogue has been conducted in blank verse, apart from the concluding lines to each speech, which have taken the form of a couplet. Now, however, as an argument develops between Biron and the King, blank verse gives way to couplets, the right vehicle for snip-snap repartee in which the participants seek to score points off one another, until Biron produces a definition of the proper end of study which, if accepted by the others, would turn the whole idea of the academy upside down and inside out, leading the King to say:

> These be the stops that hinder study quite,
> And train our intellects to vain delight.
>
> (1.1.70–1)

Hereupon, Biron, taking this statement as a challenge to his dialectical virtuosity, and slipping easily into quatrains in alternate rhyme, which allow of a more fluid movement than do end-stopped couplets, catches up the King's last two words and expatiates on them for the next twenty lines. At first sight it may well seem that he is using far more words than are necessary, especially as some of them are the same words, though employed in senses that are constantly shifting. The whole outpouring appears to be wide open to the charge Sir Francis Bacon would soon bring against the Renaissance Latinists, whom he would accuse of paying more attention to 'copie' [i.e. copiousness] than 'weight', and then go on to say: 'Here therefore is the first distemper of learning, when men study words and not matter'.[1] Doctor Johnson was certainly of this opinion. Picking out the line 'Light, seeking light, doth light of light beguile', he comments:

The whole sense of this gingling declamation is only this, that *a man by too close study may read himself blind*, which might have been told with less obscurity in fewer words.[2]

---

[1] *The Advancement of Learning*, ed. William Aldis Wright (Oxford, 1900), p. 30.
[2] *Johnson on Shakespeare*, ed. Walter Raleigh (Oxford, 1908), p. 86.

But might it? Is not the total significance of the line richer than Johnson allows? What Biron is saying runs something like this: 'A man seeking for understanding solely by reading books fails to find the illumination he looks for. Instead, he becomes muddled and confused, and, ultimately goes blind.' The play on the word *light* enforces the paradox that the misguided effort defeats the attainment of the laudable objective it has in view.

Doctor Johnson should have cheered. The sentiments are very much his. He found fault with Milton for looking at life 'through the spectacles of books', and in his *Rasselas* the sage, Imlac, tells the Abyssinian prince: 'It seems to me, that while you are making the choice of life you neglect to live.'[1] But Johnson was put off by the word-play. Nevertheless, that word-play is an extremely important element in the comedy. From this point onwards there is one reference after another to *light*, *eyes*, and *books*. The interplay between them is complex and subtle, but, broadly speaking, their main significance is much as follows: light is understanding, and especially understanding of life; but it is also that which enables us to see, in the metaphorical as well as the literal sense of that word, and that which dazzles us and makes us incapable of seeing when there is too much of it. The eye is, of course, the organ through which light is perceived, but, where men and women in love are concerned, it is also, in the sense of the beloved's eye, the book that is studied and interpreted, sometimes rightly and sometimes wrongly.

Biron's manner of expressing all this is clever, intricate, and ostentatiously artificial; but his message is plain, simple, and sensible, a plea for the exercise of common sense and for heeding the promptings of nature. When the King accuses him of being a kill-joy, because he is so critical of the forcing-house that the academy threatens to become, his answer comes back clearly and unequivocally:

> Why should proud summer boast
> Before the birds have any cause to sing?
> Why should I joy in any abortive birth?
> At Christmas I no more desire a rose
> Than wish a snow in May's new-fangled shows,
> But like of each thing that in season grows.
> ($1.1.102–7$)

---

[1] *Johnson: Prose and Poetry*, selected by Mona Wilson (1950), pp. 837 and 444–5.

Far more simple and direct than anything Biron has said hitherto, these lines announce a theme that will continue to run as a sort of bass through the rest of the play's course and finally emerge as its dominant strain in the songs of Spring and Winter with which the comedy ends: a deep feeling for the connections between the human world and the world of nature, together with a recognition of the vital importance of seasonal rhythms. If it is to succeed, a proposal, including a proposal of marriage, must be rightly timed. By the end of the play, the four men are just beginning to learn this. The women have known it from the start.

But, while *Love's Labour's Lost* shares this concern with Shakespeare's other comedies, the movement of its action is, in one respect at least, unique. Instead of ending with the coming into being of a new society, it concludes with a reversion to a much older one. Beginning by trying to fit himself for the role of philosopher–king, Navarre, and his lords with him, finally accepts that of the medieval knight who wins the hand of his lady by service. The magical phrase 'a twelvemonth and a day', so reminiscent of *Sir Gawaine and the Green Knight*, 'The Wife of Bath's Tale', and romance in general, occurs twice in the last hundred lines of *Love's Labour's Lost*, and nowhere else in the whole of Shakespeare's writings.

It is, appropriately enough, Biron, the man with whom facts count, who now notices and points out that one part of the King's Utopian dream is already out of date and impracticable. Since the Princess of France is already on her way to Navarre to negotiate about matters of state, the King must perforce break his newly-taken oath not to talk with a woman for the next three years. From this moment the idea of the academy, already badly shaken, is in ruins, though the men are reluctant to admit it. It is plain, as it should have been from the first, that the King cannot abandon his royal duties and obligations in favour of living as a recluse without making proper arrangements for the conduct of affairs during his retirement from public life. Trying to make the best of a bad job, Navarre pleads necessity as a reason for infringing his own decree; and Biron draws the logical consequences:

> Necessity will make us all forsworn
>   Three thousand times within this three years' space;
> For every man with his affects is born,
>   Not by might mastered, but by special grace.

$$(1.1.148-51)$$

Much of the subsequent development of the action, and of the play's total significance, is implicit in those lines. *Love's Labour's Lost*, for most of its course, dances lightly on its way; there is nothing solemn or portentous about it; but, like all good comedy, it is not without its serious concerns. Foremost among them are two: first, the conviction that man is a passional being, incapable of controlling his 'affects', his instinctive urges and desires, without divine assistance; and, secondly, the recognition that oaths, the bonds of civil society, are, or at least should be, binding. They are not to be taken rashly and then brushed aside casually, as the King seems to think, or made in the full knowledge that they will not be kept, which is what Biron does when, in complete defiance of his own eminently rational demurs, he sets his name to the articles.

With the matter of the oath-taking settled for the time being, a fresh interest is needed. Biron opens the way for it by asking: 'is there no quick recreation granted?' The King replies by giving a full-length 'character' of Armado in which he describes that 'refinèd traveller of Spain' as

> One who the music of his own vain tongue
> Doth ravish like enchanting harmony.
>
> (1.1.165–6)

The words apply equally well to the four students, and particularly well to Biron; but blissfully blind to this fact, the King goes on to say:

> How you delight, my lords, I know not, I,
> But I protest I love to hear him lie,
> And I will use him for my minstrelsy.

The minstrel was, among other things, the story-teller; and the stories the King apparently expects Armado to relate are tall stories of the kind Falstaff would soon be telling, tales of great deeds done and daring enterprises about to be undertaken—all of them fictional and having no more substance than the boasts made about the 'invincible' Spanish Armada with which both Armado's name and his nationality connect him. Biron approves of the plan, characterizing Armado as 'A man of fire-new words,

27

fashion's own knight', and Longueville adds his mite of expository information:

> Costard the swain and he shall be our sport,
> And so to study three years is but short.
>
> (1.1.178–9)

From all this it would appear that the King and his followers are arranging a programme of entertainment for themselves, which we shall see carried into action. That impression is seemingly confirmed at once, for, pat on the cue provided by his name, Costard makes his entry, escorted by Constable Dull who has him in custody and bears a letter for the King recounting the heinous offence with which Costard is charged. It is, one notes admiringly, marvellously right that we should hear Armado, the author of the letter, before we actually see him, for the essence of the man is in what he says, or rather in his way of saying it.

The reading-out of the letter is delayed by Costard, who insists on giving his own version of his misdemeanour. Employing the legal terminology and the verbal quibbles he regards as proper for the occasion, much as the Gravedigger would do in *Hamlet* five or six years later, he reveals that he was caught in the act of consorting with Jaquenetta in the royal park, an action which he stoutly defends on the grounds that it was perfectly natural. The preposterousness of the academy and, still more, of the King's attempt to force its restrictions on his dependents, is emphatically underscored. Eventually, however, the letter is read out by the King, while his rehearsal of its polysyllabic periphrases is punctuated by terse monosyllabic interruptions from Costard. So far as matter goes, the letter adds nothing whatever to Costard's own account of his delinquency, but the manner of it is utterly different. Armado, to impress the King with his dutiful devotion, and, as he hopes, to elevate the clown's 'hearkening after the flesh' into a major crime, uses dozens of words to say what Costard says in one.

The letter is deliciously and consistently ridiculous. But what, precisely, is Shakespeare, as distinct from Armado, doing in it? He is, surely and above all else, enjoying himself enormously. The missive is written *con amore*; its composition a labour of love. Fvery word in it has been chosen with care and discrimination; every construction elaborated in conformity with a set pattern.

Often labelled satire, it is really nothing of the kind. The playwright's aim is not to attack the extravagant copiousness of much
Elizabethan narrative prose, especially of the pastoral variety, and
destroy it by concentrating on its absurdities, but rather to build
up, in a spirit of creative play, an insubstantial and fantastic
edifice of words and figures of speech, which he and his audience
in the theatre can then stand back from and admire with amused
amazement as they see so much being made out of so little. If
Shakespeare himself played a part, as seems quite likely, in the
early performances of *Love's Labour's Lost*, it should have been
that of Armado.

By the time the first scene is over, we think we know how
Armado will continue to be used. The King and his party will
encourage him to indulge his fondness for unrelenting circumlocution, something we have now heard him doing, and his
compulsion to brag and tell lies, something we have been told
he does but have not yet heard him doing, and will find entertainment in his posturings. In fact, we are quite wrong on both
counts. It is true that Boyet, the know-all attendant on the Princess,
keeps up the fiction by telling her in the fourth act:

> This Armado is a Spaniard that keeps here in court,
> A phantasime, a Monarcho, and one that makes sport
> To the Prince and his book-mates.

$$(4.1.97-9)$$

But the fact remains that Armado never appears on stage with
the King and his courtiers until about four hundred lines from the
end of the play, and, when he does so, it is to hand the King the
'plot' or programme, as it would be today, for the Pageant of
the Nine Worthies which he has commissioned and in which he is
about to take part. Moreover, he does not brag in the manner the
King has led us to expect he will. He talks, and writes, in high-
flown terms that are admirably sustained, some of them fire-new
from the neological mint, some of them bits of treasure-trove from
the ancient fields of romance, but he tells no boasting tales either
about himself or others. The nearest he comes to doing so is when
he insinuates, in 5.1, that he is on intimate terms with the King.
Shakespeare, it seems clear, changed his mind about Armado.
Having written that first letter, he knew that he wanted to
compose more letters and speeches in the same exuberantly

7. John Neville as Don Armado in the Stratford, Ontario production of 1984, directed by Michael Langham.

fantastic vein. He therefore jettisoned the notion of Armado as the braggart of theatrical tradition, and turned him into a brilliant parody of the King and his followers. Like them, Armado falls in love, thus breaking his promise to 'study three years' with them; like them, he writes a love letter to the idol of his affections; and, most significant of all, he puts his trust in words and their power to move and prove. He even has a tiny court of his own. It consists solely of his page Moth, who is as critical of his master's poses and plans as Biron is of the King's, and who, again like Biron, is much given to word-play.

The second scene of the first act, where we actually see Armado in person, is in no small measure a preview of much that will follow in the main action. Already in love with Jaquenetta, the Spaniard has adopted the melancholy pose thought proper to that condition. Confessing his love, he asks Moth to provide some precedents for such unsoldierly behaviour, much as the King will ask Biron to find some justification for his falling in love in 4.3; and, when Jaquenetta herself appears, he declares his love for her and is rebuffed by her, much as Biron will be rebuffed by Rosaline in 2.1. Similarly the superb self-regarding soliloquy with which he closes 1.2 anticipates the way in which all the students will become sonneteers, while at one point—so thin is the line that separates the mock-heroic from the true heroic—it even has more than a touch of Othello's farewell to his 'occupation' (*Othello* 3.3.352–62) when it ends thus:

Adieu, valour; rust, rapier; be still, drum; for your manager is in love; yea, he loveth. Assist me, some extemporal god of rhyme, for I am sure I shall turn sonnet. Devise, wit; write, pen; for I am for whole volumes in folio.

Like his letter to the King, Armado's soliloquy is an ostentatious parade of affectation. It says little; but that little is, in its own peculiar manner, exquisitely phrased and cadenced. It has musical properties and affinities. Grammar is transformed into notes on a scale as the positive *base* inevitably leads on to the comparative *baser*, and that, in turn, to the superlative *basest*. Furthermore, the triple pattern thus established is renewed in 'Love is a familiar; Love is a devil. There is no evil angel but Love', and again in 'Adieu, valour; rust, rapier; be still, drum'. In Armado's case the style—and he has style—is indeed the man, and it comes into full flower in the letter he writes to Jaquenetta, which is read out by Boyet in 4.1. In it the pattern of graduated triple repetition is dominant, and even acquires a classical sanction when Armado takes over Caesar's '*Veni, vidi, vici*', a statement so laconic that it provides the material for his next twenty lines or so as he translates it into his own idiosyncratic kind of English. But this dominant triple rhythm is now complicated by the interplay with it of double antitheses, such as 'The magnanimous and most illustrate King Cophetua set eye upon the penurious and indubitate beggar Zenelophon', and 'I am the King, for so stands the comparison; thou the beggar, for so witnesseth thy lowliness'. The letter might well be described as variations on a theme by Caesar.

Armado's part, then, changes and grows as Shakespeare first perceives and then realizes and exploits the possibilities latent in it. It also seems to have led him to the creation of two other figures, who were not, perhaps, envisaged in his original conception of the comedy—Holofernes the pedant, and Sir Nathaniel the curate. They, unlike Armado, are not introduced by character sketches that precede their appearance on stage. Indeed, there has not been so much as a hint of their existence before they suddenly pop up, as it were, in the stage direction that initiates the action of 4.2, that is to say about one third of the way through the play, and not long after the disappearance from it of the two nameless lords attending on the Princess. Called for by the stage direction that opens 4.1, these two speak not a word in the scene and make their exit from it, along with the Princess, about forty lines before it ends. It looks very much as though Shakespeare phased them out because by this time he had come to see that he could make much better use of the two actors playing these supernumerary parts by giving them new roles. The introduction of the parson and the schoolmaster has a double effect. First, it fills out and completes the village community, represented hitherto by Costard, Dull, and Jaquenetta; and, secondly and more importantly, it provides the playwright with the means to carry much further that exploration and exploitation of linguistic fads and eccentricities which he had begun through his creation of Armado.

A talker, if he is to show his paces—and both Armado and Holofernes are bent on doing so—must have an audience. Armado is furnished with a sharply critical one in Moth; Holofernes with an effusively adulatory one in Sir Nathaniel. Both talkers are expert in making much of little; but their ways of doing it differ widely. The Spaniard's great stand-by is the periphrasis; whereas the pedant relies mainly on the synonym, of which George Puttenham had remarked in his *The Art of English Poesy* (1589) that an abundance of them 'doth much beautify and enlarge the matter'.[1] The first speech Holofernes makes shows conclusively that he is of the same mind as Puttenham. Addressing Sir Nathaniel, he says:

The deer was, as you know, in blood, *sanguis*, ripe as the pomewater, who now hangeth like a jewel in the ear of *caelum*, the sky, the welkin, the heaven, and anon falleth like a crab on the face of *terra*, the soil, the land, the earth. (4.2.3–7)

Armado, it is true, also makes play with synonyms on occasions, as when he writes, for instance, of the ink 'which here thou

[1] Ed. Gladys D. Willcock and Alice Walker (Cambridge, 1936), p. 215.

viewest, beholdest, surveyest, or seest' (1.1.238–9), but with him they are only one item in a large store of decorative devices. Holofernes, however, is a speaking dictionary, and a polyglot dictionary at that. Moreover, he has a head full of Latin tags and familiar quotations, prefers long Latinate words of the inkhorn variety to plain English terms, and finds lists irresistible. Yet figure of fun though he is, he too, like Armado, has his moments of felicity that bring him close to his creator. When he graciously accepts the curate's praise of his painfully excogitated lines on the death of the deer, he hymns his own inventive faculty in a way that suggests he has the root of the matter in him, and that looks forward to Falstaff's tribute to the stimulating effect sack can have on the imagination (*2 Henry IV* 4.2.93–9); and his admiring quibbling reference to Ovid may well express something of Shakespeare's own attitude to the Roman poet whose work meant so much to him:

for the elegancy, facility, and golden cadence of poesy … Ovidius Naso was the man. And why indeed 'Naso' but for smelling out the odoriferous flowers of fancy, the jerks of invention? (4.2.121–4)

Improvisation, so evident in Shakespeare's treatment of Armado and in his invention of Holofernes and Sir Nathaniel, has also left its mark on the play as a whole. Both the masque of Muscovites and the Pageant of the Nine Worthies look very much like afterthoughts, as distinct from integral parts of the playwright's original plan. A mere glance at the way in which similar material is handled in *A Midsummer Night's Dream* is instructive. In it the 'tedious brief scene of young Pyramus | And his love Thisbe: very tragical mirth' (5.1.56–7) is an essential part of the structure, something built into it from the outset. Within a dozen lines of the opening Theseus orders Philostrate to 'Stir up the Athenian youth to merriments'; and no sooner is the first scene over than a consequence of that order is before our eyes as the mechanicals gather to discuss their play and take up the roles Quince has allotted them. The masque in *Love's Labour's Lost*, on the other hand, is never so much as mentioned until the end of the climactic scene 4.3, where the King suggests that he and his men devise some entertainment for the Princess and her ladies, and Biron, being a little more specific, sees four possibilities: 'revels, dances, masques, and merry hours' (4.3.354). Even so, however, the final scene is well advanced before the audience learns that a masque has been decided on. As for the Pageant, the first we hear about it is in 5.1, when Armado asks the schoolmaster for his assistance in providing the King with 'some delightful ostentation, or show, or pageant, or antic, or firework'. *Love's Labour's Lost* exerts a peculiar fascination of its own because it positively invites one to look over Shakespeare's shoulder, as it were, and watch him in the act of composition, coping with difficulties as they arise.

Yet the main outlines of the play, and especially of the closely interrelated conflicts with which it deals, never waver. So definite are they that they almost cry out to be formulated in abstract terms. The dominant motif is that of antithesis and reversal. Already present in the first scene, it becomes crystal clear in the second where it takes visual form as the tiny page Moth, whose diminutive stature is insisted on throughout, and his tall gaunt master, as most producers rightly make him, appear on stage for the first time. Between them these two form 'a little academe' of their own as well as a little court. But in this school the relationship of teacher to taught is inverted. It is Moth who instructs and provides the examples and definitions—'Define, define, well-educated infant', says Armado to him at one point (1.2.90); while the boy addresses his master as 'Negligent student' at another (3.1.32)—and the definitions themselves are much concerned with hair-splitting. Logic flourishes, especially in its extreme form, arithmetic, and so does paradox, as when Moth 'proves' that lead, far from being 'a metal heavy, dull, and slow', is 'swift' (3.1.54–9). But Moth's most telling way of going to work is by repeating and, in the process, reversing whatever Armado says, as he does in the following exchange:

ARMADO How canst thou part sadness and melancholy, my tender juvenal?
MOTH By a familiar demonstration of the working, my tough señor.
ARMADO Why tough señor? Why tough señor?
MOTH Why 'tender juvenal'? Why 'tender juvenal'?
ARMADO I spoke it, tender juvenal, as a congruent epitheton appertaining to thy young days, which we may nominate tender.
MOTH And I, tough señor, as an appertinent title to your old time, which we may name tough.

$(1.2.7–15)$

The incisive and insistent pattern set up by these exchanges is the very backbone of the comedy's dialogue, running right through it to culminate in the perfectly balanced songs with which Spring and Winter take up an old dispute that neither can win. *Love's Labour's Lost* is, in fact, the dramatization of a whole collection of closely interrelated oppositions: young men versus young women; artifice versus nature; study versus love; Plato versus Ovid; books versus eyes; words versus deeds; and deliberately cultivated neologizing speech versus plain idiomatic speech.

The most important of these 'contraries', as William Blake might have called them, is the first, the battle of the sexes. Implicit in the King's opening speech, and made quite explicit in the first two articles of his edict, is the notion of women as the enemy. From this point onwards the relationship between the two sexes is repeatedly seen and referred to by both sides as a kind of warfare. The dialogue is shot through and through with military terminology in a manner that goes back at least as far as Ovid, who had begun the ninth elegy of his First Book with the words '*Militat omnis amans, et habet sua castra Cupido*',[1] and then developed the analogy between the lover and the soldier through the rest of his poem. This use of the language of war becomes even more pronounced in the soliloquy with which Biron concludes 3.1, and reaches a sustained climax, that carries over into 5.2, at the end of 4.3. There the King, swept off his feet by Biron's eloquent praise of love, cries out: 'Saint Cupid, then! And, soldiers, to the field!', to which Biron himself adds:

> Advance your standards, and upon them, lords!
> Pell-mell, down with them! But be first advised
> In conflict that you get the sun of them.
>
> (4.3.342–4)

In its bawdy innuendo that speech sounds more like the prelude to a rape of the Gallic women than to a masque—soon to become a massacre—of Muscovites. The women are more than equal to the challenge. Told by Boyet, whom she addresses as 'scout', that the men are approaching 'Armèd in arguments', the Princess responds by saying 'Saint Denis to Saint Cupid!' (5.2.81–8).

The war is, as Boyet says, waged with arguments and with

---

[1] Every lover is a soldier, and Cupid has his tents.

repartee. Whenever the men and women meet wit combats ensue, usually in the form of stichomythic thrusts, parries, and counterthrusts. Words become weapons, and very sharp weapons at that. Boyet sums up this aspect of it all when he remarks:

> The tongues of mocking wenches are as keen
>   As is the razor's edge invisible,
> Cutting a smaller hair than may be seen;
>   Above the sense of sense, so sensible
> Seemeth their conference; their conceits have wings
> Fleeter than arrows, bullets, wind, thought, swifter things.
>   (5.2.256–61)

As the last line and a half make plain, words can be missiles as well as swords and daggers. Moreover, the women, like the men, play war-games to keep their hands in, as it were. They spend much of their time whetting their wits on one another's and on Boyet's; while Biron, from the very outset, is always ready to take on his fellow-students, or even himself. In speech after speech, whether it be a soliloquy such as that with which he ends 3.1, a diatribe, such as his castigation of the other three in 4.3, or his two flyting attacks on Boyet in 5.2, he piles up dismissive item on dismissive item in what becomes a positive hailstorm of picturesque abuse, made up to a large extent of freshly coined compound nouns. *Carry-tale*, for which the *OED* can find only one precedent, together with *please-man*, *mumble-news*, and *trencher-knight*, for which it can cite none, and *zany*, borrowed either from the French or the Italian, all appear in the course of a mere two lines (5.2.463–4).

The linguistic vigour and fertility so evident in these lines and in the entire speech from which they come is, of course, typical of the play as a whole. *Love's Labour's Lost* contains, as Alfred Hart showed more than forty years ago,[1] a larger number of new words—new in the sense that Shakespeare had not used them before—than any other play, with the single exception of *Hamlet*, that he wrote; and *Hamlet*, it has to be remembered, is nearly half as long again as the comedy. Armado and Holofernes between them are responsible for the majority of these new words; but Biron is the third most important contributor to the total; and,

[1] 'Vocabularies of Shakespeare's Plays' and 'The Growth of Shakespeare's Vocabulary', *RES* 19 (1943), 128–40 and 242–54.

while their new words smell of the inkhorn, his do not. They appear as natural growths from the native soil of plain English usage. They need no gloss and have never needed one.

In this respect they tie up with and complement another less noticed yet equally striking feature of Biron's speech, his recourse to proverbial lore, which tends to be the language of common experience and common sense. The figures concerning this phenomenon, as set out by R. W. Dent in his *Shakespeare's Proverbial Language*,[1] are highly illuminating. *Love's Labour's Lost*, with a total of 189, makes more use of proverbs than does any other of the comedies, its nearest rival being *Twelfth Night*, with 150, and is outdone by only two of the other plays, both of them tragedies: *King Lear*, with 197, and *Romeo and Juliet*, with 223. No fewer than 47 of these proverbial phrases by my count, i.e. one quarter, come from the lips of Biron.

The range and variety of Biron's vocabulary are a pointer to what is simultaneously his main strength and his main weakness. A true child of the Renaissance, he sets great store, as do his fellow-students, by eloquence, which Samuel Daniel would soon invoke in his *Musophilus* (1599) in the following terms:

> Power above powers, O heavenly *Eloquence*,
>   That with the strong rein of commanding words,
>   Dost manage, guide, and master th'eminence
>   Of men's affections, more than all their swords.[2]

Like Daniel, the four young men regard the power of words as unlimited. Having fallen in love, they all turn to the writing of verse as the recognized and appropriate means of persuading the ladies to love them in return. Moreover, all four think that words, properly handled, can prove anything, even that black is white. It is true that when Biron says of the dark Rosaline, 'I'll prove her fair, or talk till doomsday here' (4.3.271), the other three protest against his sophistry, but within a dozen lines the King is requesting him to do the impossible: ' good Biron, now prove | Our loving lawful and our faith not torn'. It is an absurd demand. The men have broken their initial vows; and nothing they can do will alter that fact. Still less will anything they can say. Costard knows better. He is not taken in when Armado gives him three

---

[1] Berkeley, Los Angeles, London, 1981, pp. 3–4.

[2] *Poems and 'A Defence of Ryme'*, ed. A. C. Sprague (1950), p. 96, ll. 939–42.

farthings by way of 'remuneration'. For him three farthings remain three farthings, despite the imposing, six-syllable, Latinate name Armado chooses to give them, and, as such, elevenpence farthing inferior to Biron's two-syllable 'guerdon' of one shilling (3.1.127–38).

Nevertheless, Biron complies with the King's request, and puts on a sparkling display of rhetorical and, it must in fairness be added, poetical pyrotechnics, that grows out of his similar performance at the play's opening (1.1.72–93). Addressing his fellows as 'affection's men-at-arms', and thus implying that they have now enlisted under the banners of those same natural impulses they originally set out to 'conquer', he begins by arguing along pseudo-logical lines. But as he warms to his work, and moves on to the subject of women's eyes, the prompters of love, his verse takes off, so to speak. It becomes musical, singing with lyrical grace and rhapsodical fervour, and rising to a climax in the lines:

> For valour, is not Love a Hercules,
> Still climbing trees in the Hesperides?
> Subtle as Sphinx, as sweet and musical
> As bright Apollo's lute, strung with his hair;
> And when Love speaks, the voice of all the gods
> Make heaven drowsy with the harmony.
>
> (4.3.315–20)

There is more than a touch of Marlowe about it all, of the Marlowe who had written of men's souls 'Still climbing after knowledge infinite', and of the poet ever searching for the perfect word and image that always elude him (*1 Tamburlaine* 2.1.24 and 5.2.98–110). But it also has its own peculiar 'Promethean fire', with *Promethean* meaning 'life-infusing', as it does again in *Othello*, at 5.2.12, the only other place where the word appears in Shakespeare's writings. Having soared into the empyrean, however, Biron must eventually come back to earth. He does so by returning to the dialectical legerdemain with which he began, and by concluding with the rhetorical question, 'Who can sever love from charity?', that assumes the answer 'No one', but really deserves the answer 'Anyone who knows the difference between pagan *amor* and Christian *caritas*'.

For a moment Biron is as much intoxicated by his own virtuosity as are the other three, but before the scene is over he has begun to sober down. Nevertheless, much has yet to happen to bring him to a proper understanding of the limits of language. Even after the masque of Muscovites has turned into a fiasco, he still attempts to win Rosaline's love by harping on his favourite conceit about *eyes*, *light*, and the dazzling effect of the *sun* (5.2.374–6); and it is not until the women reveal that they knew all along who the masquers were that he begins at last to see something of the inadequacy of words. The palinode in which he does so: 'Thus pour the stars down plagues for perjury ... sans crack or flaw' (5.2.394–415), is a superbly paradoxical performance by a master of paradox. Biron rejects verbal artifice, to which he has hitherto pinned his faith, in favour of plain homespun language, or so at least he says. Yet the terms in which he does it are a compelling demonstration of the force and energy figurative speech is capable of. Its power to wound is vividly conjured up in the four lines he devotes to Rosaline's wit:

> Here stand I, lady, dart thy skill at me,
>   Bruise me with scorn, confound me with a flout,
> Thrust thy sharp wit quite through my ignorance,
>   Cut me to pieces with thy keen conceit.

But so also is its capacity to delight. The sensuous pleasure to be derived from it becomes palpable in the soft rich materials with which he clothes his figures, 'Taffeta phrases, silken terms precise', and so on. In love with them still, he lingers fondly over them in the very act of abjuring them, and then undercuts all he has said so far by his inability to resist the attractions of the gallicism *sans*.

Even at this late stage Biron is far from cured of his infatuation with words. He will still go on to make his abusive attack on Boyet (5.2.460–81); to preface an appeal to the ladies with the statement, 'Honest plain words best pierce the ear of grief', and then launch into yet another word game, playing upon *eyes* and juggling with the meanings of the words *false* and *true* (5.2.743–64). Moreover, in the very speech where he finally capitulates and asks Rosaline to 'Impose some service' on him he is still talking about 'the window of my heart, mine eye'. Only when she has laid down her conditions does he admit that there are indeed things that words cannot do:

> To move wild laughter in the throat of death?
> It cannot be, it is impossible.
> Mirth cannot move a soul in agony.
>
> (5.2.837–9)

Biron is obviously the dominant figure among the men, their leader, as they acknowledge when the King, seconded by Longueville and Dumaine, calls on him to 'prove' that they have not been guilty of perjury. He is also the most interesting of them, because he has a certain complexity. Capable, on the one hand, of genuine poetic flight, notably in his hymn to love, he can, on the other, be self-critical, making himself the object of his own wry mockeries, and even cynical. There are times, particularly in the soliloquy with which he ends 3.1 and in its companion soliloquy with which he opens 4.3, when he reminds one of the young John Donne who was a student at Lincoln's Inn between 1592 and 1594, where he may have written such poems as 'Woman's Constancy' and 'The Triple Fool'.[1] In the first Donne plays tricks with the words 'true' and 'false' much as Biron does at 5.2.760–4, while he begins the second with the lines:

> I am two fools, I know,
> For loving and for saying so
> In whining poetry.

I am not suggesting that Biron is to be identified with Donne, but rather that the roundness his character takes on may owe something to the contacts Shakespeare seems to have had with the young men of the Inns of Court in the early 1590s (see pp. 45–7), which was also, interestingly enough, the time when, according to Sir Richard Baker, Donne was 'a great visitor of ladies, a great frequenter of plays, a great writer of conceited verses'.[2] If the playwright ever depicted a typical Inns of Court man, then Biron is he.

Biron's counterpart among the women and, simultaneously, his antithesis is not, as one would expect, Rosaline. She is altogether too much like him, especially when she looks forward with such keen anticipation to 'torturing' him (5.2.60–8), to fulfil that role. The opposing voice to his is that of the Princess, who, unlike the King, exerts a natural unquestioned authority

[1] See R. C. Bald, *John Donne: A Life* (Oxford, 1970), p. 71.

[2] Quoted from Bald, p. 72.

over her followers. It is a quiet reasonable voice, free from the assertive argumentativeness that characterizes so many of Biron's speeches, but it is also firm and confident. The first exchange between her and the King tells us much. 'Fair Princess, welcome to the court of Navarre', says he, mouthing the polite formula he thinks appropriate to the occasion and, no doubt, expecting a similar formula in return. He does not receive it. Instead, the Princess replies: ' "Fair" I give you back again, and welcome I have not yet' (2.1.91–2). It is already clear that for her words are not things to be twisted, turned, and given as much or as little weight as the speaker chooses. They should be the instruments of society, the servants of truth, and correspond with facts. Forced into facing his own discourtesy, Navarre tries to gloss it over, but only succeeds in making it worse, as the Princess points out by saying:

> I hear your grace hath sworn out housekeeping.
> 'Tis deadly sin to keep that oath, my lord,
> And sin to break it.
>
> (2.1.103–5)

Her clear-eyed perception of the dilemma the men are now in and the attitude she adopts towards it remain hers to the end. When the King, having decided to abandon his initial position, eventually invites her to enter his court, her answer is as unequivocal and uncompromising as it was at their first interview:

> This field shall hold me, and so hold your vow.
> Nor God nor I delights in perjured men.
>
> (5.2.345–6)

A mirror of manners—her reception of the Pageant in particular is a rebuke to the uncouth and unruly responses to it of the King's men—the Princess is the standard by which the men are measured and found wanting. She is the play's still centre, exercising an influence on its outcome and characters that goes far beyond anything the mere size of her part might lead one to expect.

Love, the mischievous amoral Dan Cupid, who thinks women are to be won 'with revels, dances, masques, and merry hours', and, above all else, with sophistries and flatteries, stands no chance of prevailing against one for whom 'the right true end of love' is marriage, and marriage 'a world-without-end bargain'.

As Ver, '[maintained] by the cuckoo', and Hiems, 'maintained by the owl', renew an ancient debate, we are transported out of the rarefied atmosphere and artificial ambience of the royal park into the genuine countryside. The 'war of wits' is over; and with it have gone the sharp ripostes, the dazzling word-play so like sword-play, the puns, the 'taffeta phrases', the 'silken terms precise', the lexicographical lists, and the circling periphrases. Specious dialectic no longer rears its head. From a world in which words have an almost independent life of their own, fighting and dancing with one another, we move into another where they are intimately related to the things they denote—flowers, birds, the wind that blows, the cold that freezes, and simple yet essential human activities. The two seasons, like the two sexes, not only oppose one another but also balance one another. Spring is a time of love and delight, but it also brings its attendant misgivings typified by the voice of the cuckoo. Winter is a time of coughs and red noses, but it also has its compensations, the roasted crab-apples hissing in the bowl and the merry note of the staring owl. The two songs, so antiphonally connected, establish the point of balance on which the play has come to rest.

The Date and 'Sources'

The earliest text of *Love's Labour's Lost* that we have, the First Quarto, was published, its title-page tells us, in 1598, and thus provides a definite *terminus ad quem* for the date of its composition. That same title-page also states that the play had been 'presented before her Highness this last Christmas'. At first sight this looks like a reference to the Christmas of 1597, thus pushing the latest time for composition back by a year; but then one realizes that the First Quarto might have come out during the first three months of what we now call 1599, so that the Christmas in question could still be that of 1598. One other bit of external evidence can be gleaned from the title-page. It says that the text it offers has been 'Newly corrected and augmented', thus implying that there had been a previous edition which could not conceivably have been published later than 1598. If there had been, however, no copy of it has ever come to light. The two earliest mentions of the play—one in Robert Tofte's *Alba*, cited at pages 1-2, and the other in Francis Meres's *Palladis Tamia* (see pp. 81-2)—do not help in establishing any other date by which it must have been written, since both occur in works first published in 1598. Some scholars have argued that the word 'once' in the first line of Tofte's account of his visit to the theatre means 'a long time ago', but, in view of what he says about his experience there, 'on a particular occasion' seems a far more likely interpretation of it.

In these circumstances internal evidence becomes all important, and it, by its very nature, tends to be subjective. It is obviously so in the opinion hazarded by Charles Gildon in 1710, which runs thus: 'since it is one of the worst of Shakespeare's Plays, nay I think I may say the very worst, I cannot but think it is his first' (Furness, p. 327). Not all critics of the eighteenth century were so ready to condemn the comedy as Gildon was, but most of them did concur with him in regarding it as very early, i.e. as belonging to 1590 or thereabouts. Edmond Malone, the first scholar to make 'An Attempt to ascertain the Order in which the Plays of Shakespeare were written' (1778), pointed the way to a more objective method. Taking a high incidence of rhymed verse as an index to plays composed early in the playwright's career, he began by suggesting 1591 as the date of *Love's Labour's Lost*, but then later revised it to read 1594, though he still thought of the play as 'one of [Shakespeare's] earliest essays' in the writing of comedy (Furness, p. 328). It was, however, the notion of earliness, rather than the specific date of 1594, that appealed to scholars and critics in the nineteenth century and well on into the twentieth. Then, as the play began to rise in critical estimation, its chronological place in the canon was assessed afresh with results that are well summarized by E. K. Chambers in his *William Shakespeare*, where he writes of *Love's Labour's Lost*: 'The versification is extremely adroit, and certainly not that of a beginner. I regard the play as the earliest of the lyrical group which includes *Midsummer Night's Dream*, *Romeo and Juliet*, and *Richard II*, and I put it in 1595' (i. 335).

There are verifiable grounds for bringing these four plays together and thinking of them as a separate group. They are not only lyrical, as Chambers says, but also their lyricism is evident in the extensive use they make of rhyme. No fewer than 43.1 per cent of the total lines in *Love's Labour's Lost* and 45.5 per cent of those in *A Midsummer Night's Dream* are rhymed. No other of Shakespeare's comedies comes anywhere near to approaching them in this respect. Their closest rival is *The Comedy of Errors*, with 21.5 per cent. Similarly, *Richard II* has far more rhymed verse—19.1 per cent—than any other of the history plays; and *Romeo and Juliet*, with 16.6 per cent, more than any other of the tragedies (the figures are taken from Harbage, p. 31).

Other links between the four plays reinforce the idea that they are connected with one another and belong to roughly the same stage in the playwright's career. Those connecting *Love's Labour's Lost* with *A Midsummer Night's Dream* are particularly strong, and do much to suggest that the latter play grew, to some extent, out of the former. Both contain a play-within-the-play, or rather, in the case of *Love's Labour's Lost*, shows-within-the-play, in their last acts. But, while the Masque of Muscovites and the Pageant of the Nine Worthies look like bits of improvisation on the part of the playwright, the 'tedious brief scene of young Pyramus | And his love Thisbe' has been carefully prepared for from the very opening of *A Midsummer Night's Dream.* Moreover, Shakespeare himself positively invites us to contrast these two comedies with one another. Near the end of *Love's Labour's Lost* Biron remarks: 'Our wooing doth not end like an old play: | Jack hath not Jill'; whereas Robin Goodfellow concludes the third act of *A Midsummer Night's Dream* with the words:

> Jack shall have Jill,
> Naught shall go ill,
> The man shall have his mare again, and all shall be well.

Whether or not 'Pyramus and Thisbe' is meant as a burlesque of *Romeo and Juliet*, the temptation to see it as one is strong; and there is a distinct possibility that Rosaline in *Love's Labour's Lost* grew out of the unseen presence, also called Rosaline, who haunts the opening scene of the tragedy. As for *Richard II*, its hero is as eloquent as Biron, puts his trust in words, as Biron does, and eventually discovers their inadequacy as a means of dealing with the practical difficulties of life.

Assuming, then, that the four plays are indeed a group, and that, as seems likely, either *Love's Labour's Lost* or *Romeo and Juliet* is the earliest of them, what light does this throw on the date when *Love's Labour's Lost* came into being? It seems to show that

all four had been produced by 1597, for in that year two of them—
Romeo and Juliet and *Richard II*—appeared in print, each bearing on
its title-page the statement that it had been publicly acted by
Shakespeare's company, and, in the case of *Romeo and Juliet*, 'often
(with great applause)', which almost certainly implies that it had
been in existence for some considerable time before that date.
Indeed, had that First Quarto been a legitimate publication, as the
First Quarto of *Richard II* was, printing a text obtained from the
company, it would be possible to say, with a fair measure of
certainty, that the play was considerably more than a year old.
Elizabethan acting companies did not normally allow their plays to
be printed until well after they had ceased to draw an audience.
The case of Ben Jonson is an interesting one in this connection, for
he, unlike most of his fellow-dramatists, saw to it that the printed
versions of his plays specified the year in which a particular drama
was first put on. Of the nine plays he wrote between 1598 and
1611, only *Catiline*, the last of them, came out in the same year as
that in which it was first staged; and it, significantly, had been a
complete flop. It seems reasonable, therefore, to think that the
group of Shakespeare's plays to which *Love's Labour's Lost* belongs
had been written by 1596 at the latest.

Is there, then, a date before which these four plays are unlikely
to have been written? There is such a date, and it is the spring of
1594, for it was not until then that the worst outbreak of plague
in the whole of Elizabeth's reign came to an end. It had begun in
August 1592, and had kept the theatres closed, except for brief
intervals, for the best part of two years. During this time acting
companies fell into disarray and broke up, while Shakespeare
himself devoted some at least of his energies to the writing of his
two narrative poems: *Venus and Adonis*, published in 1593, and
The Rape of Lucrece, published in 1594. With the end of the plague
came a time of reorganization and rebuilding in the acting
profession; and Shakespeare became a 'sharer' in a newly formed
company, the Lord Chamberlain's Men, as they were called, with
which he was to remain for the rest of his career. *Love's Labour's
Lost*, which frequently echoes both narrative poems, could well
have been one of the first plays he wrote for this new company;
and the date 1594–5 the likeliest for its composition.

An even more precise dating would be possible if only it could
be shown conclusively that Shakespeare was indebted to the

8. *Maroccus Extaticus*, a pamphlet celebrating the
many talents of Moth's 'dancing horse' (1.2.53),
was published in 1595, at roughly the same time
as the first performances of *Love's Labour's Lost*.

Gray's Inn Revels of Christmas 1594–5 for the idea of the Masque
of Muscovites in 5.2 of his comedy. On this particular occasion
the Revels were of an unusually elaborate kind; and the Lord
Chamberlain's Men were almost certainly involved in them. On
the night of 28 December the Lord of Misrule at Gray's Inn, or
Prince of Purpoole as he was called, received an 'Ambassador'
from the Inner Temple in what was evidently meant to be a scene
of mock-pageantry. However, as might be expected of ceremonies
presided over by a Lord of Misrule, things got out of hand. The
audience invaded the stage; and the 'Ambassador' left in a huff,
taking his train with him.

After their departure the throngs and tumults did somewhat cease,
although so much of them continued as was able to disorder and
confound any good inventions whatsoever. In regard whereof, as also for
that the sports intended were especially for gracing of the *Templarians*, it
was thought good not to offer any thing of account, saving dancing and
revelling with gentlewomen; and after such sports, a Comedy of Errors
(like to *Plautus* his *Menechmus*) was played by the players. So that night
was begun, and continued to the end, in nothing but confusion and
errors; whereupon, it was ever afterwards called, *The Night of Errors*.[1]

[1] *Gesta Grayorum 1688*, ed. W. W. Greg (Oxford, 1915), p. 22.

The comedy must have been *The Comedy of Errors*, and the 'players' of it the Lord Chamberlain's Men.

A few days later, on Twelfth Night, a further entertainment was put on. In it another 'Ambassador', purporting to come from 'the mighty Emperor of Russia and Muscovy', appeared on stage at Gray's Inn, 'in attire of Russia, accompanied with two or three of his own country, in like habit', to praise some English knights for having defeated some Bigarian and Negro-Tartars who had invaded the Emperor's dominions.[1] The likelihood of a connection between the Revels and *Love's Labour's Lost* becomes a near-certainty at this point, for when the men make their entrance in 5.2, disguised as Muscovites, they are preceded by '*blackamoors with music*'; but the question of who borrowed from whom still remains open, and there seems to be no way of arriving at a definite answer to it. Moreover, the Masque of Muscovites is simply an episode in the comedy, it does not provide the overall structure of it, and in this respect, as well as in its inconclusiveness, it is typical of the 'sources' that have been, at one time or another, suggested for the play.

It is, for instance, quite likely but far from certain that the initial idea of four young men withdrawing from the world for a time in order to study reached Shakespeare through Pierre de la Primaudaye's *L'Académie française*, first published in 1577, and translated into English by T. Bowes in 1586. Dedicating his work to Henry III of France, de la Primaudaye writes of four young gentlemen of Anjou who were placed under the tuition of a master in order that they might learn Latin, Greek, and, above all, 'the moral philosophy of ancient sages and wise men', thus becoming familiar with 'the doctrine of good living'. These young men do not, however, take any rash oaths; and, when their studies are interrupted, it is not by the appearance of ladies in their retreat, but by an outbreak of civil war (Bullough, i. 434–5).

In fact, no source in the proper sense of that word, i.e. a story or record of a series of events that corresponds with the main outlines of Shakespeare's plot, has been discovered, or seems likely to be. The latest attempt to suggest one, that by Glynne Wickham in his article '*Love's Labour's Lost* and *The Four Foster Children of Desire*, 1581',[2] falls down on two counts at least.

---

[1] Ibid., pp. 45–6.
[2] *Shakespeare Quarterly*, 36 (1985), 49–55.

There is nothing in the entertainment, put on in the tiltyard at Whitehall about fourteen years before the comedy was written, to correspond to the death of the King of France, which is the climactic event in Shakespeare's play. Furthermore, one cannot have it both ways. If, as Wickham argues, *Love's Labour's Lost* is the playwright's 'riposte to Sidney's strictures on "mongrel tragi-comedy" ', a deliberate and defiant mingling of kings and clowns, then it should, to be consistent, also make fun of the neo-classical unities of time and place, since the popular drama's complete disregard of them counted for at least as much in Sidney's attack on it as did its 'mongrel' nature. In fact, however, the comedy, either by accident or design, observes both these 'unities', and its doing so cannot be casually dismissed as mere 'lip-service'.

It is in perfect keeping with the general nature of this particular comedy, so preoccupied with the *cacoethes loquendi*, which it simultaneously indulges and holds up to ridicule, that the one source for it about which one can reasonably feel certain should account for no more than a name, and that the name of a minor character who, nevertheless, has a decisive effect on the play's outcome and whose importance for the whole is in inverse proportion to the size of his part—a mere twenty-eight words. Monsieur Marcadé, as J. M. Nosworthy[1] and Anne Barton[2] recognized and pointed out independently of each other, had his origins in a play by Robert Wilson, *The Cobbler's Prophecy*, first published in 1594 but probably composed several years earlier. Samuel Schoenbaum dates it *c.*1589–1594. In this comedy the god Mercury plays a large part; but Ralph the Cobbler, who has evidently not enjoyed the benefit of a grammar-school education, refers to him as 'Markedy' (lines 129, 169), 'Markedie' (lines 242, 652), and 'Merkedy' (line 1356).[3] 'Here then', writes Nosworthy, 'is the apparent source from which Shakespeare derived his name for a human *deus ex machina* who, at the same time, transparently fulfils two of the functions of the god Mercury—those of the messenger and psychopomp' (p. 109). But, while the debt to Wilson is there, it sheds no fresh light on the date of *Love's Labour's Lost*, since Shakespeare could well have

[1] 'The Importance of Being Marcade', *Shakespeare Survey* 32 (1979), 105–14.
[2] *The Times Literary Supplement*, 24 November 1978.
[3] Malone Society Reprint (Oxford, 1914).

seen a performance of *The Cobbler's Prophecy* long before its ap-pearance in print in 1594.

One large question remains: how far is *Love's Labour's Lost* a topical comedy, dealing with and reflecting on persons and events contemporary with it? In part at least it is. It stands alone among Shakespeare's plays in that some of the leading characters in it are, nominally at any rate, historical figures who were walking this earth at the time when it was written. The King is, in some respects, Henry of Navarre (1553–1610), who had become Henry IV of France on the assassination of Henry III in 1589 and had eventually, after a protracted struggle with the Catholic League and with Spain, made his own position secure and brought peace to a land that had been torn by religious wars ever since 1562 by abjuring Protestantism and becoming a Catholic in 1593. Even then, however, he had to wait another two years before the Pope finally lifted the sentence of excommunication which had been in force against him for the previous ten years. The fact that the King of Navarre in the play is called Ferdinand, not Henry, would in no way have hindered this identification by the original audiences, since the name Ferdinand never occurs in the dialogue, being found only in some of the stage directions and speech headings.

The King's fellow-students also had their counterparts in real life. The Duc de Longueville fought for the King during the later stages of the religious wars; and so did two Birons, father and son. Which of the two Shakespeare had in mind is not altogether clear. Armand de Gontaut, Baron de Biron, was killed in 1592, by which time he was sixty-eight years old, whereas his son Charles de Gontaut, Duc de Biron, was only thirty. If the play belongs to 1594–5, the son seems the more likely of them. Dumaine is the odd man out in this company, though he, like Henry himself, had already appeared, under precisely this name, on the English stage in Marlowe's *The Massacre at Paris* (1593). Historically he was Charles de Lorraine, Duc de Mayenne (1554–1611), who had taken over the leadership of the Catholic League after the assassination of his elder brother, Henry, Duc de Guise, in 1588. The most inveterate of Henry IV's opponents, he carried on the struggle until January 1596, when he at last made his peace with the King. The Dumaine of the play is and, equally evidently, is not de Mayenne. Similarly, the Princess of France is and is not

Marguerite de Valois, whom Henry married in 1572. Shallow, frivolous, and morally lax, Marguerite was almost the obverse of Shakespeare's Princess; and her marriage to Henry was one of convenience not of affection and esteem.

In *Love's Labour's Lost* there is not so much as a hint of the horrors and the savagery of the religious wars. Set in a sunlit park, the only war it dramatizes is that of the sexes. There is something of the pastoral about it all, including the intrusion of the *memento mori*, with its message *et ego in Arcadia vixi*, represented by Monsieur Marcadé. Yet the action it deals with has its historical side. Most of Henry IV's life was spent in warfare and business of state. He was already serving as a soldier and taking part in battles at the tender age of fourteen. Nevertheless, he did enjoy one holiday. In 1576, after spending the four years that followed the St. Bartholomew's Day massacre of 1572 as a virtual prisoner at the French court in Paris, he escaped and made his way back to south-western France and Navarre. And there, in 1578, he was visited at his ancestral home of Nérac by Marguerite, from whom he had been separated for the best part of three years. At Nérac Henry, who resumed conjugal relations with his wife for a time, passed his days in hunting, playing tennis, paying visits, and pursuing women. The vows he makes at the opening of Shakespeare's play—'Not to see ladies, study, fast, not sleep'— would have met with nothing but derision from him. Marguerite brought with her not only her mother Catherine de Medici but also, knowing her husband's tastes and proclivities, a train of beautiful young women, including a former mistress of his with whom he renewed his relationship and the fair Victoria d'Ayole Dayolle, whom he soon made his mistress. Marguerite did not mind, since the arrangement left her free to enjoy herself with young men of her own choice. In fact, as Lord Russell of Liverpool puts it, 'the royal couple lived their own lives and had their own lovers and mistresses, and there was no secret about it'.[1] In the evenings there was dancing and performances of Italian comedies. In 1582, however, Marguerite returned to the court in Paris; and soon thereafter Henry had to resume his campaigning.

It seems likely that the festive atmosphere of life at Nérac— even though Shakespeare could only have learned about it

---

[1] *Henry of Navarre* (1969), p. 58.

through gossip and rumour—contributed something to the festive nature of his comedy, which can be seen as a delicate, glancing comment on that life. Nor would an Elizabethan audience in the mid-1590s have missed the parallel between the men's perjuries in the play and Henry IV's abjuring of Protestantism in 1593, an action that came in for some harsh censure in England, where he had hitherto been regarded as something of a hero, and from which he had received a measure of support in the shape of military forces as well as money.

But, while Shakespeare positively invites his audience to identify the King and his three courtiers with living figures by the names he gives them, this cannot be said about the characters in his sub-plot, where the names are patently fictional. Nevertheless, this fact has not deterred scholars and critics from making erudite guesses and even assertions. As early as 1747 William Warburton wrote: 'By Holofernes is designed a particular character, a pedant and schoolmaster of our author's time, one John Florio, a teacher of the Italian tongue in London' (Furness, p. 351). Warburton's description of Florio is deliberately slanted to make the identification fit. Florio was indeed a schoolmaster, in the sense that he taught Italian, but far from being a pedant, he was a man of great distinction, the author of, among other things, an Italian–English dictionary, entitled *A World of Words*, published in 1598, and the translator of Montaigne's *Essays*, which came out in 1603. Enjoying the patronage of men such as the Earl of Pembroke and the Earl of Southampton, and eventually becoming tutor to Prince Henry, the son of James I, Florio is a far cry indeed from Shakespeare's country dominie, who is, according to Warburton, a satirical portrait of him. Doctor Johnson was 'inclined to doubt' the whole idea, as were many others, but once started speculation continued throughout the eighteenth and the greater part of the nineteenth century, until, in 1884, it reached the heights of irresponsible absurdity in F. G. Fleay's article 'Shakespeare and Puritanism'.[1] Fleay dismissed Warburton's identification as a 'crude theory' deserving 'no consideration', but then proceeded to add: 'it does not follow that there is no truth in the notion that he [Holofernes] represents somebody. If he does, however, the whole group to which he belongs must also be

[1] *Anglia*, 7 (1884), 223–31.

personal portraits' (Furness, p. 7). Thinking, as most critics did at the time, that *Love's Labour's Lost* was written in 1590, Fleay had looked around for a suitable historical event with which to connect it, and had, he thought, found it in the Martin Marprelate controversy of 1588–90. Holding that Shakespeare at this stage in his career was on the side of Martin and the Puritans, Fleay identified the characters of the sub-plot with those who wrote against Martin or acted in plays attacking him. Armado becomes a caricature of John Lyly; Holofernes of Thomas Cooper, the Bishop of Winchester; Sir Nathaniel of Robert Greene; Costard of the actor William Kempe; Moth of Thomas Nashe; and Anthony Dull of Anthony Munday. Jaquenetta, however, true to her character, proved more than a match even for Fleay's misplaced ingenuity, so he quietly ignored her.

Fleay's wild guessing had at least one salutary effect: it put an end for a time to the merry game of unmasking the characters; but not for good and all. In 1923, nearly forty years after the appearance of his article, Sir Arthur Quiller-Couch and John Dover Wilson published their Cambridge edition of the play, and in their Introduction to it, after asserting confidently and twice over their conviction that *Love's Labour's Lost* was written 'as a *topical* play' (pp. xvi and xviii), they continued thus:

if the Marprelate Controversy be extended over the dispute between Gabriel Harvey and Thomas Nashe, which grew out of it, Fleay's general aim was perhaps not wholly wide, and one of his arrows (we are convinced) hit the mark. 'Is not Moth,' he asks, 'Thomas Nashe, "the young juvenal," the tender boy, the ready pamphleteer, the sarcastic satirist?' To this we answer, 'Yes, and almost beyond a doubt.' (p. xx)

Wilson still maintained this position in the Preface to his second edition, published in 1962 (p. xiii); so it seems worth while to examine the 'proofs' he and Quiller-Couch originally offered for their assertion. First, they quote Moth's speech at 3.1.10–23, which, they say, is in Nashe's manner. So it is, especially in its sustained use of reductive comparisons and its headlong pace; but the passage remains an isolated one; Moth never speaks in this vein again or at this length. His normal mode of discourse is made up of sharp questions and quick answers. As further evidence the two editors point to the dialogue that opens 1.2, in which Armado addresses his page as 'my tender Juvenal', and

Moth retorts by addressing him as 'my tough señor', thus leading in to a 'set of wit' in which the two phrases are bandied to and fro. Of this they say:

Now some have disputed that Nashe is the 'young Iuuenall, that byting Satyrist' referred to by Greene in the famous passage of *A Groatsworth of Wit* (1592) wherein he warns his fellow-dramatists against the 'Upstart Crow': but there can be no question that Meres hails him as 'sweet Tom,' and 'gallant young Juvenal' in his *Wit's Treasurie* (1598) ... The epithet 'tender', moreover, is not to be overlooked. Neshe was a recognized variant of the surname Nashe, and 'nesh' or 'nash' at that time = 'soft, delicate, pitiful, tender.' (p. xxii)

To this they add: 'Puns upon "purse", "pen", "penny" obtrude themselves throughout the play when Moth is assailed or retorts: all of them meaningless (so far as we can discover) unless referable to Nashe's *Pierce (i.q. Purse) Penilesse.*' Then comes the 'clue' provided by Hercules' killing of 'Cerberus, that three-headed Canis', which they interpret as a reference to 'Nashe's prowess in 1589 against the three-headed Martin—Martin Marprelate, Martin Senior and Martin Junior' (p. xxiii). And, finally, to clinch the argument comes 'the discovery ... that "Moth" is, by Elizabethan spelling, just Nashe's familiar Christian name reversed.'

It is all very erudite and ingenious, no doubt, but what has it to do with *Love's Labour's Lost*, a play written for a theatre audience in the mid-1590s, not for a group of scholars spending their days in the British Museum in the 1920s? Greene's pamphlet is 'famous'—or 'infamous'—now for its attack on Shakespeare, the first reference we have to him as a dramatist, and it did cause something of a stir in its own day. But that stir seems to have been short-lived. Published first in 1592, the pamphlet did not go into a second edition until 1596, which means that probably not more than 500 copies of it were in circulation when Shakespeare wrote his play.[1] The likelihood that any significant number of people in the earliest audiences would be reminded of Greene's advice to Nashe is, therefore, small. Nor is there any good reason for thinking that a theatre-goer of the day would say 'Nashe' on hearing the word 'tender' applied to Moth. In fact, Nashe, as his

[1] See Edwin H. Miller, *The Professional Writer in Elizabethan England* (Cambridge, Mass., 1959), p. 155.

opponents were quickly made to realize, was anything but tender. As for the 'Puns upon "purse", "pen", "penny" [that] obtrude themselves ... when Moth is assailed or retorts', 'purse' occurs once only (5.1.66) with no punning intent that I can see, while 'pierced' and 'piercing' (4.2.81–5) belong to a scene in which Moth has no part. 'Pen(s)' are more plentiful, but again I see no punning on them, nor do I find any in the three uses of 'penny' (3.1.25, 135; and 5.1.63). Moreover, if the statement were true, which it patently is not, it would prove nothing. Proverbs about purses and pennies were part of the small change of daily intercourse in Shakespeare's England. Still less likely is it that anyone would have exclaimed 'Martin!' on hearing of the 'three-headed Canis', or thought of Thom spelled (more or less) backwards at a mention of Moth.

Plays do not work in the way the Cambridge editors seem to have imagined. There is, as it happens, a trilogy in which Nashe does appear. The work of an anonymous author, it was written for a special audience, the students of Cambridge University in general and of St. John's College in particular, Nashe's own college. There the first play, *The Pilgrimage to Parnassus*, was put on at Christmas 1598–9; the second, *The First Part of the Return from Parnassus*, at Christmas 1599–1600; and the third, *The Second Part of the Return from Parnassus* at Christmas 1601–2, and again at Christmas 1602–3. One of the leading characters in it, Ingenioso, who appears in all three parts, was identified with Nashe by Fleay as long ago as 1891.[1] Characteristically Fleay offered little evidence. There is, however, no shortage of it, and it is set out in detail by the play's most recent editor, J. B. Leishman, who devotes nine pages of his Introduction to it.[2] It is essentially of two kinds:

firstly, the fact that much that we hear of and from Ingenioso corresponds very closely with the known facts of Nashe's life; secondly, the fact that the author of the Parnassus Plays reveals a very close acquaintance with his writings, modelling ... numerous passages upon them, and sometimes borrowing from them whole phrases, a large number of which he puts in the mouth of Ingenioso. (p. 72)

Leishman's identification of Ingenioso with Nashe is a solid structure on a firm foundation. Compared with it, the Cambridge

---

[1] *A Biographical Chronicle of the English Drama*, 2 vols. (1891), ii. 348.

[2] *The Three Parnassus Plays* (1949).

editors' identification of Moth with Nashe has no more foundation than the proverbial castle in the air.

They have an even more insubstantial foundation for their
main and very influential contention to which their suggested
Moth–Nashe connection is but a prelude. It consists of four words
only, which are, as they print them, 'the School of Night'. They
occur in the great climactic scene 4.3, and they are spoken by the
King. Biron has been rhapsodizing about Rosaline's dark beauty
and has concluded his speech with the following words, quoted
here in the spelling and punctuation of the Quarto:

> O who can giue an oth? Where is a booke?
> That I may sweare Beautie doth beautie lacke,
> If that she learne not of her eye to looke:
> No face is fayre that is not full so blacke.

Outraged by this piece of sophistry, the King retorts:

> O paradox, Blacke is the badge of Hell,
> The hue of dungions, and the Schoole of night ...
>
> (4.3.247–52)

Many editors ever since the time of Theobald had been troubled
by the word 'Schoole' in this context and had sought to emend it
in various ways, none of them really convincing. Quiller-Couch
and Dover Wilson, however, let it stand because they thought it
'not only right but illuminating' (p. xxix), provided that the
punctuation of the relevant lines was altered and the word 'night'
given an initial capital. So in their edition the two lines read:

> O paradox! Black is the badge of hell,
> The hue of dungeons and the School of Night.

The King's three parallel statements have been reduced to two,
with the second of them now meaning 'Black is the hue of
dungeons and (also the hue of) the School of Night'. The
troublesome 'Black is ... the school of night' has been eliminated,
provided, that is, that there was something called 'the School of
Night'. Quiller-Couch and Dover Wilson were convinced that
there was. Adopting a theory first set out by Arthur Acheson in
his *Shakespeare and the Rival Poet* (1903), they agreed with him
'that a School of Night really existed, that Chapman's *Shadow of
Night* (1594) was a product of this School, and that the Academe

of Navarre is Shakespeare's satire upon it' (p. xxx). Their grounds for doing so, even though no other reference to 'the School of Night' has ever been found, amount to this: that there was what the Jesuit Robert Parsons, writing in 1592, had dubbed 'Sir Walter Ralegh's school of atheism', a group of men deeply interested in mathematics, astronomy, and unorthodox speculation. As well as Ralegh, who was its leader, it included George Chapman, the Earl of Derby, the Earl of Northumberland, Sir George Carey, Matthew Roydon, Thomas Harriot the famous mathematician, and, possibly, Christopher Marlowe. Opposed to this group, the Cambridge editors hypothesize, was another that included Shakespeare's patron the Earl of Southampton, Southampton's friend the Earl of Essex, and, of course, Shakespeare himself. Whereas the first group was devoted to abstract and arcane ideas and set a high value on the study of books, the second favoured common sense and natural behaviour. Biron sums up the essential opposition for us when he dismisses close study as 'leaden contemplation' and states his preference for a doctrine derived 'from women's eyes'.

How an audience could possibly have gathered all this from a single mention of 'the school of night' is something the Cambridge editors do not explain. Nevertheless, the notion was widely accepted among scholars, especially after it had been developed in much greater detail and with far more circumspection by Frances A. Yates in her *A Study of 'Love's Labour's Lost'* (Cambridge, 1936), and held the field until 1941, when it was decisively challenged by E. A. Strathman. Engaged at the time on his very important work *Sir Walter Ralegh: A Study in Elizabethan Skepticism*,[1] Strathman published some interim findings in the form of an article entitled 'The Textual Evidence for "The School of Night" '.[2] In it, after meticulously examining the evidence used by the Cambridge editors, he concludes thus:

That Chapman's *Shadow of Night* and the speeches of Berowne present contrasting philosophies is true; that Ralegh and Northumberland were patrons of scientific learning is true; that the Ralegh coterie was accused of unorthodox beliefs is true. But there is no independent evidence ... to establish the Q reading 'Schoole of night' as an allusion to Ralegh and his associates. (p. 186)

[1] New York, 1951.
[2] *Modern Language Notes*, 56 (1941), 176–86.

The final blow to the whole tottering edifice of conjecture and speculation came in 1956 when C. J. Sisson pointed out that 'a plain sense resides in the original [reading], which in fact offers no crux. *Black is the school of night,* in the sense that night is the scholar or pupil of blackness, darkness ...'[1] It might be added that the idea of student and teacher lying behind the statement has already been adumbrated in Biron's assertion: 'beauty doth beauty lack, | If that she [beauty] learn not of her [Rosaline's] eye to look' (4.3.248–9), and is repeated and endorsed when he refers to the ladies as 'beauty's tutors' (4.3.298).

The Text

The earliest text we have of *Love's Labour's Lost* is a quarto of 1598, henceforward referred to as Q, of which fourteen copies have survived.[2] Its title-page, reproduced here in facsimile, is of considerable interest on several scores. First, the description of the play that it offers is a remarkably accurate one, for the most distinctive feature of this comedy is precisely its 'pleasant conceited', meaning 'delightfully clever and witty', quality. Secondly, the title-page carries Shakespeare's name, something none of his plays published before it does; and, thirdly, it makes two further statements, both designed to catch the prospective purchaser's interest and attention: one of them, if taken literally, patently untrue, and the other tantalizingly unverifiable. The text of Q cannot be a faithful version of the comedy 'As it was presented before her Highnes | this last Christmas', because it is, as it stands, unactable; and if the words 'Newly corrected and augmented' are intended to imply, as many scholars think they are, that there had been an earlier and, perhaps, inferior quarto, as they undoubtedly do on the title-page of the Second Quarto of *Romeo and Juliet* (1599), which claims its text to be '*Newly corrected, augmented, and | amended*', they can neither be completely verified nor completely refuted, since no copy of any such quarto has ever come to light.

Q is unactable for a number of reasons. First, it is plagued by a superfluity and confusion of names. Of its twenty characters, only

---

[1] *New Readings in Shakespeare* (Cambridge, 1956), p. 115.

[2] Their locations are given by Paul Werstine in his 'Variants in the First Quarto of *Love's Labor's Lost*', *Shakespeare Studies*, 12 (1979), 35–47.

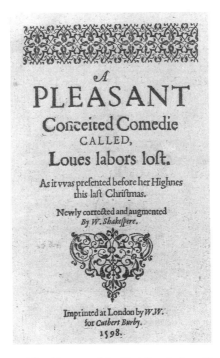

A

PLEASANT

Conceited Comedie
CALLED,

Loues labors lost.

As it vvas presented before her Highnes
this last Christmas.

Newly corrected and augmented
By *W. Shakespere.*

Imprinted at London by *W.W.*
for *Cutbert Burby.*
1598.

9. The title-page of the First Quarto (1598).

six—Longueville, Dumaine, Biron, Boyet, the Forester, and Marcadé—have each a single consistent speech-prefix for their parts. The others come on, speak their lines, and go off again under various names and titles. The King, for instance, makes his initial entry at the play's opening as 'Ferdinand K. of Nauar'; and his first speech is headed '*Ferdinand.*' After that he is '*Ferd.*' or '*Fer.*' for the rest of the scene. On his next appearance, however, at 2.1.89.1, he is '*Nauar.*', and, for his subsequent speeches, '*Nauar.*' or '*Nau.*', until, at line 127, he suddenly becomes '*Ferd.*' once more and remains so up to his exit line which is headed '*Nau.*' He is not seen again until 4.3, where, at line 19.2, the direction reads: '*The King entreth*'. His first words are headed '*King.*'; and '*King.*' or '*Kin.*' he then continues to be to the end of the play. There are also, it is worth noting, four occasions in the first two acts when other characters refer to him as 'the Duke'. In similar fashion the Princess is '*Princesse*' when she makes her initial entrance at the beginning of 2.1; but her first speech is headed '*Queene.*', a title that is not properly hers until she hears the news of her father's death in 5.2. For her second speech in 2.1 she becomes '*Prince.*', and thereafter, to the end of the scene, her speech-prefixes are abbreviations of '*Princesse*'. It is under this title that she comes on at the opening of 4.1; but the first speech she makes after doing so is prefixed '*Quee.*', and '*Queen.*' or '*Quee.*' she remains for the rest of the play, except at 5.2.552, where her speech thanking Costard for his performance in the role of Pompey is headed '*Lady.*' Even such minor figures as Dull and Jaquenetta enjoy the luxury of two other names apiece in stage directions and speech-prefixes: he is also '*Anthonie*' and '*Constable*', while she is also '*Maid*' and '*Wench*'.

Such variations in nomenclature as these are, of course, common enough in a dramatist's early drafts, where he is naturally more concerned with a character's relation to others on stage than with that character's often arbitrary personal name, and they strongly suggest that Q represents the play in a pre-performance state, before the speech-prefixes and the like had been regularized by the bookkeeper. Confirmation that such is indeed the case is provided by a characteristic feature of the stage directions noted and documented by W. W. Greg. 'Everywhere', he writes, 'they illustrate the author's uncertainty how to describe his characters and, particularly in the last act, his vague definition of groups' (*SFF*, p. 221). Typical examples of the phenomenon he has in mind, all culled from the final scene, are the following: '*Enter the Ladyes*' (5.2.0.1); '*Enter the King and the rest*' (l. 309.1); '*Enter the Ladies*' (l. 336.1); and '*Enter all*' (l. 871.1), where '*all*' must mean 'all those members of the cast who are not already on stage'.

This multiplicity of names would not, of course, in itself make the play impossible to stage. Moth, for example, should have no difficulty in answering to the call '*Boy*' as well as the call '*Page*'; but things would obviously run more smoothly if he had but one of them to keep in mind. It is the confusion of names that is really damaging. It appears in its simplest and most readily explicable form at 5.2.242–55, a 'set of wit' in which the players are Katherine and Longueville. There can be no question about their identity, since their duologue begins at a point where the three other mismatched couples—Rosaline and the King, the Princess and Biron, and Maria and Dumaine—having played their 'sets', are all busy talking to one another. Nevertheless, every one of Katherine's speeches has the prefix, either in full or abbreviated, of '*Maria*.' The mistake cannot be the compositor's. There is no likelihood of a manuscript '*Kath*.' being read as '*Maria*.'. The error must, therefore, be the author's. Shakespeare has allowed his pairing of Longueville and Maria, which is right for the rest of the play, to obscure the fact that at this point Longueville is speaking, not to Maria, but to Katherine disguised as Maria. It is a mistake which can easily be corrected, but it must be put right before the play can be staged.

Much more serious is the muddle in 2.1 over the names of two of the ladies in attendance on the Princess. When they first speak, all three of the ladies do so as nameless numbers. 1. *Lady* gives an admiring character sketch of Longueville, whom she met at a 'marriage feast' celebrating the union of 'L. *Perigort* and the bewtious heire | of *Jaques Fauconbridge*'; 2. *Lady* does the same thing for Dumaine, whom she saw 'at the Duke *Alansoes* [Alençon's] once'; and 3. *Lady* for Biron, who was with Dumaine on that occasion.

At this point the King and his three courtiers appear; and the Princess wastes no time in making it amply clear that she is highly displeased by the King's decision to lodge her and her ladies 'in the field'. She then goes on to present him with a letter from her father that is, we later discover, both long and complicated; and in order to give Navarre at least a token time in which to read and digest it Shakespeare has Biron make advances to one of the attendant ladies, whose speech-prefix is '*Kather*.' or '*Kath*.', in an attempt to establish her identity as someone he danced with 'in *Brabant* once'. She, however, skilfully parries his probes until, thwarted in his efforts, he gives up. As this encounter ends, the King and the Princess spend the next fifty lines or so in arguing about the rather tiresome business of Aquitaine; and, when they have done, the King makes his exit, which is clearly marked, and presumably takes Dumaine with him, for some twelve lines later that character is required to enter. It also looks as though Longueville too leaves. Biron, however, remains on stage to take part in a duologue with a lady whose speech-prefix is '*Ros*.' Like his earlier exchanges with Katherine, these are made up of stichomythic thrust and parry that begins as prose but then slips into three-beat couplets. In fact, this set of wit looks like a continuation of the previous one, except for the difference in the lady's name. It concludes with Biron making his exit. A piece of formal patterning of the kind so frequent in this comedy follows. No sooner has Biron gone than Dumaine returns to ask Boyet: 'What Ladie is that same?' To this Boyet replies: 'The heire of *Alanson*, *Rosalin* her name', thus equating her with '2. *Lady*.' Satisfied, Dumaine goes off. He is immediately succeeded by Longueville enquiring about the name of another Lady whom he refers to as 'she in the white'. Some verbal sparring ensues, but eventually Boyet replies: 'She is an heire of *Falconbridge*', i.e. '1. *Lady*.', or, as she will be named at line 213, '*Lady Maria*.'. Finally, to complete the sequence, Biron comes back to put his query: 'Whats her name in the capp?', to which Boyet answers: '*Katherin* by good happ.'

All now seems clear, or nearly so. '1. *Lady*.', acquainted with Longueville, is Maria; '2. *Lady*.', acquainted with Dumaine, is Rosaline; and '3. *Lady*.', acquainted with Biron, is Katherine. But we are left with the awkward question of why the lady whom Biron addresses in his second battle of wits with a woman, which reads so much like a continuation of his first, should be called Rosaline not Katherine. It looks as though the playwright is dithering over the two names; and confirmation that such is indeed the case is provided by what follows. After Biron has gone the next speaker is '*Lady Maria*.', and at line 217 '*Lady Ka*.' joins in, but then for the rest of the scene the three personal names disappear completely and are replaced by such indeterminate prefixes as '*La*.', '*Lad*.', '*Lad*. 2', and '*Lad*. 3.' Then, at 3.1.161, Biron entrusts Costard with the delivery of a letter addressed to Rosaline. After that there is no more confusion of the two names Rosaline and Katherine. Shakespeare has at last made up his mind. Beginning by thinking, perhaps, that the name of the heroine of *The Taming of the Shrew* would be the right name for a woman capable of holding her own with Biron, he then allows Rosaline, the name of the 'pale hard-hearted wench' with the black eyes in *Romeo and Juliet* (2.3.4 and 13), to take over for a few moments at 179–90, and then completely at 3.1.161. Having settled the matter, he presses on with his play, leaving the tidying-up to be done in a fair copy which has, by this time, become indispensable.

This seems the simplest and most likely solution to the

problem and therefore dictates the course followed in this edition, where 'Rosaline' replaces 'Katherine' at 114–25 and 208 and 'Katherine' replaces 'Rosaline' at 193. But there are other ways of dealing with the 'tangle', as it has often been called. Dover Wilson, building on a suggestion by Capell, and on an elaboration of that suggestion by H. B. Charlton,[1] takes the view that Shakespeare initially intended the three ladies to wear masks— the Katherine of Q certainly has one, whether she is wearing it or not, at 122–3—but then, to avoid anticipating the use of mistaken identities in 5.2, dropped the idea and with it both the duologue between Biron and Katherine at 113–26 and that between Biron and Rosaline at 178–91. However, the compositor failed to recognize his cancellation marks and so printed what he should have suppressed. There are at least two difficulties in the way of accepting this explanation: first, there is no direction for the ladies to mask; and, secondly, there is nothing in the form of action or dialogue to cover the King's perusal of the letter.

John Kerrigan's treatment of the crux comes nearer to that adopted in this edition.[2] He holds that Shakespeare in his first draft wrote the exchanges between Biron and Katherine because at this stage he meant to pair the two of them. Then, having decided that Rosaline would, after all, be a better name for Biron's love, he wrote the second duologue on a separate sheet of paper to take the place of the first. The compositor, however, printed both, instead of replacing the first with the second as he should have done. In keeping with this hypothesis, Kerrigan prints the second duologue where the first stands in Q, and relegates the first to the commentary. This procedure effectively disposes of the business of masking but also creates difficulties of its own. The symmetry, so evident in exchanges between Biron and a lady while the King reads the letter and further exchanges between Biron and a lady after the meeting between the King and the Princess is over, is destroyed. Moreover, Kerrigan leaves himself with some awkward stage business: he has to give Dumaine an exit along with the King in order to bring him back on stage immediately.

Stanley Wells, in his edition of the play for the *Complete Oxford*

---

[1] *Love's Labour's Lost*, ed. John Dover Wilson and Sir Arthur Quiller-Couch (Cambridge, 1923), p. 119.

[2] 'Shakespeare at Work: The Katherine–Rosaline Tangle in *Love's Labour's Lost*' *RES*, NS 33 (1982), 129–36.

Shakespeare, takes much the same line about the issue as does this edition, which is much indebted to his, but with some important differences in the way of explanation. He thinks that 'in writing the lines as they stand in Q, Shakespeare paired Biron with Katherine and at a later stage, having decided on a change of name, altered the prefix correctly at [180–93], but failed to make the necessary changes elsewhere' (*TC*, p. 271). It is, of course, possible that this is what happened, but it seems unlikely. Revision and a failure to revise make awkward bedfellows. As an alternative to this theory he goes on to suggest that 'the second duologue may be a later addition composed to give further prominence to Biron and Rosaline after Shakespeare had made his final decision about her name' (ibid.). This also could be true; but symmetry is such a marked feature of the play that two matching duologues could well have been part of its original structure. On the whole, then, the notion of authorial havering over the two names accounts for more than any other hypothesis and accounts for it more readily and economically.

Further troubles with nomenclature are still to come. There is a very bad muddle in 4.2, and again at one point in 5.1, over the names of the Curate and the Schoolmaster. They make their first entrance at the opening of 4.2, where the stage direction reads: 'Enter *Dull*, *Holofernes*, the *Pedant* and *Nathaniel*', an ambiguous statement in itself, since it is not clear whether it covers four characters or only three. In fact, it covers three because Holofernes and the Pedant are one and the same. There is some slight irregularity in the speech-prefixes to begin with. Nathaniel, the first to speak, does so as '*Nat.*'; but his second speech is headed '*Curat Nath.*'; and Holofernes says his first line as '*Ped.*' After that, however, all is plain sailing up to line 64, with the speeches of the three characters involved headed '*Holo.*', '*Nath.*', and '*Dul.*' respectively. Then, suddenly and for no apparent reason, everything goes wrong. At line 65 a speech that clearly belongs to Holofernes is headed '*Nath.*', while the reply to it, which should be Nathaniel's, is headed '*Holo.*' From this point onwards, for the next eighty lines or so, every speech assigned to Nathaniel really belongs to Holofernes and *vice versa*. But there are also two speeches by the Schoolmaster which carry the prefixes '*Pedan.*' and '*Ped.*'; and in both cases (118–19 and 134–40) the assignment is correct. There are, moreover, other curious irregularities and puzzles. At line 104, where the Curate starts to read Biron's sonnet, there is no speech-prefix at all, though one is badly needed; and, when the reading is over, the Schoolmaster, now speaking as '*Pedan.*', makes a two-line comment on it which is rightfully and properly his, but then loses his next seven lines to '*Nath.*' Furthermore, at line 120, where the prefix is '*Ped.*', he actually addresses Nathaniel as 'Sir *Holofernes*', something he will do again at 5.1.107. It is not until line 146 that the scene gets back on course through a series of exchanges in which the Schoolmaster is consistently '*Ped.*' or '*Peda.*' and properly addresses the Curate as 'Sir *Nathaniel*' (l. 148).

The simplest and, in many ways, the most attractive solution to the puzzle is Gary Taylor's. He thinks 'that as Shakespeare composed the second half of his play he became muddled about the clergyman's and schoolmaster's names and, to make things easier for himself, used occupational names instead' (Kerrigan, p. 192). This suggestion works perfectly for 5.1 and 5.2, where the speech-prefixes for Holofernes and Nathaniel are rightly and consistently *Pedant* and *Curate* respectively; but it does not explain how Shakespeare could suddenly become confused about the personal names of the two characters roughly one third of the way through 4.2 after using them quite correctly up to that point. At least it does not do so for those who think of Shakespeare as a playwright who did his composing while sitting in his study, if he ever had one, and who looked back carefully over what he had written already. It might well have happened, however, that having written the first third of 4.2, he realized how best to continue the scene while he was away from his lodgings in London, touring somewhere in the provinces perhaps, reached for the nearest sheet of paper, and jotted the continuation down, caring little whether he had the names right or wrong, since he knew any necessary adjustment could be made in the fair copy.

The confusion of names is not the only confusion in the relevant part of 4.2. Two of Jaquenetta's speeches in it cannot be reconciled with one another. At line 88 she asks the Curate, whom she addresses as 'Good M. Parson', to 'be so good as read me this letter, it was geuen me by *Costard*, and sent me from *Don Armatho*'. Later, however, when the Schoolmaster asks her: 'Was this directed to you?', she replies: 'I sir from one mounsier *Berowne*, one of the strange Queenes Lordes' (128–9). This answer is, as it stands and where it stands, sheer nonsense. It not only contradicts her previous statement but is also badly astray in its description of Biron. It looks, in fact, like a garbled version of Holofernes' comment in the next speech, where he says: 'this *Berowne* is one of the Votaries with the King, and here he hath framed a letter to a sequent of the stranger Queenes' (134–6). It would be in keeping with the general character of Q for Shakespeare to have written Jaquenetta's speech as it stands, then to have recognized its inconsistency with her earlier answer and cancelled the words after 'I sir' with a marking unknown to the compositor, who, consequently, left them standing.

That possibility is made all the likelier by what can now be regarded as a fortunate and enlightening accident: at least two passages in the play are duplicated. First in 4.3, and then again in 5.2, what is evidently a false start is followed, immediately in the first case and fifteen lines later in the second, by a revised and much expanded version of the same matter, which is, in both instances, manifestly superior to the first shot. The writing of the new versions should have led, of course, to the deletion of the false starts; but, either because Shakespeare in the heat of composition failed to mark them for deletion, or because he used for that purpose theatrical markings familiar to the bookkeeper but not to the compositor, they survived, and are to be found in Appendix A to this edition. They have their own peculiar fascination, since a comparison between them and the final versions enables us to observe Shakespeare at work, changing his mind, and changing it for the better, charging Biron's initial praise of women's eyes with mythological matter that transforms it into a glowing hymn to Love, and converting five rather tame lines, in which Rosaline lays down the conditions on which she will accept Biron, into a much more detailed and harsher sentence moved into a position where it ceases to be a mere item in a list of such conditions and becomes, instead, a fitting and powerful climax to that list.

All the features of Q dealt with so far not only make it unactable but also point unequivocally in one direction—to the author's foul papers as the 'copy' from which it was set up. So do the strange and unusual spellings with which it is replete, and which led Dover Wilson to describe it as 'a mine for students of Shakespearian spelling' and to compile 'a brief list of the archaic and peculiar forms' to be found in it (p. 103). Some of his examples do not, it should be pointed out, stand up to a close scrutiny. The form 'bed-red' (1.1.137), for instance, is not only older than 'bed-rid', which has now displaced it, but persisted, according to *OED*, into the eighteenth century, while 'deus' (1.2.46) for 'deuce' was still current in the nineteenth. Other seemingly odd spellings look more like compositorial errors than authorial idiosyncrasies: 'dooters', i.e. 'doters', at 4.3.257, is probably the result of a misreading of 'doaters'; and 'rayse' (4.3.26) could well come from a transposition by the compositor of the last two letters in 'rayes'. All the same, there is a considerable residue of what might fittingly be called 'racked ortagriphie' (5.1.19); and it can be added to. Very strange indeed, for example, are 'abhortive' (1.1.104) and 'mouce' (5.2.19), spellings not recognized at all by *OED* because in the Folio text of the play, on which it relies, they have already been corrected to 'abortive' and 'mouse'. Moreover, at least one word in Wilson's list, 'annothanize' (4.1.67), which he regards as a partial misprint of 'anothomize', found at Q *2 Henry IV*, Ind.21, could well be a Shakespearian coinage, combining the senses of 'anatomize', i.e. 'analyse', and 'annote', i.e. 'explain', a word not used elsewhere by Shakespeare himself but current in his day.

So far, then, the case for authorial foul papers as the 'copy' from which Q was set seems a wholly convincing one. There is, however, a large obstacle in the way of its acceptance: the four words 'Newly corrected and augmented' which appear on its title-page. Five other plays by Shakespeare came out in quartos that carried some such statement on their title-pages: *Romeo and Juliet* Q2 (1599), 'Newly corrected, augmented, and amended'; *1 Henry IV* Q2 (1599), 'Newly corrected'; *Richard III* Q3 (1602), 'Newly augmented'; *Hamlet* Q2 (1604–5), 'Newly imprinted and enlarged to almost as much againe as it was, according to the true and perfect Coppie'; and the two-part play of *The Whole Contention* Q3 (1619), 'newly corrected and enlarged'. But, though they look similar, these claims, when examined, vary greatly in their validity, ranging from the blatantly misleading to the almost mathematically accurate. At one end of the scale, *Richard III* Q3, purporting to be 'Newly augmented', has no augmentation whatsoever. It is simply a reprint of Q2 (1598), which is, in its turn, a reprint of Q1 (1597). At the other, *Hamlet*

Q2 is indeed nearly twice as long as *Hamlet* Q1 (1603). In fact, 'Newly corrected and augmented', or 'enlarged', seems to have been a rather elastic formula, but a formula used only in connection with plays that had already appeared in print, irrespective of whether that earlier appearance had been as a good quarto, like *1 Henry IV* Q1 (1597), as a 'goodish' quarto, like *Richard III* Q1 (1597), or as a bad quarto, like *Romeo and Juliet* Q1 (1597) and *Hamlet* Q1 (1603). It may, therefore, reasonably be assumed that, even though so far as we know, no copy of it has survived, there had been an edition of *Love's Labour's Lost* prior to the publication of the quarto of 1598.

In these circumstances, we do not and cannot know for a certainty whether the lost quarto was good or bad. However, most scholars, following the lead given by A. W. Pollard in 1909,[1] have inclined to the latter alternative, for three reasons: first, Q *Love's Labour's Lost* and *Romeo and Juliet* do resemble one another in the claims they make on their title-pages; secondly, neither of them was entered on the Stationers' Register; and, thirdly, both came from the house of the same publisher. Nevertheless, their case is not so strong as it looks at first sight. There is what could well be a significant difference between the wording on the title-page of *Romeo and Juliet* Q2 and that on the title-page of Q *Love's Labour's Lost*: the latter does not say, as *Romeo and Juliet* Q2 does, that the text it offers has been 'amended', which, in this context should mean something like 'substantially altered for the better', as indeed the text of *Romeo and Juliet* Q2 has been when compared with that of Q1. Had it been possible to make such a claim for the 1598 quarto of *Love's Labour's Lost*, it seems likely that Cuthbert Burby, the publisher of both the quartos concerned, would have made it. Furthermore, it does not follow that because *Romeo and Juliet* Q1, not entered in the Stationers' Register, was a bad quarto, the lost edition of *Love's Labour's Lost*, also not entered, must likewise have been bad. It has to be remembered 'that many books were quite openly and regularly published without entrance', and that 'the proportion of works published that were entered ... appears to have been on the average about two-thirds' (Greg, *SFF*, pp. 34–5).

The question of whether the lost quarto was good or bad

---

[1] *Shakespeare's Folios and Quartos* (1909), pp. 70–1.

cannot, it should now be clear, be decided on the strength of analogies alone. If a stress on the analogy of Q with *Romeo and Juliet* Q2 leads to the conclusion that it was bad, a stress on the analogy with *1 Henry IV* Q2 leads to the opposite conclusion, that it was good. Something more objective in the form of evidence is badly needed. Fortunately, a splendid start in providing it has been made by Paul Werstine in a meticulously documented and very persuasive study published in 1984.[1] His point of departure is the fact that twenty books printed between 1598 and 1600 in the shop of William White, the 'W.W.' of the Q title-page, have survived. Twelve of them were printed from manuscript, while four, including three plays—Shakespeare's *The True Tragedy of Richard Duke of York* Q2 (1600), George Peele's *The Famous Chronicle of King Edward I* Q2 (1599), and Thomas Kyd's *The Spanish Tragedy* Q3 (1599)—were reprints. There were also three editions of Samuel Rowlands's *The Letting of Humour's Blood* (1600), which Werstine excludes from his survey, since he is not sure whether they were set from manuscript or not, and, finally, the 1598 quarto of *Love's Labour's Lost.* A careful analysis of some of the spellings in the seventeen works he considers leads Werstine to conclude that White's compositors 'demonstrated nearly absolute consistency in maintaining their preferences for the spellings of a number of common words whenever they worked from manuscript copy. Only when they were faced with printed copy did their constancy waver as they transferred from printed books spellings that they almost never used in setting from manuscript' (pp. 54–5). For example, the word *any* occurs 283 times in the books set from manuscript, and on 282 of these occasions it is spelled *any*; only once does the alternative spelling *anie* appear. In the reprints and in Q *Love's Labour's Lost*, however, the tally is a different one. In *The Spanish Tragedy* Q3 the ratio of *any* to *anie* is 10/4, in *The Famous Chronicle* it is 22/2, and in Q *Love's Labour's Lost* 10/2. Similarly, the ratio of *eye* to *eie* in works set from manuscript is 117/3, whereas it is 8/7 in the *True Tragedy*, 9/10 in *The Famous Chronicle*, 17/9 in *The Spanish Tragedy*, and 63/10 in *Love's Labour's Lost.* Three other common words—*fayth/faith*, *many/manie*, and *very/verie*—tell much the

[1] 'The Editorial Usefulness of Printing House and Compositor Studies', *Play-Texts in Old Spelling*, ed. G. B. Shand and Raymond C. Shady (New York, 1984), pp. 35–64.

same story, as does the less common word *mayd(en)/maid(en)*. As Werstine puts it with modest caution, 'While six pairs of spelling variants from LLLQ1 are too few for any conclusive demonstration that LLLQ1 is a reprint of an earlier quarto, they are enough to indicate that LLLQ1 may be a reprint' (pp. 57–8). And this possibility opens up another, for 'if the first printing of LLL served as copy for the entire first extant quarto, the first printing must have been a good quarto, not a bad one', providing 'a better, not a worse, text of the play' (p. 61).

Before Werstine's paper came out in its final form his intimate knowledge of White's printing house, and of all the extant copies of Q, evident in his article 'Variants in the First Quarto of *Love's Labour's Lost*',[1] had enabled him to deal decisively with the view expressed by George R. Price,[2] to the effect that any hypothesis suggesting the use of printed copy in the setting-up of Q is 'untenable' (p. 434). Price gives two reasons for his verdict: first, 'the difficulties experienced by the compositors [of Q] in casting off, as revealed by irregularities in the setting of the pages', which, he thinks, could not have occurred had they been setting from print; and, secondly, 'the very abundance of the typographical errors left uncorrected'. Replying to this statement,[3] Werstine points out that 'exactly the same irregularities in the setting of pages appears in White's reprint of *The True Tragedie*. If faulty casting off drove White's compositor to limit A4 of LLLQ1 to thirty-six lines [instead of the normal thirty-eight] in order to avoid setting a centered stage direction at the bottom of the page, an error in casting off forced the compositor of C3 of *The True Tragedie* to set only thirty-five lines to avoid ending that page with a stage direction'. As for the 'abundance of typographical errors' in Q, Werstine, who counts sixty-seven of them, shows that this total is very much in keeping with those to be found in the three plays that are reprints. 'White's compositors', he writes, 'introduced at least sixty-eight such errors into the reprint of *Edwarde the first*, seventy-four into the reprint of *The True Tragedie*, and fifty-nine into the reprint of *The Spanish Tragedie*' (p. 494).

A third theory about the nature of the copy used in the setting

---

[1] *Shakespeare Studies*, 12 (1979), 35–47.

[2] 'The Printing of *Love's Labour's Lost* (1598)', *Papers of the Bibliographical Society of America*, 72 (1978), 419–34.

[3] *Papers of the Bibliographical Society of America*, 73 (1979), 493–4.

of Q is set forth by Manfred Draudt in his 'Printer's Copy for the Quarto of *Love's Labour's Lost* (1598)'.[1] His hypothesis is that the copy was mixed, some of it printed, the rest manuscript. He sees the quarto as falling into two parts: Acts 1 to 3, occupying sheets A to C/D, and Acts 4 and 5, occupying sheets C/D to K. Accepting, but not verifying, Price's statement that sheets A, B, and C are passably free of errors, but with D the remaining sheets become much worse, he argues that this 'worsening' is due to a change-over from printed copy to manuscript copy which the compositors found much harder to cope with. In fact, however, as Werstine conclusively shows, many of the errors in question are of a kind that compositors are prone to—transposition of letters, and the like—and are not to be attributed to any difficulties caused by a puzzling handwriting ('Editorial Usefulness', p. 52). Moreover—and this observation is crucial—the crop of errors in Q, says Werstine, can be paralleled by 'scores of similar errors ... in books set by White's compositors from clear printed copy' (p. 53).

It is hard to escape the conclusion that Draudt has been over-impressed by the similarities in wording between the title-page of Q and the title-page of *Romeo and Juliet* Q2, especially as he pushes that analogy to include *Hamlet* Q2 as well. His basic assumption is that because *Romeo and Juliet* Q2 was printed mainly from manuscript but with some use of Q1, and because *Hamlet* Q2, though printed from manuscript, was affected to some degree by Q1, which the printers consulted, Q *Love's Labour's Lost* must have had much the same kind of printing history and depended in part on the lost quarto, which, again by reason of analogy, he takes to have been 'bad'. Nowhere does he so much as mention the possibility that it could equally well have been good.

Of the three hypotheses, Werstine's, resting as it does on patiently gathered verifiable evidence, seems by far the most persuasive and acceptable. Moreover, it can be supported by considerations other than those already taken into account. The recognized bad quartos of Shakespeare's plays, different though they are in other respects, have one thing in common: all of them present versions of plays that are very decidedly plays of action, with a pronounced story interest; and the general tendency of the

---

[1] *The Library*, VI, 3 (1981), 119–31.

bad quartos is to increase the emphasis on action by cutting or entirely dispensing with passages of narration, description, or reflection. But *Love's Labour's Lost* is not a play of this kind at all. It has less story interest than any other play that Shakespeare ever wrote. Reduced to its action alone, it would offer thin fare indeed. Closely connected with this consideration is another. The bad quartos are bad because the texts they present are not directly and immediately related to the author's manuscript or to any authoritative transcript of that manuscript. All of them rest on reports, on what one or more people could remember of the words spoken on the stage. But any reporter who knew his business would have seen at once that *Love's Labour's Lost* was not a play that lent itself readily to memorial reconstruction. Both its unusual vocabulary and, still more, its intricate word-play would have militated against its being recalled with any precision. But these same qualities might well have made a sound version of it, legitimately acquired from the company, very attractive to a reader. From its pages he would have been able to work out at his leisure the fine details of many an exchange which had caught his attention but eluded his full comprehension when spoken in the theatre.

The most reasonable and acceptable theory with regard to the copy for Q is that set out by Stanley Wells, who writes:

Although the use as copy of a mixture of bad quarto and foul papers cannot be disproven, it remains to be proven, and all evidence so far produced is compatible with the simpler hypothesis that Q is a straight reprint of a lost 'good' quarto, itself set directly from Shakespeare's foul papers.[1]

Three attempts have been made to identify the compositor or compositors responsible for setting Q. Draudt thinks that only one was involved, but gives no reason for so thinking ('Printer's Copy', pp. 121–2). Price, on the other hand, bringing a whole battery of tests into play, eventually but rather hesitantly concludes that the work was carried out by three compositors, of whom the first set seventeen pages, the second thirty-two pages, and the third twenty-five pages. But both the criteria he uses and the way in which he applies them have met with some damaging criticism from Werstine ('Editorial Usefulness', pp. 42–54), who

---

[1] *William Shakespeare: A Textual Companion* (Oxford, 1986), p. 270.

has made his own identifications which do not correspond at all with Price's, apart from the fact that he too thinks that three compositors worked on the setting of Q. Relying for his evidence on the well-tried test of preferred spellings, Werstine finds that William White employed five workmen in all during the years 1598 to 1600. Two of them had no hand whatever in the composing of Q, while another, whom he labels R, was responsible for one page only—B1 (1.1.221–66). The remainder of the work was, he thinks, divided very unequally between Compositor S and Compositor T, with S setting a mere seven pages—A2–3ᵛ (1.1.143) and F1–2 (4.3.181–7)—and thus leaving sixty-six pages out of the total of seventy-four to Compositor T.

These findings ('Editorial Usefulness', pp. 37–8), backed up, as they are, by a mass of detail, carry far more conviction than do Price's; and, in their suggestion that one compositor set more than nine-tenths of the text, are consonant with what is, perhaps, the most marked characteristic of Q as a piece of printing: 'its uniform badness', as Dover Wilson called it more than sixty years ago. So struck was he by the sheer incompetence of the workmanship that he remarked, 'it is charitable to suppose that the printing-office was hardly in working order when the job was begun'—White had only recently acquired his business at the time—and then went on to express his belief that the task was carried out by one man alone, since such a botched job could 'hardly be the product of two men setting up alternately'. As for the compositor concerned, Wilson labels him 'the veriest tyro at his craft', and writes of his 'prentice-hand' (p. 100).

This 'prentice-hand' betrays itself, Wilson notes, in several different kinds of elementary error. First, the text is plastered with 'literals', especially in the form of turned letters or foul case. Here are some examples chosen from the beginning and the ending of the play: 'publibue' for 'publique' (1.1.130), 'inchannting' for 'inchaunting' (1.1.166), 'Contempls' for 'Contempts' (1.1.188), 'Gfficer' for 'Officer' (1.1.258), 'Conqueronr' for 'Conquerour' (5.2.567), 'Flder' for 'Elder' (5.2.599), '*Eeter*' for '*Enter*' (5.2.623.1), 'interrnpptest' for 'interrupptest' (5.2.706), and 'rherefore' for 'therefore' (5.2.779). Secondly, missing letters are common. Q has 'thee' for 'three' (1.1.24), 'pome' for 'pompe' (1.1.31), 'wost' for 'worst' (1.1.269), 'prosperie' for 'prosperitie' (1.1.300), 'measue' for 'measure' (5.2.222), 'Loke' for 'Looke'

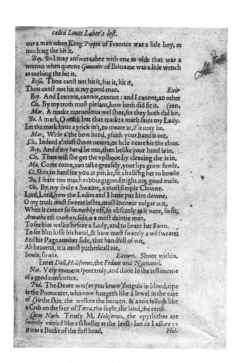

10. Sig. D4 of the First Quarto.

(5.2.251), 'thy' for 'they' (5.2.500), and 'intiled' for 'intitled' (5.2.800). Thirdly, the punctuation is anything but helpful. As Wilson says, it is 'not only frequently absurd but greatly over-weighted throughout, especially in the matter of full-stops, which occur in great profusion' (p. 104). There is no need to go further than the first page of Q (1.1.1.–30) to verify the accuracy of this observation. There line 5 ends with 'buy:' at a point where no stop at all is needed and where the colon is positively distracting. The same thing can be said about 'desires.' at the end of line 10 and about 'delyghts:' at the end of line 29. Even pages that have, as Werstine shows ('Variants', pp. 39–40), been subjected to some scrutiny, still contain glaring errors. Signature D4 will serve to make the point: see Fig. 10. In line 10, the proof-reader rightly and properly changed 'hid hit', the uncorrected reading, to 'did hit', and, in a pernickety mood, altered 'a' to 'a' ' twice in consecutive lines (13 and 14). Yet he allowed far more serious mistakes to stand. Having replaced 'hid' with 'did', he still failed to complete the line he was setting. The correct reading, dictated by sense, rhythm, and rhyme, is 'did hit it'; but the compositor, having no space left in his line, or in the line above, or in the line below, for the recalcitrant 'it', adopted the Procrustean solution to his difficulty by leaving 'it' out entirely, just as, for precisely the same reason, he omitted the full stop that should close line 18. Moreover, two other errors remain uncorrected. At line 16, the compositor has picked up the words 'is in' from the end of the previous line and used them again, instead of printing 'pin', as he should have done. And, finally, at line 28, he has omitted the word 'a' from the phrase 'it is a most patheticall nit'.

The general badness of Q as a specimen of the printer's craft raises two important questions. First, how far was it proof-read and corrected; and, secondly, how far is it to be trusted when it presents bad Latin and garbled Italian? The answer to the first question is that it was certainly subjected to proof-reading in parts. As long ago as 1957, W. W. Greg, in the introduction to his facsimile edition of Q,[1] listed seven known variants, due to stop-press correction. The full extent of the corrective process, in so far as it can be determined, was not established, however, until 1979, when Paul Werstine published his valuable study 'Variants in the First Quarto of *Love's Labor's Lost*'. In it he demonstrates that seven of the play's nineteen formes were proof-read: the outer forme of sheet A, and both the inner formes and the outer formes of sheets C, D, and E. Whether proof-reading continued beyond the end of E it is impossible to say, since no extant copy of Q shows any variants from the rest after this point.

Noting that the corrections, which are collated in this edition, fall into two groups, being scanty in outer A and in C but more numerous in D and E, Werstine deduces, fairly enough, that editors should be circumspect about emending words and passages in D and E, and agrees with those, such as H. H. Furness and Richard David, who hold that it is the characters, not the printer, who are responsible for 'the grossest corruptions of foreign languages in the play' (p. 42). However, a further look at the facsimile of D4 makes one question the validity of this latter view. In the first line he speaks the Pedant, as he is called at this point, remarks that the deer the Princess shot was 'sanguis in blood'. The words are sheer nonsense, of course, and have been much discussed, yet they admit of a simple explanation: the compositor, trying to carry too much in his head, has transposed 'sanguis' and 'in blood'. The right reading (see Commentary) is 'in blood, sanguis', which makes perfect sense and is couched in what we soon come to recognize as Holofernes' personal idiom. Moreover, this is not an isolated instance of Compositor T's tendency to transpose. At 4.3.173, the King says bitterly to Biron: 'Are we betrayed thus to thy over-view?', to which Biron replies in Q: 'Not you by me, but I betrayed to you', an answer which, as Capell noticed, is more to the point and takes on the right antithetical bite if it reads: 'Not you to me, but I betrayed by you'. Nor does Compositor T restrict his transposing habit to single words and phrases. On one occasion at least (5.2.876–7) he transposes whole lines, printing the second and third lines of the cuckoo song in reverse order. Even '*Celo*' in the same initial speech, which many have seized on as evidence of the school-master's incompetence as a Latinist because it is in the wrong case, the ablative instead of the nominative, could equally well be 'a misreading of a manuscript "*Celũ*" ("e" was acceptable in renaissance Latin for "ae", and the tilde over the "u" stood for "m")' (Kerrigan, pp. 188–9). Furthermore, it is abundantly clear that the worst piece of corruption in the entire text is compositorial, and in no way reflects badly on Holofernes. At 5.1.26, Nathaniel, in answer to a question put to him by Holofernes, replies: '*Laus deo, bene intelligo.*' It is good grammatical Latin, yet it is met with what must be a reproof, that runs thus: '*Bome boon for boon prescian*, a little scratcht, twil serue.' Whatever those first four words are supposed to mean, they certainly cannot be the words Shakespeare gave Holofernes to speak. Indeed, it is not even clear what language or languages they are intended to represent. This passage alone—and it does not stand alone, for Holofernes has already been saddled with another piece of gibberish on the subject of Venice at 4.2.95–6—is sufficient in itself to make one sceptical, as Dover Wilson had become in his second edition of 1962 (pp. viii–xi), of the view that errors in the use of foreign languages are deliberately designed by the playwright to expose the emptiness of their speakers' pretensions to learning. It also leaves one equally sceptical about the title-page's claim that the text has been 'Newly corrected'. Such correction as it has undergone can only have been of the most cursory and casual kind.

What, then, is the validity of 'augmented'? In one sense, it is indubitably and demonstrably true. The evidence is there in the two duplicated passages. At 4.3.293, twenty-three lines of a first draft have been expanded into a revised version of forty-eight lines; and at 5.2.819 the thirty-five lines of dialogue between Biron and Rosaline that follow are clearly meant to replace a mere six lines of dialogue between them that began originally at 5.2.805. Whether these revised lines are the augmentations that whoever was responsible for the wording on the title-page had in mind it is not possible to say; but they do raise two crucial and interrelated questions. First, are they, as Dover Wilson (p. 125) averred, part of 'a drastic revision' of the play as originally composed; and, secondly, when were they written? Like most critics before him, Wilson had no doubt that there was such a revision and that it was made in preparation for the performance the Queen saw during the Christmas season of 1597–8. Yet, as has already been demonstrated at some length (pp. 57–65), if there was such a revision and it resulted in the text of Q, it still left the play unactable. To this editor, as to Chambers (*William Shakespeare*, i. 335) and Greg (*SFF*, p. 220), both the first version of 4.3.293–340 and the first version of 5.2.805–53 look like 'false starts', which Shakespeare had no sooner written than he recognized their inadequacy, and promptly replaced them with fuller and better versions. They belong naturally with so much else in the play that bears witness to the playwright's discovery of his comedy as he proceeds with the writing of it: his difficulty in deciding on the right names for two of the ladies, for instance, and his introduction of three French lords into the cast at the opening of 2.1, only to find that one of them, Boyet, is enough for his purposes, whereupon he unobtrusively drops the other two before the end of 4.1.

Nevertheless, the notion that there was a revision of some kind in 1597 has been slow to die, largely owing to an influential article by J. W. Lever, published in 1952.[1] In it Lever argues, in a way many have found convincing, that the first stanza of the spring-song at the end of the play was heavily indebted to a

---

[1] 'Three Notes on Shakespeare's Plants', *RES*, NS 3 (1952), 117–29.

passage in John Gerard's *Herbal*, which first appeared in 1597. Abbreviated, the relevant passage in that work runs thus:

Milk-white Lady-smocks hath stalks rising immediately from the root ... The flowers grow at the top, made of four leaves of a yellowish colour. ... These kinds of cuckoo-flowers grow in moist meadows, [and they flower] in April and May when the cuckoo doth begin to sing her pleasant notes without stammering. ... They are commonly called in Latin *flos Cuculi*, for the reason aforesaid ... it is called ... in English cuckoo-flowers; in Norfolk, Canterbury bells; at the Nantwich in Cheshire, where I had my beginning, Lady-smocks, which hath given me cause to christen it after my country fashion.[1]

From this statement Lever deduced 'that the Cheshire name "Lady-smocks" came into standard English through Gerarde's idiosyncrasy, and that Shakespeare took it straight from the *Herball*', along with 'the meadows', and so on.

So things stood until 1982, when John Kerrigan demolished the whole theory in his '*Love's Labor's Lost* and Shakespearean Revision',[2] where, starting from Mats Rydén's noticing that the word 'Lady-smocks' was already in literary use by 1593,[3] when it appeared in Michael Drayton's *The Shepherd's Garland*,[4] Kerrigan comes to the irrefutable conclusion 'that if one Warwickshire man [Drayton] could write about "Lady-smocks" in the early to mid-1590s, another [Shakespeare] surely could' (p. 339). Shakespeare's lines are then, as one instinctively feels, the fruit of his observation, not of his reading. They throw no light on the date of the play or on the question of whether it was revised or not.

So far, then, it is clear that Q must be the control-text for an edition of the comedy, since the copy from which it was set was either the author's foul papers or the lost Quarto which had itself been set from those same foul papers. But there is a complication. The next appearance of *Love's Labour's Lost* in print, after 1598, was in the First Folio edition of Shakespeare's plays, hence-forward referred to as F, published in 1623, seven years after the playwright's death, where it occupies pages 122–44 of the

---

[1] Book II, Chap. xviii, p. 203.

[2] *Shakespeare Quarterly*, 33 (1982), 337–9.

[3] 'Shakespeare's Cuckoo-buds', *Studia Neophilologica*, 49 (1977), 25–7.

[4] 'The Fourth Eclogue', l. 153; *Poems of Michael Drayton*, ed. John Buxton (1953), i. 58. 153.

comedies (signatures L1ᵛ–M6ᵛ); and the text printed in F, though manifestly set from a copy of Q, differs in some significant ways from that of Q. The most obvious and immediately perceptible of these differences, though by no means the most important, is summarized thus by W. W. Greg:

F introduces a division into acts only (misprinting the fifth 'Actus Quartus') of monstrously disproportionate lengths—509, 257, 207, 710, and 1104 lines respectively. Probably it was made at the time of printing, for in this case the note 'Finis Actus Primus' ... looks as though it had been added merely to fill up the space at the foot of a column. (*SFF*, p. 223)

The act divisions of F are patently absurd. Nevertheless, they have been preserved in this edition, along with the scene divisions introduced by editors in the eighteenth century, purely for convenience of reference.

The other major difference between F and Q, and by far the most important one, is that F adds six words, 'You that way; we this way', to the very end of the play and assigns them, together with the entire speech they conclude, to Armado, whereas Q's enigmatic final comment, 'The words of Mercury are harsh after the songs of Apollo', is not assigned to anyone. To many critics 'You that way; we this way', endorsing the fact that this comedy ends with partings not unions, has seemed the perfect conclusion. But what authority does it have? Is this addition the work of Shakespeare himself, or is it, as Greg unhesitatingly asserts, 'the editor's desperate attempt to fit the final words of Q into the structure of the play' (*SFF*, p. 223)?

To reach any kind of conclusion about the authenticity of those final words peculiar to F and of the other variants from Q that it offers, it is necessary to take a closer look at F as a whole. That it was indeed set from a copy of Q is beyond doubt. The proof is, as Dover Wilson acutely pointed out (p. 186), that it prints the word 'venewe', at 5.1.55, as though it were two words, 'vene we', thus perpetuating an error that originates in Q, where it was caused by the accidental loosening and shifting of the type after it had been set. For more evidence of the dependence of F on Q, one need only turn to F's treatment of Q's D4 (see Figure 10). F repeats at least three of Q's patent mistakes: 'did hit' for 'did hit it', 'the is in' for 'the pin', and 'it is most' for 'it is a most' (4.1.128, 135, and 147). Moreover, F adds two gratuitous errors of its own. It shifts the stage direction '*Exit*' from the end of Rosaline's speech at line 125 to the end of Boyet's speech at line 127, where it is clearly out of place, since he remains on stage; and it omits the word 'And' from the beginning of that same speech. At the same time, however, it makes good one omission from Q by supplying the full-stop that is needed at the end of line 137.

The Folio compositor responsible for setting its version of Q's D4, Compositor D,[1] was also guilty of omitting nine lines of dialogue, 80–8, from 3.1. One can see how it came about. It occurs in the course of the exchanges between Armado and Moth in which the jingle, 'The fox, the ape, and the humble-bee | Were still at odds, being but three', is spoken no fewer than three times in a mere twelve lines. Faced with this repetitive pattern, D allowed his eye to skip from the words introducing the first instance to those introducing the third. This is not to say, however, that omission is the prerogative of Compositor D. His fellow-worker C, for example, leaves out the word 'quite' (1.1.27) on the first page; while B completely ignores the moving sentence, 'When he breathed, he was a man' (5.2.652–3), in Armado's spirited defence of the dead Hector.

The Folio compositors also imported other kinds of corruption into their text. They are prone to modernize. At 1.1.130 D turns 'can possible' into 'shall possibly', and at 1.1.157 'other' into 'others'; while C, for his part, changes 'a' to 'he', and thus starts a trend towards the less colloquial which becomes quite pronounced. Moreover, all three are ready to alter a word, or even leave it out altogether, in order to justify a line of type. For this reason C replaces 'fitteth' (1.2.40) with 'fits'; D reduces 'Maister, will' (3.1.7) to 'Will'; and B cuts 'to her thither' down to size by omitting 'thither' (5.2.312). They are also given to transposing words. At 1.2.164–5 C prints 'yet *Sampsoun* was' for 'Yet was *Sampsoun*', and at 2.1.175 'we shall' for 'shall we'; and B, at 5.2.324, turns 'kist his hand, a way' into 'kist away his hand'.

These examples—a few out of many—confirm that MacD. P. Jackson is right when he generalizes to the following effect: 'The

[1] F was set by three compositors, working as follows: C set L1ᵛ, D set L2, C set L2ᵛ–L4, D set L4ᵛ–6ᵛ, C set M1–3ᵛ, B set M4–6ᵛ. See Charlton Hinman, *The Printing and Proof-Reading of the First Folio of Shakespeare*, 2 vols. (Oxford, 1963), ii. 514.

79

similarities between the three compositors are more notable than the differences. Each corrupted the text with definite errors or with unauthorized alterations at the rate of about six per Folio page.'[1] And, since *Love's Labour's Lost* occupies 23 Folio pages, Jackson's count of corruptions in F, 138, corresponds almost exactly with the total of 137 arrived at by Dover Wilson (p. 189). Wilson notes further that F allows no fewer than 59 errors in Q to stand while making sound corrections of some 117 errors in that text, most of the mistakes concerned being of a kind that an experienced workman would recognize at once: 'missing, transposed, or wrong letters'. Even some of F's more striking changes, such as 'Importunes' for Q's 'Importuous' (2.1.32), 'vnpeopled' for 'vnpeeled' (2.1.88), 'indiscreet' for 'indistreel' (4.2.29), and the like, would not be beyond these compositors' capability and purview.

There are also, however, other alterations that can hardly have originated with the printers. Wilson puts the matter thus: 'No compositor would have changed "Clymbe ore the house to vnlocke the little gate" (Q.) into "That were to clymbe ore the house to vnlocke the gate" (F.), which occurs at 1.1.109'; and he then goes on to list 'seven other variants of the same kind'. They are 'parts' for 'peerelsse' (2.1.44), 'stab'd' for 'stable' (5.2.80), 'Ioue' for 'God' (l. 316), 'Zanie' for 'saine' (l. 463), 'manager' [it should be 'manage'] for 'nuage' (l. 482), 'doth least' for 'doth best' (l. 513), and 'euer' for 'herrite' (l. 804). It is, perhaps, not purely coincidental that the last six of these alterations occur in the final scene of the play, and the last five of them in the stint that was set by Compositor B, who has become almost notorious for his high-handed treatment of copy. But, however that may be, it seems clear that the copy of Q used by the printers of F had undergone some annotation before it went to them from the playhouse.

What is not clear is whether the annotator consulted a playhouse manuscript in making his alterations. The evidence is contradictory. In substituting 'Ioue' for 'God' he could well have been using his own initiative, since all he was doing was to bring the text into line with the requirements of the Act of 1606 prohibiting profanity on the stage, something he signally failed to do with the other twenty instances of 'God' in Q; but in replacing

[1] MacD. P. Jackson, 'Compositors B, C, and D, and the First Folio Text of *Love's Labour's Lost*', *Papers of the Bibliographical Society of America*, 72 (1978), 61–5.

'herrite' with 'euer' he must have been guessing; and why he chose to alter his text at 1.1.109 is beyond the wit of man. Yet the other five changes, assuming that the word he substituted for the unintelligible 'nuage' was indeed 'manage' which Compositor B misread as 'manager', are all sound. On balance, therefore, it does look as though he had access, when he chose to avail himself of it, to a better text than that provided by Q, and that he did turn to it when scanning the last part of Q, to which he paid more attention than he seems to have done to the rest of it. In these circumstances the case for the authenticity of F's final sentence becomes a strong one.[1]

In view of what has been said already (pp. 60–3) about the confusion of names in 2.1, it would be helpful to the case set out there if the same claim to authenticity could be made for F's alteration of the speech-prefix '*Kather⟨ine⟩*' at lines 114–25 to '*Rosa⟨line⟩*'. Unfortunately, it cannot. The other changes of speech headings in F forbid it, for they are either obvious corrections of mis-spellings in Q, such as '*Clo.*' for that text's '*Col.*' (1.1.286), or the abortive effort in 1.2 to regularize '*Armado*' to '*Braggart*' and the equally abortive attempt to provide personal names for Q's indecisive '*Lad.*', '*Lad. 2.*', '*Lad. 3.*', '*Lad.*', and '*Lad.*' in the closing lines of 2.1.

Behind the text of *Love's Labour's Lost*, as we have it in the Quarto of 1598, lurks the ghost of an earlier 'lost' quarto. It is in keeping with the comedy's teasing ending and with its pronounced symmetry of form that behind it there lurks another ghost, that of a 'lost' play by Shakespeare entitled *Love's Labour's Won*. The only evidence, prior to 1953, that it ever existed was provided by its appearance in the celebrated list of Shakespeare's works given by Francis Meres in his *Palladis Tamia: Wit's Treasury* of 1598, where Meres writes:

As *Plautus* and *Seneca* are accounted the best for Comedy and Tragedy among the Latines: so *Shakespeare* among the English is the most excellent in both kinds for the stage; for Comedy, witnes his *Gentlemen of Verona*, his *Errors*, his *Loue labors lost*, his *Loue labours wonne*, his *Midsummers night dreame*, & his *Merchant of Venice*: for Tragedy his *Richard the 2. Richard the 3. Henry the 4. King Iohn, Titus Andronicus* and his *Romeo* and *Iuliet*. (Quoted from Chambers, *William Shakespeare*, ii. 194)

---

[1] See Stanley Wells, 'The Copy for the Folio Text of *Love's Labour's Lost*', *RES*, NS 33 (1982), 137–47.

However, no copy of *Love's Labour's Won* has ever come to light; and up to 1953 scholars tended to think that there were three possible explanations for Meres's statement. First, and most likely, that *Love's Labour's Won* was simply some other known comedy by Shakespeare under another name: *The Taming of the Shrew*, for instance, or *Much Ado About Nothing*, neither of them in Meres's list. Secondly, there was the possibility that *Love's Labour's Won* was merely an alternative title for *Love's Labour's Lost* itself, and that Meres had failed to realize this. Thirdly, it was suggested that Meres had invented the title *Love's Labour's Won* in order that he might have six comedies to balance the six 'tragedies' he cites.

Then, late in 1953, two leaves of paper, covered with Elizabethan handwriting, were found in the backing used to strengthen the spine of a copy of Thomas Gataker's *Certaine Sermons* published in 1637–8. Happily, this find was shown at once to the well known American scholar T. W. Baldwin, who immediately recognized its significance, proceeded to work on it, and, two years later, published an exhaustive account of his findings: *Shakspere's 'Love's Labor's Won'* (Carbondale, 1957). The leaves were, he discovered, from the ledger of a stationer in Exeter, and the jottings noted various items the stationer had sold during the month of August 1603, together with a list of books he had in stock at the time. Part of that list was made up of '[inte]rludes & tragedyes', and it concludes with the following items:

> marchant of vennis
> taming of a shrew
> knak to know a knave
> knak to know an honest man
> loves labor lost
> loves labor won.

In print by 1603 at the very latest, *Love's Labour's Won* was no fictitious play invented by Meres for the sake of symmetry; nor can it have been an alternative name for *The Taming of a/the Shrew*, or *The Merchant of Venice*, or *Love's Labour's Lost* itself. It was also distinct, Meres's testimony assures us, from *The Two Gentlemen of Verona*, *The Comedy of Errors*, and *A Midsummer Night's Dream*. There is no other comedy thought to have been written by Shakespeare before 1598 with which to equate it. It seems beyond doubt, therefore, that it did exist, that it was published, and that it has since disappeared. Further than that it is not possible to go.

EDITORIAL PROCEDURES

FOR the reasons set out in the Introduction the control text for this edition is the Quarto of 1598, since it was printed either from Shakespeare's manuscript or from a lost quarto based on that same manuscript. It is further assumed that the manuscript in question must have been in the form of 'foul papers', that is to say in a state from which a 'fair copy', suitable for use as a prompt-book and the drawing up of actors 'parts', could be made and would have to be made before the play could be staged. On the hypothesis that the text of F, which is in all essentials a reprint of Q, may have been influenced by some cursory and unsystematic consultation of such 'fair copy', some of its readings, including its last line, which does not appear at all in Q, are adopted here, but, apart from its corrections of obvious printers' errors, only very rarely. It is, however, substantially collated. So far as words and passages in foreign languages, and especially in Latin, are concerned, errors in them have been corrected because, to this editor, they look far more like compositorial mistakes than an attempt on the part of the playwright to pillory Holofernes' Latin as bad. Pedants are often tiresomely pernickety but rarely wildly inaccurate.

The general principles governing the modernization of the text are those set out by Stanley Wells in his *Modernizing Shakespeare's Spelling* (Oxford, 1979); and, in keeping with them, passages from authors of the sixteenth and early seventeenth centuries, quoted in the introduction and commentary, have also been modernized even when they have been taken from editions using old spelling. Old spellings are, however, retained in documentary evidence, for much of the matter dealt with in that part of the introduction devoted to the text, and in the collations, where the lemma takes the modernized form but the rest of the entry is given in the original spelling.

Since directions such as 'aside' or 'to' another character, together with act and scene divisions, are all editorial, they are not attributed in the collations. Changes or variations in the punctuation are noted only where they are significant. Speech headings have been silently normalized.

85

Quotations from the Bible are taken, unless otherwise stated, from the Bishops' Bible of 1568. References to other works by Shakespeare are keyed to Oxford.

Words are normally defined only when they first appear or when they convey a significantly different meaning from that which they had on their first appearance. All words that are glossed are listed in the index.

Abbreviations and References

The following abbreviations are used in the textual part of the introduction, in the collations, and in the commentary. The place of publication is, unless otherwise specified, London.

EDITIONS OF SHAKESPEARE

Q	*A* PLEASANT Conceited Comedie CALLED, Loues labors lost. As it was presented before her Highnes this last Christmas. Newly corrected and augmented *By W. Shakespeare.* ... 1598
Q2	Loues Labours lost. A WITTIE AND PLEASANT COMEDIE, As it was Acted by his Maiesties Seruants at *the* Blacke-Friers *and the* Globe. By WILLIAM SHAKESPEARE. ... 1631.
F	The First Folio, 1623
F2	The Second Folio, 1632
F3	The Third Folio, 1663
F4	The Fourth Folio, 1685
Alexander	Peter Alexander, *Complete Works* (1951)
Cambridge	W. G. Clark and W. A. Wright, *Works*, The Cambridge Shakespeare, 9 vols. (Cambridge, 1863–6)
Capell	Edward Capell, *Comedies, Histories, and Tragedies*, 10 vols. (1767–8)
Collier	John Payne Collier, *Works*, 8 vols. (1842–4)
Collier 1853	John Payne Collier, *Plays* (1853)
Collier 1858	John Payne Collier, *Comedies, Histories, Tragedies, and Poems* (1858)
David	Richard David, *Love's Labour's Lost*, new Arden Shakespeare (1951)
Delius	Nikolaus Delius, *Werke*, 7 vols. (Elberfeld, 1854–61)

Dyce	Alexander Dyce, *Works*, 6 vols. (1857)
Furness	Horace Howard Furness, *Love's Labour's Lost*, A New Variorum Edition (Philadelphia, 1904)
Globe	W. G. Clark and W. A. Wright, *Works*, The Globe Edition (1864)
Halliwell	James O. Halliwell, *Works*, 16 vols. (1853–65)
Hanmer	Thomas Hanmer, *Works*, 6 vols. (Oxford, 1743–4)
Harbage	Alfred Harbage, *Complete Works*, The Pelican Shakespeare (1969)
Hart	H. C. Hart, *Love's Labour's Lost*, Arden Shakespeare (1906)
Hudson	H. N. Hudson, *Works*, 11 vols. (Boston, 1851–6)
Johnson	Samuel Johnson, *Plays*, 8 vols. (1765)
Johnson and Steevens	Samuel Johnson and George Steevens, *Plays*, 10 vols. (1778)
Johnson and Steevens 1785	Samuel Johnson, George Steevens, and Isaac Reed, *Plays*, 10 vols. (1785)
Keightley	Thomas Keightley, *Plays*, 6 vols. (1864)
Kerrigan	John Kerrigan, *Love's Labour's Lost*, New Penguin Shakespeare (Harmondsworth, 1982)
Knight	Charles Knight, *Works*, Pictorial Edition, 8 vols. (1838–43)
Malone	Edmond Malone, *Plays and Poems*, 10 vols. (1790)
Marshall	Henry Irving and Frank A. Marshall, *Works*, The Henry Irving Shakespeare, 8 vols. (1888–90)
Oxford	Stanley Wells and Gary Taylor, *Complete Works* (Oxford, 1986)
Pope	Alexander Pope, *Works*, 6 vols. (1723–5)
Pope 1728	Alexander Pope, *Works*, 10 vols. (1728)
Rann	Joseph Rann, *Dramatic Works*, 6 vols. (Oxford, 1786–94)
Ridley	M. R. Ridley, *Love's Labour's Lost*, The New Temple Shakespeare (1934)
Riverside	G. B. Evans (textual editor), *The Riverside Shakespeare* (Boston, 1974)
Rowe	Nicholas Rowe, *Works*, 6 vols. (1709)
Rowe 1714	Nicholas Rowe, *Works*, 8 vols. (1714)
Singer	Samuel Weller Singer, *Dramatic Works*, 10 vols. (1856)

Sisson	Charles Jasper Sisson, *Complete Works* (1954)
Steevens	George Steevens and Isaac Reed, *Plays*, 15 vols. (1793)
Theobald	Lewis Theobald, *Works*, 7 vols. (1733)
Theobald 1740	Lewis Theobald, *Works*, 8 vols. (1740)
Warburton	William Warburton, *Works*, 8 vols. (1747)
White	Richard Grant White, *Works*, 12 vols. (Boston, 1857–66)
Wilson	Sir Arthur Quiller-Couch and John Dover Wilson, *Love's Labour's Lost*, The New Shakespeare (Cambridge, 1923)
Wilson 1962	John Dover Wilson, *Love's Labour's Lost*, The New Shakespeare (Cambridge, 1962)

OTHER WORKS

Abbott	E. A. Abbott, *A Shakespearian Grammar*, second edition (1870)
Arcadia, The	Sir Philip Sidney, *The Countess of Pembroke's Arcadia*, ed. Albert Feuillerat (Cambridge, 1939)
Binns	J. W. Binns, 'Shakespeare's Latin Citations: the Editorial Problem', *Shakespeare Survey* 35 (1982), 119–28
Bullough	Geoffrey Bullough, *Narrative and Dramatic Sources of Shakespeare*, 8 vols. (1957–75)
Chambers, *William Shakespeare*	E. K. Chambers, *William Shakespeare*, 2 vols. (Oxford, 1930)
Chapman	*The Plays of George Chapman*, ed. T. M. Parrott, 2 vols. (1910–14)
Chaucer	*The Works of Geoffrey Chaucer*, ed. F. N. Robinson (Boston, 1933)
Dent	R. W. Dent, *Shakespeare's Proverbial Language: An Index* (1981)
Farmer	Richard Farmer, in *Works*, ed. Johnson and Steevens (1773)
Grosart	*The Life and Complete Works ... of Robert Greene*, ed. A. B. Grosart, 15 vols. (1881–6)
Harvey Wood	The Plays of John Marston, ed. H. Harvey Wood, 3 vols. (1934–9)
Helicon	*England's Helicon* (1600)
Malcontent, The	*The Malcontent* [by] John Marston, ed. G. K. Hunter (1975)

Nashe	*The Works of Thomas Nashe*, ed. R. B. McKerrow (1904–10) ... With supplementary notes ... by F. P. Wilson, 5 vols. (Oxford, 1958)
OED	*The Oxford English Dictionary, being a corrected re-issue of A New English Dictionary on Historical Principles*, 13 vols. (Oxford 1933), and Supplements 1–3 (1972, 1976, 1982)
Onions	C. T. Onions, *A Shakespeare Glossary*, second edition revised (Oxford, 1966)
Partridge	Eric Partridge, *Shakespeare's Bawdy* (1968)
Pilgrim	*The Passionate Pilgrim* (1599)
Schmidt	Alexander Schmidt, *A Shakespeare Lexicon*, fourth edition (revised by G. Sarrazin), 2 vols. (Berlin and Leipzig, 1923)
Schoenbaum	*Annals of English Drama 975–1700*, by Alfred Harbage, revised by S. Schoenbaum (1964)
SFF	W. W. Greg, *The Shakespeare First Folio* (Oxford, 1955)
Shakespeare's England	*Shakespeare's England*, ed. C. T. Onions, 2 vols. (Oxford, 1932)
Sisson, *New Readings*	C. J. Sisson, *New Readings in Shakespeare*, 2 vols. (Cambridge, 1956)
TC	Stanley Wells and Gary Taylor with John Jowett and William Montgomery, *William Shakespeare: A Textual Companion* (Oxford, 1987)
Thomson	J. A. K. Thomson, *Shakespeare and the Classics* (1952)
Tilley	M. P. Tilley, *A Dictionary of the Proverbs in England in the Sixteenth and Seventeenth Centuries* (Ann Arbor, 1950)
Tyrwhitt	Thomas Tyrwhitt, *Observations and Conjectures upon Some Passages of Shakespeare* (1766)
Walker, W. S.	W. S. Walker, *A Critical Examination of the Text of Shakespeare*, 3 vols. (1860)
Webster	*The Works of John Webster*, ed. F. L. Lucas, 4 vols. (1927)
Wells, *Re-Editing*	Stanley Wells, *Re-Editing Shakespeare for the Modern Reader* (Oxford, 1984)

Love's Labour's Lost

THE PERSONS OF THE PLAY

FERDINAND, King of Navarre

BIRON

LONGUEVILLE   }   lords in attendance on the King

DUMAINE

THE PRINCESS OF FRANCE

ROSALINE

MARIA   }   ladies in attendance on the Princess

KATHERINE

BOYET, a French lord in attendance on the Princess

TWO OTHER FRENCH LORDS, also in attendance on the Princess

MONSIEUR MARCADÉ, a messenger

DON ADRIANO DE ARMADO, a braggart from Spain

MOTH, his page

HOLOFERNES, a schoolmaster

NATHANIEL, a curate

DULL, a constable

COSTARD, a rustic

JAQUENETTA, a dairymaid

A FORESTER

Attendants on the King

Love's Labour's Lost

1.1   *Enter Ferdinand, King of Navarre, Biron, Longueville, and Dumaine*

KING

Let fame, that all hunt after in their lives,
Live registered upon our brazen tombs,
And then grace us in the disgrace of death;

Love's Labour's Lost] *A PLEASANT* Conceited Comedie CALLED, Loues labors lost. Q (*title-page*); *A pleasant conceited Comedie: called Loues Labor's lost* Q (*running titles*); Loues Labour's lost. F (*head-title; running titles*); Loues Labour lost. F (*table of contents*).
    1.1.0.1 *Biron*] QF (Berowne)   0.1 *Longueville*] QF (Longauill)   1 KING] ROWE; *Ferdinand* QF

Love's Labour's Lost It is far from certain what Shakespeare intended his play to be called. Its name, as it appears on the title-page of Q, is 'Loues labors lost', which is ambiguous. It can mean either 'the labour of love is lost' or 'the lost labours of love'. However, the running title of Q— '*A pleasant conceited Comedie: called Loues Labor's lost*'—seems to settle the issue, especially as it has the support of F, where the running title is '*Loues Labour's lost*' and the head-title 'Loues Labour's lost'. But there are complications. In the Catalogue of the plays included in F it is listed as '*Loues Labour lost*', and this is the name by which Robert Tofte refers to it in his *Alba* of 1598 (see Introduction, p. 1). Francis Meres, however, in his *Palladis Tamia: Wit's Treasury*, also published in 1598, calls it '*Loue labors lost*'. *Love's Labour's Lost* is probably right, but *Love's Labours Lost* has its attractions, particularly in a play where the name *Hercules* occurs no fewer than eleven times.

Like much else in the comedy, the title has a proverbial ring to it. 'To lose one's labour' (Tilley L9) goes back to the early 16th century; and Dent (L555.1) gives good reasons for thinking that although Shakespeare's title is the first recorded instance of the precise phrase it may well have been current earlier. *Love* is, of course, Cupid, who is mentioned more often in this play than in any other that Shakespeare wrote, though *Much Ado About Nothing*—another comedy with a proverbial title—runs it close in this as in many other respects.

1.1.0.1 *Ferdinand, King of Navarre* There never was a king of Navarre called Ferdinand; and no one in the play ever refers to him by that name. It is used, however, in the speech-prefixes of 1.1 and 2.1. After that his speeches are headed '*King*'.
    Biron See Introduction, p. 49. Shakespeare, like Nashe (ii.182), spells the name 'Berowne', and rhymes it with 'moon' (4.3.229).
    Longueville See Introduction, p. 49. Spelling this name 'Longauill', 'Longauil', and 'Longauile', Shakespeare makes it rhyme with 'ill' (4.3.121), with 'compile' (4.3.131), and even extracts some puns on 'veal' and 'well' from it (5.2.247).
    Dumaine See Introduction p. 49. The name is an Anglicized version of the Duc de Mayenne.
1.1.1–7 **Let ... eternity** As many critics and commentators have noticed, there are marked similarities between these lines and some of the Sonnets, especially 19, 55, 63–5, and 100.
  2 **brazen tombs** tombs bearing inscribed brass plates
  3 **grace ... death** make us honoured and admired even when we have been physically disfigured by death—a version of the Latin tag '*Vivit post funera virtus*' (Tilley V74). Compare *Lucrece* 1319–21: 'When sighs and groans and tears may grace the fashion | Of her disgrace,

95

When, spite of cormorant devouring Time,
Th'endeavour of this present breath may buy
That honour which shall bate his scythe's keen edge,
And make us heirs of all eternity.
Therefore, brave conquerors—for so you are,
That war against your own affections
And the huge army of the world's desires—   10
Our late edict shall strongly stand in force.
Navarre shall be the wonder of the world;
Our court shall be a little academe,
Still and contemplative in living art.
You three, Biron, Dumaine, and Longueville,
Have sworn for three years' term to live with me,
My fellow-scholars, and to keep those statutes
That are recorded in this schedule here.
Your oaths are passed, and now subscribe your names,
That his own hand may strike his honour down   20
That violates the smallest branch herein.

5 buy ∧] F2 ; ∼ : QF   10 desires—] ROWE (*subs.*) ; ∼ . QF

the better so to clear her | From that
suspicion which the world might bear
her.'

4 **spite** in spite
  cormorant ravenous. For Shakespeare
  and his age the cormorant was an emblem of consuming greed.
  devouring Time 'Time devours all things'
  was proverbial (Tilley T326).
5 **Th'endeavour ... breath** our efforts while
  we are alive
6 **bate** blunt, dull
  his scythe's keen edge Erwin Panofsky
  has a fascinating chapter on the evolu-
  tion of the figure of Father Time, complete
  with scythe or sickle, in his *Studies in
  Iconology* (Oxford, 1939; repr. New York
  and Evanston, 1962), pp. 69–93. It
  throws much light on this particular
  passage.
8 **brave conquerors** The King rashly but
  characteristically assumes that he and
  his fellow-students have already accomplished the arduous task on which they
  are only now about to embark.
9 **affections** passions, natural impulses

11 **late** recent
13 **academe** academy. Not used by Shakespeare in any other of his writings, this
   'poetic' form of the older word *academy*
   appears to have originated in this passage. Imitations of Plato's Academy came
   into being first in Florence during the mid
   15th century and then in other parts of
   Europe. *L'Académie française* by Pierre de
   la Primaudaye, a fictional account of
   such an institution published in 1577,
   had been translated into English by
   Thomas Bowes in 1586 under the title of
   The French Academy and was widely
   known. See Introduction p. 47.
14 **Still and contemplative in** calmly and
   steadily studying (hendiadys)
   living art The phrase seems to combine
   two ideas in one: (1) the art of living—the
   ars vivendi of the Stoic philosophers; (2)
   vital learning, learning that has a practical bearing on the whole business of
   living.
17 **keep** observe
   statutes terms, conditions
19 **passed** pledged
21 **branch** clause, detail

If you are armed to do as sworn to do,
Subscribe to your deep oaths, and keep it too.
LONGUEVILLE
I am resolved. 'Tis but a three years' fast.
The mind shall banquet though the body pine.
Fat paunches have lean pates, and dainty bits
Make rich the ribs but bankrupt quite the wits.
    He signs
DUMAINE
My loving lord, Dumaine is mortified.
The grosser manner of these world's delights
He throws upon the gross world's baser slaves.   30
To love, to wealth, to pomp, I pine and die,
With all these living in philosophy.
    He signs
BIRON
I can but say their protestation over.
So much, dear liege, I have already sworn,
That is, to live and study here three years.
But there are other strict observances:
As not to see a woman in that term,
Which I hope well is not enrollèd there;
And one day in a week to touch no food,
And but one meal on every day beside,   40
The which I hope is not enrollèd there;
And then to sleep but three hours in the night,
And not be seen to wink of all the day,

---

24 resolved] F (resolu'd); resolued Q   three] F; thee Q   27 bankrupt quite] Q (bancrout quit); bankerout F   27.1 *He signs*] *not in* QF   30 slaves.] F (slaues:); ~ ∧ Q   31 pomp] Q (pome), F   32.1 *He signs*] *not in* QF   43 day,] ROWE (*subs.*); ~ . QF

22 **armed** prepared, ready
23 **deep** grave, serious
26 **Fat ... pates** i.e. fat-bellied men have poor headpieces. The idea was an old one, but Shakespeare's phrasing of it made it proverbial (Tilley P123). He contradicted it, of course, when he created Falstaff. **bits** morsels (synonymous with 'bites')
28 **mortified** dead to worldly pleasures
29 **manner** sort, kind
32 **With ... philosophy** i.e. finding a more than adequate substitute for love,

wealth, and pomp in the study of philosophy
37 **not to see a woman** David notes that Robert Greene, in his *The Royal Exchange* (1590), says: 'Plato admitted no auditor in his academy but such as while they were his scholars would abstain from women; for he was wont to say that the greatest enemy to memory was venery' (Grosart, vii. 314).
43 **wink of all** close one's eyes during the whole of

When I was wont to think no harm all night,
And make a dark night too of half the day,
Which I hope well is not enrollèd there.
O, these are barren tasks, too hard to keep:
Not to see ladies, study, fast, not sleep.

KING

Your oath is passed to pass away from these.

BIRON

Let me say no, my liege, an if you please.   50
I only swore to study with your grace,
And stay here in your court for three years' space.

LONGUEVILLE

You swore to that, Biron, and to the rest.

BIRON

By yea and nay, sir, then I swore in jest.
What is the end of study, let me know?

KING

Why, that to know which else we should not know.

BIRON

Things hid and barred, you mean, from common
        sense?

KING

Ay, that is study's god-like recompense.

BIRON

Come on then, I will swear to study so,
To know the thing I am forbid to know: 60

57 common] Q (cammon), F   59 Come on] F; Com'on Q

44 **think ... night** i.e. think there was no
harm in sleeping all the night—an allusion to the proverb 'He that drinks well
sleeps well and he that sleeps well thinks
no harm' (Tilley H169)
49 **pass away from** abandon, give up
50 **an if** if
54 **By yea and nay** 'a formula of asservera-
tion in the form of, and substituted for, an
oath' (*OED, yea*, 3b). This common oath,
derived from Matthew 5: 37: 'let your
communication be Yea, yea; Nay, nay',
is applied equivocally by Biron to suggest
that he swore and did not swear.
57 **Things ... sense** There is a distinct echo
here, as David points out, of Ovid's
description of Pythagoras and his teach-

ings (*Metamorphoses*, xv. 60–272). In
Golding's translation (1565) the relevant
part of it relates how Pythagoras 'taught
his silent sort [group of disciples] | (Which
wondered at the heavenly words their
master did report) | The first foundation of
the world; the cause of everything; |
What Nature was, and what was God;
whence snow and lightning spring; |
And whether Jove or else the winds in
breaking clouds do thunder; | What
shakes the earth; what law the stars do
keep their courses under; | And what-
soever other thing is hid from common
sense.'
57 **common sense** ordinary or untutored
perception (*OED*, 2c)

As thus—to study where I well may dine,
    When I to feast expressly am forbid;
Or study where to meet some mistress fine,
    When mistresses from common sense are hid;
Or, having sworn too hard-a-keeping oath,
Study to break it and not break my troth.
If study's gain be thus, and this be so,
Study knows that which yet it doth not know.
Swear me to this, and I will ne'er say no.

KING

These be the stops that hinder study quite,   70
And train our intellects to vain delight.

BIRON

Why, all delights are vain, but that most vain
Which, with pain purchased, doth inherit pain:
As painfully to pore upon a book
    To seek the light of truth, while truth the while
Doth falsely blind the eyesight of his look.
    Light seeking light doth light of light beguile;
So, ere you find where light in darkness lies,
Your light grows dark by losing of your eyes.
Study me how to please the eye indeed   80
    By fixing it upon a fairer eye,
Who dazzling so, that eye shall be his heed,

---

62 feast] THEOBALD; fast QF   72 but] Q; and F

65 **too hard-a-keeping oath** an oath that is too hard to keep
70 **stops** obstacles (*OED*, *sb.*² 7)
71 **train** entice, allure (*OED*, *v.*¹ 4)
73 **pain** (a) effort, pains (b) suffering
purchased obtained, won
inherit pain bring trouble and suffering with it
74 **As** for instance (Abbott 113)
painfully laboriously, painstakingly
76 **falsely** treacherously
his look [the eyesight's] ability to see. *His* is the normal form for the possessive of *It* as well as of *He* in Shakespeare (Abbott 228).
77 **Light ... beguile** i.e. the eye seeking for intellectual illumination through reading robs itself of the power to see, or, as Dr Johnson puts it, 'a man by too close study may read himself blind'.
Light Shakespeare can refer to the eyes as

light because it was believed in his day that they emitted 'eyebeams' by means of which they saw. Compare Donne's 'The Ecstasy', ll. 8–9: 'Our eyebeams twisted, and did thread | Our eyes upon one double string'.
78 **darkness** obscurity (of learned books)
80 **Study me** study, I say. This is an instance of the so-called 'ethic dative' in which *me* originally meant 'for me'. By Shakespeare's time, however, it had become little more than a means by which the speaker drew attention to himself. See Abbott 220.
81 **a fairer eye** i.e. the eye of a beautiful girl
82–3 **Who ... by** i.e. and the man whose eyesight is thus made ineffective will find that fairer eye to be his salvation, since it will give real light to him whose eyesight was at first blinded by it.
82 **dazzling** To *dazzle* was 'to lose the faculty

99

And give him light that it was blinded by.
Study is like the heaven's glorious sun,
    That will not be deep-searched with saucy looks;
Small have continual plodders ever won,
    Save base authority from others' books.
These earthly godfathers of heaven's lights,
    That give a name to every fixèd star,
Have no more profit of their shining nights   90
    Than those that walk and wot not what they are.
Too much to know is to know naught but fame,
And every godfather can give a name.

KING

How well he's read, to reason against reading.

DUMAINE

Proceeded well, to stop all good proceeding.

LONGUEVILLE

He weeds the corn, and still lets grow the weeding.

BIRON

The spring is near when green geese are a-breeding.

DUMAINE

How follows that?

BIRON   Fit in his place and time.

---

of distinct and steady vision, especially
from gazing at too bright light' (*OED*, *v*.
1). Compare *Richard Duke of York* 2.1.25:
'Dazzle mine eyes, or do I see three suns?'
82 **heed** protection, means of safety
(Schmidt)

84–5 **heaven's ... looks** Compare the
proverbial saying 'He that gazes upon the
sun shall at last be blind' (Dent S971.1).
85 **saucy** insolent, presumptuous
86 **Small** little. Shakespeare often uses adjectives as nouns (Abbott 5).
    plodders drudges, purveyors of second-
hand learning. This is the first instance of
the word cited by *OED*; but it also occurs
in *The Unfortunate Traveller* (1594),
where Nashe writes of some German
scholars: 'Gross plodders they were all,
that had some learning and reading, but
no wit to make use of it' (Nashe, ii. 251.
11–13).
88–9 **These ... star** i.e. astronomers, who
give names to stars in much the same
way as godparents name children when

they are baptized
91 **wot** know
92 **Too ... fame** i.e. men acquire knowledge,
in excess of anything they can make use
of, merely to show off
95 **Proceeded** argued (*OED*, *v*. 2b).
    proceeding advancement (of learning)
    (*OED*, *vbl. sb.* 4)
96 **weeds ... weeding** pulls up the wheat and
leaves the weeds to grow. *OED* (*vbl. sb.*
1c) offers no parallel to this unusual sense
of *weeding*; and the gloss it provides,
'That which is weeded out', is patently
wrong. It should read: 'That which
ought to be weeded out but is not'.
97 **The spring ... a-breeding.** *Green geese* are
geese hatched in the autumn and eaten
in the spring, particularly May, of the
following year. Proverbially giddy and
witless, they are also synonymous with
silly young fools. Biron seems to be
equating the triplet in double rhyme
uttered by his companions to the cackling
of mating geese.
98 **his** its

DUMAINE

In reason nothing.

BIRON   Something then in rhyme.

KING

Biron is like an envious sneaping frost,   100
  That bites the first-born infants of the spring.

BIRON

Well, say I am. Why should proud summer boast
  Before the birds have any cause to sing?
Why should I joy in any abortive birth?
At Christmas I no more desire a rose
Than wish a snow in May's new-fangled shows,
But like of each thing that in season grows.
So you, to study now it is too late,
Climb o'er the house to unlock the little gate.

KING

Well, sit you out. Go home, Biron. Adieu!   110

BIRON

No, my good lord, I have sworn to stay with you.
And though I have for barbarism spoke more
  Than for that angel knowledge you can say,
Yet, confident, I'll keep what I have sworn,
  And bide the penance of each three years' day.
Give me the paper, let me read the same,
And to the strict'st decrees I'll write my name.

104 any] QF; an POPE   abortive] Q (abhortiue), F   109 Climb ... gate] Q; That were to
clymbe ore the house to vnlocke the gate F   110 sit] Q; fit F   114 sworn] QF; swore F2
117 strict'st] F2; strictest QF

99 **In ... rhyme** An allusion to the proverbial
   contrast between rhyme and reason
   (Dent R98.1).
100 **envious** malevolent
   sneaping frost nipping frost. The King is
   quibbling on *rhyme* and *rime*. Shakespeare uses the rare word *sneap* on two
   other occasions only, both referring to
   the weather: *Lucrece* 333 and *Winter's
   Tale* 1.2.13.
101 **first-born infants of the spring** earliest
   buds and flowers. Compare *Hamlet*
   1.3.39.
104 **abortive** premature (*OED*, A.1)
107 **like of** like, take pleasure in (Abbott
   177)
109 **Climb ... gate** i.e. behave in a futile

manner. To climb over the gate, especially if it is a 'little gate', in order to unlock
the house makes good sense; but to
reverse the process makes no sense at all.
The expression sounds like a proverbial
one, but there seems to be no record of
such a proverb.
   In the Folio the line reads: 'That were
to clymbe ore the house to vnlocke the
gate'. See Introduction, pp. 80–1.
110 **sit you out** i.e. take no part in (our
   scheme). The phrase comes from card
   games.
112 **barbarism** wilful ignorance, anti-intel-
   lectualism
115 **each three years' day** i.e. each day of the
   three years

KING (*handing over a paper*)

How well this yielding rescues thee from shame.

BIRON (*reads*) 'Item: that no woman shall come within a

mile of my court.' Hath this been proclaimed?   120

LONGUEVILLE Four days ago.

BIRON Let's see the penalty. (*He reads*) 'On pain of losing

her tongue.' Who devised this penalty?

LONGUEVILLE Marry, that did I.

BIRON Sweet lord, and why?

LONGUEVILLE

To fright them hence with that dread penalty.

BIRON

A dangerous law against gentility.

(*He reads*) 'Item: if any man be seen to talk with a

woman within the term of three years, he shall endure

such public shame as the rest of the court can possible   130

devise.'

This article, my liege, yourself must break;

For well you know here comes in embassy

The French King's daughter with yourself to speak—

A maid of grace and complete majesty—

About surrender up of Aquitaine

To her decrepit, sick, and bedrid father.

Therefore this article is made in vain,

Or vainly comes th'admirèd Princess hither.

KING

What say you, lords? Why, this was quite forgot.   140

BIRON

So study evermore is overshot.

While it doth study to have what it would,

It doth forget to do the thing it should;

---

118 *handing over a paper*] not in QF   119 *reads*] not in QF   127 BIRON] THEOBALD
(*Berowne*); *continued to Longueville*, QF (*with 'Ber.' before l. 132*)   gentility] F (gentilitie);
gentletie Q   128 *He reads*] not in QF   130 public] Q (publibue), F   can possible] Q; shall
possibly F   133 embassy] Q (Embassaie), F

124 **Marry** indeed (a weakened form of the   133 **in embassy** as an ambassador
        oath 'by the Virgin Mary')   135 **complete** perfect. The accent is on the
127 **A dangerous ... gentility** a decree that   first syllable.
        endangers good manners and civilized   141 **is overshot** misses its mark by shooting
        living   over the top of the target; a proverbial
130 **possible** possibly (*OED, possible*, C)   phrase (Dent O91.1)

And when it hath the thing it hunteth most,
'Tis won as towns with fire—so won, so lost.

KING

We must of force dispense with this decree.
She must lie here on mere necessity.

BIRON

Necessity will make us all forsworn
　Three thousand times within this three years' space;
For every man with his affects is born,　　　　　　　150
　Not by might mastered, but by special grace.
If I break faith, this word shall speak for me:
I am forsworn 'on mere necessity'.
So to the laws at large I write my name;
　And he that breaks them in the least degree
Stands in attainder of eternal shame.
　Suggestions are to other as to me;
But I believe, although I seem so loath,
I am the last that will last keep his oath.

　　　He signs

But is there no quick recreation granted?　　　　　160

KING

Ay, that there is. Our court, you know, is haunted
　With a refinèd traveller of Spain,
A man in all the world's new fashion planted,
　That hath a mint of phrases in his brain,

---

152 speak] Q (speake); breake F　　157 other] Q; others F　　159.1 *He signs*] *not in* QF

145 **as towns with fire** i.e. like towns taken by assault but set on fire in the process
146 **of force** perforce, necessarily
147 **lie** stay, lodge
　mere absolute, sheer
150 **affects** passions
151 **Not ... grace** Compare the injunction in the Catechism following on the ten commandments and the lessons to be derived from them: 'My good Child, know this, thou art not able to do these things of thyself, nor to walk in the Commandments of God, and to serve him, without his special grace'.
154 **at large** in general, as a whole
156 **in attainder of** condemned to, sentenced to (*OED*, 2a)
157 **Suggestions ... me** i.e. I am as suscepti-

ble to temptations as other men are. For Shakespeare *suggestion* almost invariably means *temptation*. See the examples given by Schmidt.
159 **I ... oath** (a) I, the last to sign, will keep my oath the longest (b) I, the last to sign, am the least likely to keep my oath the longest. Biron, characteristically, is being deliberately ambiguous.
160 **quick recreation** lively sport, spritely diversion
161–2 **haunted | With** frequented by
162 **refinèd** polished, highly cultivated. *OED* (*ppl. a.* 2) cites this as its earliest example of the word in this sense.
163 **planted** invested, acknowledged (as an expert)

One who the music of his own vain tongue
  Doth ravish like enchanting harmony,
A man of compliments, whom right and wrong
  Have chose as umpire of their mutiny.
This child of fancy, that Armado hight,
  For interim to our studies shall relate   170
In high-born words the worth of many a knight
  From tawny Spain, lost in the world's debate.
How you delight, my lords, I know not, I,
But I protest I love to hear him lie,
And I will use him for my minstrelsy.

BIRON

Armado is a most illustrious wight,
A man of fire-new words, fashion's own knight.

LONGUEVILLE

Costard the swain and he shall be our sport,
And so to study three years is but short.

  Enter Constable Dull with a letter, and Costard

DULL Which is the Duke's own person?   180
BIRON This, fellow. What wouldst?

---

165 One] F; On Q   179.1 *Enter ... Costard*] MALONE (*subs.*); *Enter a Constable with Costard with a letter.* QF   180 DULL] ROWE; *Constab.* Q; *Const.* F

165–6 **One ... harmony** An elaborate version of 'He loves to hear himself speak' (Dent L563).

165 **who** whom. Shakespeare often neglects to inflect *who* (Abbott 274).

167 **compliments** fashionable manners, or, perhaps, accomplishments

168 **mutiny** strife, discord

169 **child of fancy** fantastical being
  hight is called. This word, already archaic in Shakespeare's day, appears in two only of his other works: *A Midsummer Night's Dream* (5.1.138) and *Pericles* (15.18).

170 **For interim to** to make an interval in, to provide a relaxation from

171 **high-born** high-flown, lofty (perhaps 'high-borne')

172 **tawny** yellowish-brown (because sunburnt). Compare 'The ground indeed is tawny' (*Tempest* 2.1.59).
  world's debate i.e. warfare to which the world is so prone

173 **How you delight** what gives you pleasure

175 **minstrelsy** Down to the end of the 16th century story-telling was part of the minstrel's repertoire (*OED*, *minstrel*, 2).

176 **wight** person. Much used by Pistol, this rather old-fashioned word seems to have had a smack of the absurd about it for Shakespeare.

177 **fire-new** newly coined, fresh from the mint. 'Fire-new' is itself an example of the phenomenon it describes; *OED*'s earliest citation of it is from *Richard III* 1.3.254: 'Your fire-new stamp of honour is scarce current.' It is typical of the whole temper of *Love's Labour's Lost* that while it ridicules some neologisms it is extremely rich in them.

178 **Costard** A *costard* was a large kind of apple and also a slang term for the *head*.
  swain rustic labourer

180 **the Duke's own person** Since Armado, at 1.2.36, and the Princess, at 2.1.38, both refer to the King as the Duke, this slip is very likely to be Shakespeare's rather than Dull's.

DULL I myself reprehend his own person, for I am his
grace's farborough. But I would see his own person in
flesh and blood.

BIRON This is he.

DULL Señor Arm—Arm—commends you. There's villainy
abroad. This letter will tell you more.

COSTARD Sir, the contempts thereof are as touching me.

KING A letter from the magnificent Armado.

BIRON How low soever the matter, I hope in God for high   190
words.

LONGUEVILLE A high hope for a low heaven. God grant us
patience!

BIRON To hear, or forbear laughing?

LONGUEVILLE To hear meekly, sir, and to laugh moder-
ately, or to forbear both.

BIRON Well, sir, be it as the style shall give us cause to
climb in the merriness.

COSTARD The matter is to me, sir, as concerning Jaquenetta. The manner of it is, I was taken with the manner.   200

BIRON In what manner?

COSTARD In manner and form following, sir, all those

---

183 farborough] Q (Farborough); Tharborough F   186 Señor] OXFORD;
Signeour Q; Signeor F   188 COSTARD] ROWE; Clo⟨wne⟩. QF (*throughout the scene, except at ll. 219 and 221,*
where Q *and* F *read* Cost⟨ard⟩.)   contempts] Q (Contempls), F   194 laughing] CAPELL;
hearing QF

182 **reprehend** The word Dull has in mind is,
of course, *represent*. In his verbal blunders
he anticipates Dogberry in *Much Ado*.

183 **farborough** Dull's version of *tharbo-*
rough—the reading of F—itself a corruption of *thirdborough*, the lowest in rank of
petty constables. Ben Jonson, in his *A Tale*
of a Tub, includes in his list of 'The
Persons that act' a High Constable, a
Headborough, a petty Constable, and a
Thirdborough who is a tinker. Compare
The Taming of the Shrew Ind.1.10–11.

186 **commends you** What Dull should say is
'commends himself to you', a polite formula meaning 'greets you'.

188 **contempts** Costard means 'contents',
yet in a sense he is right, for Armado's
letter does express contempt for him.

189 **magnificent** splendid, impressive (*OED*,
adj. 4). The word, which Shakespeare
employs only here and at 3.1.171, is not
completely dismissive, but, rather, playfully ironical.

192 **A high ... heaven** i.e. 'high words are a
low sort of *heaven* to *hope* highly for'
(Kerrigan)

197–8 **the style ... climb** Biron puns on *style*
and *stile* as Benedick does in *Much Ado*
5.2.5–6, where he replies to Margaret's
request that he write her a sonnet by
saying: 'In so high a style, Margaret, that
no man living shall come over it'.

199 **to** about, with reference to

200 **taken with the manner** caught in the
act. *Manner* is an Anglicized form of the
Anglo-French legal word *mainour*, the
form in which it appears in *OED*, signifying 'hand-work'. Thence it came to mean
'the stolen thing which is found in a
thief's possession when he is arrested'
(*OED*, 1), and ultimately it was no longer
confined to theft but was applied to any
unlawful act.

202 **In manner and form following** Another
legal tag that found its way into common
parlance (Dent M631.1).

three. I was seen with her in the manor-house, sitting
with her upon the form, and taken following her into
the park, which, put together, is 'in manner and form
following'. Now, sir, for the manner—it is the manner
of a man to speak to a woman. For the form—in some
form.

BIRON For the 'following', sir?

COSTARD As it shall follow in my correction; and God   210
defend the right!

KING Will you hear this letter with attention?

BIRON As we would hear an oracle.

COSTARD Such is the simplicity of man to hearken after the
flesh.

KING (*reads*) 'Great deputy, the welkin's vicegerent, and
sole dominator of Navarre, my soul's earth's god, and
body's fostering patron'—

COSTARD Not a word of Costard yet.

KING 'So it is'—   220

COSTARD It may be so; but if he say it is so, he is, in telling
true, but so.

KING Peace!

COSTARD —be to me, and every man that dares not fight.

KING No words!

COSTARD —of other men's secrets, I beseech you.

KING 'So it is, besieged with sable-coloured melancholy, I

---

214 simplicity] Q (sinplicitie), F   216 *reads*] ROWE (*subs.*); *not in* QF   welkin's] Q (*welkis*), F
219, 221 COSTARD] QF (*Cost.*)   219 Costard] Q (*corr.*), F (*Costard*); *Costart* Q (*uncorr.*)

---

210 **correction** chastisement, punishment
(*OED*, 4)
210–11 **God defend the right** The standard
prayer made by a combatant before engaging in a trial by combat. Compare, for
instance, *Richard II* 1.3.101.
214 **simplicity** The Quarto reading 'sinplicitie' has been defended on the grounds
that it is a 'Freudian' slip; but there are
many literal errors in Q, and it is hard to
see how an actor can make the point. His
audience will hear the familiar word
'simplicity', no matter how careful his
enunciation is.
hearken after listen to, follow the urgings
of
216 **welkin's vicegerent** heaven's deputy—
an inflated rendering of the orthodox

16th-century political doctrine to the
effect that 'Kings are gods on earth' (Dent
G275.1). Shakespeare does not use *vicegerent* elsewhere.
217 **dominator** ruler. The only other occur-
rence of *dominator* in Shakespeare is at
Titus Andronicus 2.3.31, where it appears
in an astrological context.
earth's god god on earth
221–2 **in telling true** to tell the truth
222 **but so** merely so so, not worth much
226 **secrets** private concerns
227 **besieged with** beset by (Abbott 193)
sable-coloured black (because *melancholy*
was supposed to result from an excess of
'black bile', one of the four *humours*, or
bodily fluids that determined a man's
temperament). See note at 1.2.76.

did commend the black oppressing humour to the most
wholesome physic of thy health-giving air; and, as I am
a gentleman, betook myself to walk. The time when?   230
About the sixth hour, when beasts most graze, birds
best peck, and men sit down to that nourishment which
is called supper. So much for the time when. Now for
the ground which—which, I mean, I walked upon. It is
yclept thy park. Then for the place where—where, I
mean, I did encounter that obscene and most preposterous event that draweth from my snow-white pen the
ebon-coloured ink which here thou viewest, beholdest,
surveyest, or seest. But to the place where. It standeth
north-north-east and by east from the west corner of thy   240
curious-knotted garden. There did I see that low-spirited
swain, that base minnow of thy mirth'—

COSTARD Me?

KING 'that unlettered small-knowing soul'—

COSTARD Me?

KING 'that shallow vassal'—

COSTARD Still me?

KING 'which, as I remember, hight Costard'—

242 minnow] QF (*Minow*); minion SISSON (*conj.* Johnson)   247 me] F (mee?); mee. Q

228 **commend** commit, entrust (*OED*, *v.* 1)
    the black oppressing humour i.e. my
    melancholy
229 **physic** medicine
    as on my word as (*OED*, *adv.* 14). Com-
    pare *Richard II* 3.3.118–19: 'This swears
    he as he is a prince and just, | And as I
    am a gentleman I credit him'.
235 **yclept** called. Shakespeare uses this ar-
    chaic word, fashionable among writers of
    the late 16th century, at two places only:
    here, and in Holofernes' speech at
    5.2.591.
236 **obscene** repulsive, disgusting
236–7 **preposterous** contrary to the natural
    order of things—something the 'event'
    Armado goes on to describe certainly is
    not
237 **snow-white pen** The *pen* is a goose-
    quill; and *snow-white* was a time-ho-
    noured cliché (Dent S591.1).
238 **ebon-coloured** black. The blackness of
    ebony was proverbial (Tilley E56a).
241 **curious-knotted garden** garden laid out
    in intricately designed beds of herbs and

flowers (*OED*, *knot*, *sb.*¹ 7). Compare
Richard II 3.4.47, where the Gardener
sees England as a ruined garden in which
the *knots* are *disordered*. For a diagram
of 'a proper knot', the horticultural
counterpart to almost any speech by
Armado, see Fig. 6.
241 **low-spirited** base (*OED*, *a.* a), not 'de-
    jected'; earliest instance cited by *OED*
242 **minnow** i.e. contemptible little object.
    Compare *Coriolanus* 3.1.92 where the
    hero refers to the Roman mob as 'min-
    nows'. Costard, whom Shakespeare
    seems to have imagined as a big man, is,
    for Armado, a 'minnow' in his unimpor-
    tance. This is *OED*'s earliest example of
    'minnow' in a figurative sense; but it
    dates *Love's Labour's Lost* 1588. As David
    points out, Nashe calls Richard Harvey
    'a little minnow' in his *Have With You
    to Saffron Walden* published in 1596
    (Nashe, iii. 80. 33–4).
244 **unlettered** illiterate
246 **vassal** slavish wretch, underling

COSTARD O, me!

KING 'sorted and consorted, contrary to thy established   250
    proclaimed edict and continent canon, wherewith?
    O with—but with this I passion to say wherewith'—

COSTARD With a wench.

KING 'with a child of our grandmother Eve, a female, or,
    for thy more sweet understanding, a woman. Him I—as
    my ever-esteemed duty pricks me on—have sent to
    thee, to receive the meed of punishment, by thy sweet
    grace's officer, Anthony Dull, a man of good repute,
    carriage, bearing, and estimation.'

DULL Me, an't shall please you. I am Anthony Dull.   260

KING 'For Jaquenetta—so is the weaker vessel called—
    which I apprehended with the aforesaid swain, I keep
    her as a vessel of thy law's fury, and shall, at the least of
    thy sweet notice, bring her to trial. Thine in all compli-
    ments of devoted and heart-burning heat of duty,

                              Don Adriano de Armado.'

BIRON This is not so well as I looked for, but the best that
    ever I heard.

KING Ay, the best for the worst.—But, sirrah, what say
    you to this?   270

COSTARD Sir, I confess the wench.

KING Did you hear the proclamation?

251 wherewith?] This edition; Which with QF; with, with THEOBALD   258 officer] Q
(Gfficer), F   260 DULL] ROWE; *Anth.* QF   262 keep] Q; keeper F   269 worst] Q (wost), F

250 **sorted and consorted** associated and
    accompanied
251 **continent canon** decree enjoining sex-
    ual restraint
251–2 **wherewith?O** Q, followed by F, reads
    '*Which with, ô*'. But this makes no sense.
    The assumption behind the emendation
    is that the compositor misread an abbre-
    viated form of 'where' as an abbreviated
    form of 'which'. 'Wherewith', meaning
    'with what' and repeated later, is in
    Armado's authentic manner.
252 **passion** grieve. Compare *The Two Gentle-
    men of Verona* 4.4.164–5: 'Madam, 'twas
    Ariadne, passioning | For Theseus' per-
    jury and unjust flight'.
257 **meed** reward
260 **an't** if it
261 **the weaker vessel** 'A woman is the

weaker vessel' was a commonplace of the
time (Dent W655). Biblical in origin, it
comes from 1 Peter 3: 7, where it is
restricted to the wife; it was extended to
women in general from at least as early as
1576. The word *vessel* came to mean
person because of its use in translations of
the Bible where the human body is
thought of as the container of the soul.
263–4 **at ... notice** i.e. immediately on
    receiving your orders
269 **the best for the worst** i.e. a superb
    example of the thoroughly bad—a varia-
    tion on the common saying 'The better
    the worse' (Dent B333)
271 **confess** acknowledge the truth of the
    accusation concerning. Compare *The
    Merchant of Venice* 4.1.178: 'Do you
    confess the bond?'

COSTARD I do confess much of the hearing it, but little of
the marking of it.

KING It was proclaimed a year's imprisonment to be taken
with a wench.

COSTARD I was taken with none, sir, I was taken with a
damsel.

KING Well, it was proclaimed damsel.

COSTARD This was no damsel neither, sir; she was a   280
virgin.

⌈KING⌉ It is so varied too, for it was proclaimed virgin.

COSTARD If it were, I deny her virginity. I was taken with a
maid.

KING This maid will not serve your turn, sir.

COSTARD This maid will serve my turn, sir.

KING Sir, I will pronounce your sentence: you shall fast a
week with bran and water.

COSTARD I had rather pray a month with mutton and
porridge.   290

KING And Don Armado shall be your keeper.—
My Lord Biron, see him delivered o'er;
And go we, lords, to put in practice that
    Which each to other hath so strongly sworn.
                    Exeunt King, Longueville, and Dumaine

BIRON
I'll lay my head to any good man's hat
    These oaths and laws will prove an idle scorn.
Sirrah, come on.

COSTARD I suffer for the truth, sir, for true it is I was taken

282 KING] F (*Fer.*); *Ber.* Q   292 delivered] F (deliuer'd); deliuered Q   294.1 *Exeunt ...
Dumaine*] *not in* QF

282 KING This is the reading of F, which
heads the speech '*Fer.*', whereas Q heads
it '*Ber.*' F is followed here because an
intrusion by Biron at this point would
break the pattern of the exchanges.
  is so varied provides for that variation
285 **This maid ... turn** i.e. your recourse to
the word 'maid' will not help you out of
your troubles
286 **will serve my turn** Costard neatly gives
the King's words a bawdy application.
Compare *Antony and Cleopatra* 2.5.58–9,
where Cleopatra, hearing from the Messenger that Antony is 'bound unto Octa-

via', asks, 'For what good turn?', and
receives the answer: 'For the best turn
i'th' bed.'
289–90 **mutton and porridge** mutton broth
(hendiadys). Costard is probably quibbling on *mutton* in the slang sense of
'whore'.
295 **I'll ... hat** A variant on the common
betting formula 'My cap (hat) to a noble
(etc.)' (Dent C63.1).
298 **I suffer ... truth** With lugubrious humour Costard casts himself for the role of
martyr.

with Jaquenetta, and Jaquenetta is a true girl. And
therefore welcome the sour cup of prosperity! Affliction   300
may one day smile again, and till then, sit thee down,
sorrow!   *Exeunt*

1.2   *Enter Armado and Moth, his page*

ARMADO Boy, what sign is it when a man of great spirit
grows melancholy?

MOTH A great sign, sir, that he will look sad.

ARMADO Why, sadness is one and the selfsame thing, dear
imp.

MOTH No, no, O Lord, sir, no.

ARMADO How canst thou part sadness and melancholy,
my tender juvenal?

300 prosperity] F (prosperitie); prosperie Q   Affliction] F; affliccio Q   301 till] Q; vntill F
sit thee down] Q; sit downe F   302.1 *Exeunt*] Q; *Exit* F

1.2.0.1 *Moth*] QF; *Mote* KERRIGAN, OXFORD   1 (*and throughout the scene*) ARMADO] Q
(*Armado, variously abbreviated*); *Arma⟨do⟩. at line 1 but thereafter Brag⟨gart⟩.* F   3 (*and
throughout the scene*) MOTH] ROWE; *Boy.* QF; KERRIGAN, OXFORD *read* MOTE

299 **true** good, honest

300 **prosperity** Costard's version of 'adver-
sity'.

301–2 **sit … sorrow.** This phrase, substantially repeated at 4.3.3–4, sounds very
much like a proverb; but no source for it
has yet been found. Shakespeare was
soon to give the familiar phrase a powerful tragic resonance in his *K. John*, where
Constance, seating herself on the ground,
says: 'Here I and sorrows sit; | Here is
my throne; let kings come bow to it'
(2.1.73–4).

1.2.0.1 **Moth** See Appendix D.

1–2 **Boy … melancholy?** The answer Armado expects but does not receive is: 'It is
an infallible sign that he is in love.' Ovid
in his *Ars Amatoria*, i. 737–8, writes: '*Ut
voto potiare tuo, miserabilis esto ; | Ut qui te
videat, dicere possit, Amas.*' Francis Wol-
ferston in his version of 1661 renders
these lines thus: 'By looking melancholy
you will prove | Successful; all will say,
"This man's in love".'

5 **imp** Originally a young shoot of a tree or
plant, *imp* was then used of children,
especially boys, with no derogatory im-
plications. Eventually, however, it came
to be restricted to 'imps of hell'.
Shakespeare seems to have found it
rather absurd or comic, for he puts it in
the mouths of three characters only:

Armado, Holofernes (5.2.581), and En-
sign Pistol (*2 Henry IV* 5.5.42 and *Henry
V* 4.1.46).

6 **O Lord, sir** indeed, certainly. The phrase
was almost meaningless, as Shakespeare
emphasizes in *All's Well That Ends Well*
2.2.13–57, where it is described as 'an
answer will serve all men'.

7 **part** separate, distinguish between

8 **juvenal** youth, juvenile. Although *OED*
can cite no example of *juvenile* before
1625, and then only as an adjective, it is
evident that Shakespeare had either the
Latin *juvenilis* or the French *juvénile* in
mind when thus turning the name of the
great Roman satirist Juvenal into a common noun. Compare his playing on the
name of Ovid at 4.2.122. There is also a
distinct possibility that he was thinking of
Robert Greene's reference to, in all likelihood, Thomas Nashe in his *Greene's
Groatsworth of Wit* (1592), where Greene
writes of 'young Juvenal, that biting
satirist, that lastly with me together writ
a comedy' (Sig. F1). This does not mean
that Moth is a portrait of Nashe. Armado
uses the word again at 3.1.63; Flute
employs it in *Dream* 3.1.89; and Falstaff
in *2 Henry IV* 1.2.19. These are its only
appearances in Shakespeare, all of them
in comic contexts.

MOTH By a familiar demonstration of the working, my
    tough señor.   10
ARMADO Why 'tough señor'? Why 'tough señor'?
MOTH Why 'tender juvenal'? Why 'tender juvenal'?
ARMADO I spoke it, tender juvenal, as a congruent epithe-
    ton appertaining to thy young days, which we may
    nominate tender.
MOTH And I, tough señor, as an appertinent title to your
    old time, which we may name tough.
ARMADO Pretty and apt.
MOTH How mean you, sir? I pretty and my saying apt, or I
    apt and my saying pretty?   20
ARMADO Thou pretty, because little.
MOTH Little pretty, because little. Wherefore apt?
ARMADO And therefore apt, because quick.
MOTH Speak you this in my praise, master?
ARMADO In thy condign praise.
MOTH I will praise an eel with the same praise.
ARMADO What, that an eel is ingenious?
MOTH That an eel is quick.
ARMADO I do say thou art quick in answers. Thou heatest
    my blood.   30
MOTH I am answered, sir.
ARMADO I love not to be crossed.
MOTH (*aside*) He speaks the mere contrary—crosses love
    not him.
ARMADO I have promised to study three years with the
    Duke.

10, 11, *and* 16 señor] OXFORD; signeor Q; signeur F   13–14 epitheton] F2; apethaton Q;
apathaton F

9 **familiar** readily intelligible (*OED, a.* 6c).
    working operation, application
10 **señor** punning on 'senior'
13–14 **congruent epitheton appertaining to**
    fitting expression to describe. *Epitheton* is
    the original Greek and late Latin form
    from which *epithet* derives. It is not used
    by Shakespeare elsewhere.
15 **nominate** name, call
16 **appertinent** belonging, appropriate
18 **Pretty and apt** pretty apt (hendiadys)
21 **pretty, because little** 'Little things are
    pretty' was proverbial (Dent T188).
25 **condign** well deserved (*OED, a.* 3)

27 **ingenious** talented, clever. Compare
    Richard III 3.1.153–4, where Richard
    says of the young Duke of York: 'O, 'tis a
    parlous boy, | Bold, quick, ingenious, for-
    ward, capable.'
28 **an eel is quick** proverbial (Dent E59)
29–30 **Thou ... blood** i.e. you make me
    angry (by misinterpreting what I say)
32 **crossed** contradicted (*OED, v.* 14c)
33 **mere contrary** i.e. absolute opposite (of
    the truth)
    crosses coins (because many had a cross
    stamped on one side: *OED, sb.* 20)

MOTH You may do it in an hour, sir.

ARMADO Impossible.

MOTH How many is one thrice told?

ARMADO I am ill at reckoning. It fitteth the spirit of a   40
tapster.

MOTH You are a gentleman and a gamester, sir.

ARMADO I confess both. They are both the varnish of a
complete man.

MOTH Then I am sure you know how much the gross sum
of deuce-ace amounts to.

ARMADO It doth amount to one more than two.

MOTH Which the base vulgar do call three.

ARMADO True.

MOTH Why, sir, is this such a piece of study? Now here is   50
three studied ere ye'll thrice wink; and how easy it is to
put 'years' to the word 'three', and study three years in
two words, the dancing horse will tell you.

ARMADO A most fine figure!

MOTH (*aside*) To prove you a cipher.

ARMADO I will hereupon confess I am in love; and as it is
base for a soldier to love, so am I in love with a base
wench. If drawing my sword against the humour of
affection would deliver me from the reprobate thought
of it, I would take desire prisoner, and ransom him to   60
any French courtier for a new-devised curtsy. I think

---

40 fitteth] Q; fits F   48 do] Q; *not in* F   50 here is] Q; here's F   51 ye'll] Q (yele); you'll F

39 **told** counted
42 **gamester** gambler
43 **varnish** finishing touch, polish
46 **deuce-ace** a throw of two and a throw of one in a dice game
48 **vulgar** ordinary people (*OED, sb.* 2a)
50 **piece** masterpiece. Compare *Winter's Tale* 4.4.32: 'a piece of beauty'.
51 **studied** thoroughly investigated, mastered
53 **the dancing horse** The horse in question is almost certainly the celebrated Morocco, mentioned by writers innumerable from 1591 onwards, and the subject of a pamphlet, *Maroccus Extaticus, or Bankes Bay Horse in a Trance* (1595). As well as being able to dance, Morocco could also count by beating out numbers

with his hoof. See Fig. 8.
54 **figure** (a) figure of speech, which is what Armado means (b) numeral, the sense in which Moth takes it
55 **cipher** nonentity, nothing. 'He is a cipher among numbers' was proverbial (Dent C391).
57 **base** unbefitting, morally reprehensible
57–8 **base wench** wench of low birth
58–9 **humour of affection** i.e. inclination to fall in love
59 **reprobate** depraved, sinful (*OED, a.* 2). Compare *Lucrece* 300–1: 'By reprobate desire thus madly led | The Roman lord marcheth to Lucrece' bed'.
61 **new-devised curtsy** i.e. latest thing in fashionable bows
61–2 **think scorn** disdain

scorn to sigh; methinks I should outswear Cupid.
Comfort me, boy. What great men have been in love?

MOTH Hercules, master.

ARMADO Most sweet Hercules! More authority, dear boy,
name more. And, sweet my child, let them be men of
good repute and carriage.

MOTH Samson, master. He was a man of good carriage,
great carriage, for he carried the town-gates on his back
like a porter, and he was in love.   70

ARMADO O well-knit Samson, strong-jointed Samson! I do
excel thee in my rapier as much as thou didst me in
carrying gates. I am in love, too. Who was Samson's
love, my dear Moth?

MOTH A woman, master.

ARMADO Of what complexion?

MOTH Of all the four, or the three, or the two, or one of the
four.

ARMADO Tell me precisely of what complexion.

MOTH Of the sea-water green, sir.   80

ARMADO Is that one of the four complexions?

MOTH As I have read, sir; and the best of them too.

ARMADO Green indeed is the colour of lovers. But to have a
love of that colour, methinks Samson had small reason
for it. He surely affected her for her wit.

---

62 **outswear** renounce, swear to do without.
Compare 2.1.103: 'I hear your grace
hath sworn out housekeeping.'

67 **carriage** behaviour, bearing

68 **carriage** power in carrying

69–70 **he carried ... porter.** The story of
how Samson carried off the gates of Gaza
is told in Judges 16: 3.

72 **rapier** Introduced from the Continent,
the rapier was the fashionable weapon in
England during the 1590s, and brought
with it a technical vocabulary that also
became fashionable with many and a
target for satire with many more. The
two attitudes are typified by Tybalt and
Mercutio in *Romeo and Juliet*.

76–81 **Of what complexion? ... one of the
four complexions?** The primary meaning
of *complexion* was *temperament*, as determined by the mixture of the four *humours*, blood, choler, phlegm, and black

bile, in a man's make-up. The notion is
still alive in the words *sanguine, choleric,
phlegmatic,* and *melancholy*. It was also
used, however, of the *humours* themselves; and, as these were supposed to
affect the colour of the skin, it eventually
acquired its modern meaning. Armado
uses it in its old sense, Moth in its modern
one.

80 **sea-water green** Moth seems to imply
that Delilah suffered from 'green-sick-
ness', i.e. chlorosis, a disease incident to
young women. He is certainly stuffing
Armado full of nonsense.

83 **Green ... lovers** David aptly refers to the
popular song 'Greensleeves'. The close
association of spring and its greenery
with love is a familiar feature of medieval
and 16th-century poetry.

85 **affected her for her wit** loved her for her
intelligence

MOTH It was so, sir, for she had a green wit.

ARMADO My love is most immaculate white and red.

MOTH Most maculate thoughts, master, are masked under
such colours.

ARMADO Define, define, well-educated infant.   90

MOTH My father's wit and my mother's tongue assist me!

ARMADO Sweet invocation of a child, most pretty and
pathetical!

MOTH

      If she be made of white and red,
        Her faults will ne'er be known,
      For blushing cheeks by faults are bred,
        And fears by pale white shown.
      Then if she fear or be to blame,
        By this you shall not know,
      For still her cheeks possess the same   100
        Which native she doth owe.

A dangerous rhyme, master, against the reason of
white and red.

ARMADO Is there not a ballad, boy, of the King and the
Beggar?

MOTH The world was very guilty of such a ballad some
three ages since, but I think now 'tis not to be found, or

---

88 maculate] Q; immaculate F   96 blushing] F2; blush-in QF

---

86 **green wit** immature childish mind. The
phrase was proverbial (Dent W563.1).
Compare *Winter's Tale* 3.2.180–1: 'Fan-
cies too weak for boys, too green and
idle | For girls of nine'.

88 **Most maculate** very impure (Shakespeare's only use of *maculate*)

90 **Define** i.e. explain what you mean

91 **My father's ... tongue** An ingenious
variation on two common expressions:
'mother-tongue' and 'mother-wit' (Dent
M1208.1 and .2).

93 **pathetical** moving, touching, appealing

99 **By this** i.e. from her complexion

100 **still** always
    possess the same i.e. retain the same
colour

101 **native she doth owe** is hers naturally
('owe' = 'own')

102–3 **A dangerous ... red** a little jingle
showing the danger of drawing conclu-
sions from *white*, which may merely be
ceruse, and *red*, which may be rouge

104–5 **a ballad ... Beggar** The ballad referred to is almost certainly the same as
that which Armado mentions again at
4.1.64–77, where he writes of 'King
Cophetua and the ... beggar Zenelophon'. The earliest surviving copy of it is
in Richard Johnson's *Crown Garland of
Golden Roses* (1612), where its title is 'A
Song of a Beggar and a King'. Thomas
Percy took it thence and reprinted it in his
Reliques of Ancient English Poetry (1765)
as 'King Cophetua and the Beggar-Maid'.
To judge from Moth's description of it, the
original ballad must have been far more
robust than Johnson's decorous version.
There are further allusions to the story in
Romeo (2.1.13–14), *Richard II* (5.3.78),
and *2 Henry IV* (5.3.103).

if it were, it would neither serve for the writing nor the
   tune.

ARMADO I will have that subject newly writ o'er, that I   110
   may example my digression by some mighty precedent.
   Boy, I do love that country girl that I took in the park
   with the rational hind Costard. She deserves well.

MOTH (*aside*) To be whipped—and yet a better love than my
   master.

ARMADO Sing, boy. My spirit grows heavy in love.

MOTH (*aside*) And that's great marvel, loving a light
   wench.

ARMADO I say, sing.

MOTH Forbear till this company be passed.   120
      Enter Costard, Dull, and Jaquenetta

DULL (*to Armado*) Sir, the Duke's pleasure is that you keep
   Costard safe; and you must suffer him to take no
   delight, nor no penance, but a must fast three days a
   week. For this damsel, I must keep her at the park; she
   is allowed for the dey-woman. Fare you well.

ARMADO (*aside*) I do betray myself with blushing.—Maid—

JAQUENETTA Man.

ARMADO I will visit thee at the lodge.

JAQUENETTA That's hereby.

ARMADO I know where it is situate.   130

JAQUENETTA Lord, how wise you are!

ARMADO I will tell thee wonders.

JAQUENETTA With that face?

116 love] Q (loue); ioue F   120.1 *Enter ... Jaquenetta*] THEOBALD; Enter *Clowne, Constable,
and Wench*. Q, F (*subs.*)   121 DULL] ROWE; *Const*. QF   122 suffer him to] Q; let him F   123
a] Q; hee F   125 dey-woman] F (Day-woman); Day womand Q   well.] Q; well. *Exit*. F
127–36 JAQUENETTA] ROWE; *Maide*. QF (*and throughout, variously abbreviated*)   133 that]
Q; what F

108 **serve** be acceptable
111 **example** excuse, justify by a precedent
   (*OED, v.* 3)
   digression transgression, going astray
   (*OED*, 1b)
113 **rational hind** yokel endowed with the
   faculty of reason
114 **whipped** Whipping was the punishment meted out to whores.
117 **light** (a) the opposite of *heavy* (line 116)
   (b) wanton
123 **penance** Dull's mistake for 'pleasance',
   a word Shakespeare uses in *Othello*

2.3.285.
   a colloquial form of *he*
125 **allowed for the dey-woman** approved to
   serve as the dairy-maid. The earliest
   citation of *dey-woman* in *OED*, not elsewhere in Shakespeare.
129 **hereby** close by. Since the rest of Jaquenetta's answers are well worn bits of
   rustic repartee, 'That's hereby' should be
   of the same kind. But, if it is, its significance remains to be discovered.
133 **With that face?** Really?

ARMADO I love thee.

JAQUENETTA So I heard you say.

ARMADO And so farewell.

JAQUENETTA Fair weather after you.

⌈DULL⌉ Come, Jaquenetta, away.

⌈*Exeunt Dull and Jaquenetta*⌉

ARMADO Villain, thou shalt fast for thy offences ere thou
be pardoned.   140

COSTARD Well, sir, I hope when I do it I shall do it on a full
stomach.

ARMADO Thou shalt be heavily punished.

COSTARD I am more bound to you than your fellows, for
they are but lightly rewarded.

ARMADO Take away this villain. Shut him up.

MOTH Come, you transgressing slave, away!

COSTARD Let me not be pent up, sir, I will fast being loose.

MOTH No, sir, that were fast and loose. Thou shalt to
prison.   150

COSTARD Well, if ever I do see the merry days of desolation
that I have seen, some shall see—

138 DULL] THEOBALD; *Clo.* QF   138.1 *Exeunt . . . Jaquenetta*] THEOBALD; *Exeunt.* QF   141 (*and for the rest of the scene*) COSTARD] ROWE; *Clo.* QF   146 ARMADO] Q (*Ar.*); *Clo.* F

135 **So . . . say** A rough equivalent of 'you
   don't say so'.

137 **Fair weather after you** proverbial (Tilley
   W217)

138 DULL Both Q and F read '*Clo⟨wne⟩.*', and
   both end the line with the stage direction
   '*Exeunt.*' This direction cannot cover Armado, Moth, or Costard, since all three
   remain behind to continue the scene. The
   line must therefore, as Theobald was the
   first to recognize, be spoken by Dull. It
   looks as though the Q compositor misread
   a manuscript '*Co.*', short for '*Constable*', as
   '*Clo.*' His error was perpetuated by the F
   compositor, who had already—either on
   his own initiative or on that of the annotator—added an '*Exit.*' for Dull at the end of
   125, where the Constable says 'Fare you
   well', but then has to remain on stage
   waiting for Jaquenetta, who is busy dealing with Armado's advances to her.

139 **Villain** (a) peasant (b) rogue

141–2 **do it . . . stomach** Referring to the
   proverb 'The belly that is full may well
   fast' (Dent B289) and quibbling on the
   phrase 'on a full stomach', meaning

'courageously'.

144 **fellows** servants

148 **pent up** (a) imprisoned (b) costive
   loose (a) at liberty (b) loose in the bowels

149 **fast and loose** A cheating trick played by
   gipsies and other vagrants. Compare
   Antony 4.13.28–9, where Antony says
   that Cleopatra 'Like a right gipsy hath at
   fast and loose | Beguiled me to the very
   heart of loss.' According to J. Brand in his
   Popular Antiquities (1873), the trick,
   which he calls 'Pricking at the Belt', was
   played thus: 'A leathern belt is made up
   into a number of intricate folds, and
   placed edgewise upon a table. One of the
   folds is made to resemble the middle of a
   girdle, so that whoever shall thrust a
   skewer into it would think he held it fast
   to the table; whereas, when he has so
   done, the person with whom he plays
   may take hold of both ends and draw it
   away' (ii. 435). Quoted from Furness.

151 **desolation** Costard probably means *jubi-
   lation*, just as by *silent* (l. 155) he means
   loquacious and by *little* (l. 157) he means
   much.

MOTH What shall some see?

COSTARD Nay, nothing, Master Moth, but what they look
upon. It is not for prisoners to be too silent in their
words, and therefore I will say nothing. I thank God I
have as little patience as another man, and therefore I
can be quiet.   *Exeunt Moth and Costard*

ARMADO I do affect the very ground, which is base, where
her shoe, which is baser, guided by her foot, which is   160
basest, doth tread. I shall be forsworn, which is a great
argument of falsehood, if I love. And how can that be
true love which is falsely attempted? Love is a familiar;
Love is a devil. There is no evil angel but Love. Yet was
Samson so tempted, and he had an excellent strength;
yet was Solomon so seduced, and he had a very good
wit. Cupid's butt-shaft is too hard for Hercules' club,
and therefore too much odds for a Spaniard's rapier.
The first and second cause will not serve my turn. The
passado he respects not, the duello he regards not. His   170
disgrace is to be called boy, but his glory is to subdue
men. Adieu, valour; rust, rapier; be still, drum; for

154 Master] F; M. Q   155 too] Q; *not in* F   158 *Exeunt ... Costard*] POPE (*subs.*); *Exit.* QF
164–5 was Samson] Q (was *Sampson*); *Sampson* was F   170 duello] F (*Duello*); *Duella* Q

159 **affect** love

159–61 **affect ... tread** 'To love (hate) the
ground another treads on' was proverbial (Dent G468).

162 **argument** proof

163 **is falsely attempted** i.e. one strives to
win by breaking one's vow (*OED, attempt, v.* 6). Compare *Timon of Athens*
1.1.127–8: 'This man of thine | Attempts
her love'.
  familiar demon, evil spirit in attendance.
Compare *1 Henry VI* 3.6.7–8: 'But where
is Pucelle now? | I think her old familiar is
asleep'.

166 **Solomon so seduced** See 1 Kings 11:
1–3.

167 **butt-shaft** a kind of arrow employed in
target practice. Having a sharp head but
no barb, it would stick in the butt
(= mark), and could then be easily ex-
tracted from it. Compare *Romeo*
2.3.14–15, where Mercutio says that
Romeo has had 'the very pin of his heart
cleft with the blind bow-boy's butt-shaft'.

169 **The first and second cause** The 1590s
saw a positive spate of books dealing with

duelling and listing the reasons for issu-
ing a challenge. Touchstone makes
splendid fun of them in *As You Like It*
5.4.49–101. One of the earliest of these
treatises, *The Book of Honour and Arms*,
attributed to Sir William Segar and published in 1590, distinguishes the two
main justifications for engaging in a duel
thus: 'I say then that the causes of all
quarrel whereupon it behoveth to use the
trial of arms may be reduced into two: for
it seemeth to me not reasonable that any
man should expose himself to the peril of
death, save only for such occasions as do
deserve death. Wherefore whensoever
one man doth accuse another of such a
crime as meriteth death, in that case
combat ought to be granted. The second
cause of combat is honour, because
among persons of reputation, honour is
preferred before life' (p. 22).

170 **passado** forward thrust with the sword,
one foot being advanced at the same time
(*OED*)
  duello duelling code (first citation by
OED)

your manager is in love; yea, he loveth. Assist me, some
extemporal god of rhyme, for I am sure I shall turn
sonnet. Devise wit; write, pen; for I am for whole
volumes in folio.   *Exit*

2.1   *Enter the Princess of France, Rosaline wearing a cap,*
        Maria in white, and Katherine, with Boyet and two
        attendant lords

BOYET

Now, madam, summon up your dearest spirits.
Consider who the King your father sends,
To whom he sends, and what's his embassy:
Yourself, held precious in the world's esteem,
To parley with the sole inheritor
Of all perfections that a man may owe,
Matchless Navarre; the plea of no less weight
Than Aquitaine, a dowry for a queen.
Be now as prodigal of all dear grace
As Nature was in making graces dear   10
When she did starve the general world beside,
And prodigally gave them all to you.

PRINCESS

Good Lord Boyet, my beauty, though but mean,
Needs not the painted flourish of your praise.
Beauty is bought by judgement of the eye,

1 76 *Exit*] Q; *Exit.* | *Finis Actus Primus.* F
    2.1.0.1–3 *Enter ... lords*] This edition: *Enter the Princesse of Fraunce, with three attending*
Ladies and three Lordes Q, F (*subs.*)   2 Consider] Q (Cosider), F   1 3 PRINCESS] F2; *Queene.* QF

1 73 **manager** controller, master (*OED*, 1;
      earliest example cited)
1 74 **extemporal god of rhyme** god of 'unpre-
      meditated verse'
1 74–5 **turn sonnet** i.e. become 'all love and
      poetry from top to toe' (Schmidt). For
      Shakespeare and his age any poem of a
      lyrical and amatory kind was a *sonnet*.
2.1.0.1–2 *Rosaline ... white* See lines 1 95
      and 207.
    1 **dearest spirits** utmost resources of will
      and intellect. For *dearest*, meaning *ut-*
      most, compare *Hamlet* 1.2.181. Kerrigan
      makes the interesting suggestion that
      there may be a playful reference to the
      idea of conjuring up devils.

3 **embassy** message (*OED*, 2)
5 **inheritor** possessor, owner
6 **owe** own
7 **plea** claim, that which is pleaded for
   (*OED*, sb. 5). All *OED* examples of *plea* in
   this unusual sense are from Shakespeare.
9 **prodigal** lavish
   dear precious
10 **dear** costly
1 1 **starve ... beside** i.e. deprive the rest of the
   world of graces
1 3 **mean** average, moderate
1 4 **painted flourish** glossy ostentatious embellishment. 'A good face needs no paint'
   was proverbial (Dent F7).

Not uttered by base sale of chapmen's tongues.
I am less proud to hear you tell my worth
Than you much willing to be counted wise
In spending your wit in the praise of mine.
But now to task the tasker. Good Boyet,   20
You are not ignorant all-telling fame
Doth noise abroad Navarre hath made a vow,
Till painful study shall outwear three years,
No woman may approach his silent court.
Therefore to's seemeth it a needful course,
Before we enter his forbidden gates,
To know his pleasure; and in that behalf,
Bold of your worthiness, we single you
As our best-moving fair solicitor.
Tell him the daughter of the King of France,   30
On serious business craving quick dispatch,
Importunes personal conference with his grace.
Haste, signify so much, while we attend,
Like humble-visaged suitors, his high will.

BOYET

Proud of employment, willingly I go.

PRINCESS

All pride is willing pride, and yours is so.   *Exit Boyet*
Who are the votaries, my loving lords,
That are vow-fellows with this virtuous Duke?

20–1 Boyet, | You] Q; *Boyet, | Prin.* You F   32 Importunes] F; Importuous Q   34 humble-
visaged] F (humble visag'd); humble visage Q   36.1 *Exit Boyet*] Q (*Exit Boy.*); *Exit* F (*both
after l. 35*)

16 **uttered** offered for sale. Compare *Romeo*
5.1.66–7: 'Such mortal drugs I have, but
Mantua's law | Is death to any he that
utters them.'
   chapmen's merchants', traders'
17 **tell** (a) speak of (b) count, reckon
18 **counted** accounted, regarded as
20 **task the tasker** impose a task on the man
who has been setting tasks (the earliest
instance of *tasker* in this sense cited by
OED, not elsewhere in Shakespeare)
21 Wells sugggests that 'F's redundant
prefix "*Prin.*" may reflect a cut in performance of the scene's previous lines'.
   fame rumour
22 **noise abroad** 'broadcast', spread the

story
23 **outwear** wear out. Shakespeare uses
outwear only with reference to time.
25 **to's** to us (colloquial)
27 **in that behalf** on that account, for that
purpose (*OED, behalf*, 2c)
28 **Bold of** confident of, trusting in (*OED, a.*
6).
29 **best-moving** most persuasive, most eloquent
   fair solicitor just advocate, reliable agent
(*OED, solicitor*, 2)
32 **Importunes** (accented on the second syllable)
   conference conversation

FIRST LORD

Lord Longueville is one.

PRINCESS   Know you the man?

MARIA

I know him, madam. At a marriage feast   40
Between Lord Périgord and the beauteous heir
Of Jaques Falconbridge, solemnizèd
In Normandy, saw I this Longueville.
A man of sovereign parts, peerless he is esteemed,
Well fitted in arts, glorious in arms.
Nothing becomes him ill that he would well.
The only soil of his fair virtue's gloss—
If virtue's gloss will stain with any soil—
Is a sharp wit matched with too blunt a will,
Whose edge hath power to cut, whose will still wills   50
It should none spare that come within his power.

PRINCESS

Some merry mocking lord belike, is't so?

MARIA

They say so most that most his humours know.

PRINCESS

Such short-lived wits do wither as they grow.
Who are the rest?

39 FIRST LORD Lord Longueville] CAPELL; *Lor. Longauill* QF   40 MARIA] ROWE; I. *Lady.* Q, F (*subs.*)   madam.] CAPELL (~;); ~ ∧ QF   41 Lord Périgord] OXFORD; L. *Perigort* QF   42 solemnizèd ∧] RANN; ~. QF   44 sovereign parts, peerless] ALEXANDER; soueraigne peerelsse Q; soueraigne parts F   45 Well ... arts] QF; In arts well fitted WHITE (*conj.* Keightley)   50 wills] ROWE; ~, QF   53 MARIA] ROWE; *Lad.* Q; *Lad.* I. F

41 **heir** heiress. *OED* gives no example of *heiress* before 1659.

42 **solemnizèd** (accented on the second syllable)

44 **sovereign parts, peerless** Q reads 'soueraigne peerelsse'; F 'soueraigne parts', The assumption behind the present reading is that the compositor of Q inadvertently omitted 'parts'. Then the annotator who prepared a copy of Q for the printing of F noticed the omission and wrote in the missing word which the compositor of F took to be a correction of 'peerelsse'. The result is a six-foot line; but *LLL* is a play of metrical variety.

45 **Well ... arms** This line would seem to be Shakespeare's rendering of the well known Latin tag *Tam Marti quam Mercurio* which the poet George Gascoigne had adopted as his motto.

45 **fitted in arts** qualified in intellectual pursuits

glorious in arms famous in war

46 **Nothing ... well** 'anything he wants to do well he does well and looks admirable for it' (Kerrigan)

47 **soil** tarnish, stain

gloss lustre

49 **matched** joined, paired

blunt a will i.e. insensitive a readiness to use it

50 **whose will still wills** i.e. and his will invariably determines

51 **his** its

53 **most his humours know** best know his moods

54 **Such ... grow** A version of 'Soon ripe soon rotten' (Tilley R133). Compare 'So

KATHERINE

The young Dumaine, a well-accomplished youth,
Of all that virtue love for virtue loved;
Most power to do most harm, least knowing ill;
For he hath wit to make an ill shape good,
And shape to win grace, though he had no wit.   60
I saw him at the Duke Alençon's once;
And much too little of that good I saw
Is my report to his great worthiness.

ROSALINE

Another of these students at that time
Was there with him, if I have heard a truth.
Biron they call him, but a merrier man,
Within the limit of becoming mirth,
I never spent an hour's talk withal.
His eye begets occasion for his wit,
For every object that the one doth catch   70
The other turns to a mirth-moving jest,
Which his fair tongue, conceit's expositor,
Delivers in such apt and gracious words
That agèd ears play truant at his tales,
And younger hearings are quite ravishèd,
So sweet and voluble is his discourse.

PRINCESS

God bless my ladies! Are they all in love,

56 KATHERINE] ROWE; 2. *Lad.* QF   60 he] Q; she F   61 Alençon's] JOHNSON and STEEVENS; *Alansoes* QF   64 ROSALINE] F (*Rossa.*); 3. *Lad.* Q   65 if] Q; as F

wise so young, they say, do never live long' (*Richard III* 3.1.79).

57 **Of** by
58 **Most … ill** i.e. because he knows little or nothing about the nature of evil, he has a great potential for doing a lot of harm
59–60 **he … wit** 'his intelligence is such that it would make up for an ugly body, and his physical endowment is such that it would make up for lack of brains' (Riverside)
62 **much too little** far too short
63 **to** compared to (*OED*, A 18). Compare *Hamlet* 1.2.139–40: 'So excellent a king, that was to this | Hyperion to a satyr'.
66 **Biron … man** David tentatively suggests

that there is a pun here on *Berowne*, the name as it is in Q, and *brown*, both pronounced to rhyme with *moon* (4.3.227 and 229). It seems highly likely, for *brown* could mean *sombre*, as in *brown study*, and would thus account for the *but*.
68 **withal** with. This emphatic form of *with* is used after the object at the end of a sentence (Abbott 196).
69 **begets occasion** spots opportunities
72 **conceit's expositor** the expounder of witty ideas (Shakespeare's sole use of *expositor*).
74 **play truant at** i.e. abandon their pursuit of serious matters in favour of listening to
76 **voluble** fluent

That every one her own hath garnishèd
With such bedecking ornaments of praise?
FIRST LORD
Here comes Boyet.
      Enter Boyet
PRINCESS   Now, what admittance, lord?   80
BOYET
Navarre had notice of your fair approach,
And he and his competitors in oath
Were all addressed to meet you, gentle lady,
Before I came. Marry, thus much I have learnt:
He rather means to lodge you in the field,
Like one that comes here to besiege his court,
Than seek a dispensation for his oath
To let you enter his unpeopled house.
Here comes Navarre.
      Enter the King, Longueville, Dumaine, and Biron
KING Fair Princess, welcome to the court of Navarre.   90
PRINCESS 'Fair' I give you back again, and welcome I have
   not yet. The roof of this court is too high to be yours,
   and welcome to the wide fields too base to be mine.
KING
You shall be welcome, madam, to my court.
PRINCESS
I will be welcome then. Conduct me thither.

---

80 FIRST LORD] Q (*Lord.*); *Ma⟨ria⟩*. F   88 unpeopled] F; vnpeeled Q   89 Here comes
Navarre] F; *Bo⟨yet⟩. Heere comes Nauar* Q   89.1 *Enter ... Biron*] QF (Enter *Nauar, Longauill,
Dumaine, & Berowne.), after l. 88*   90–110 KING] ROWE; *Nauar.* QF

78–9 **garnishèd ... bedecking ornaments**
  Compare *Henry V* 2.2.131: 'Garnished
  and decked in modest complement'.
80 **admittance** sort of reception (Schmidt)
81 **fair** Here, as so often in this play, where it
  is badly overworked, *fair* has no definite
  meaning but serves as a convenient filler
  to eke out the line.
82 **competitors** partners, associates (*OED*,
  2). This sense of *competitor* is much
  commoner in Shakespeare than its modern sense.
83 **addressed** prepared, ready
84 **Marry** a mild oath, originally the name of
  the Virgin Mary
85 **field** (a) open country (b) battlefield

88 **unpeopled house** house inadequately
  staffed with servants. Shakespeare uses
  unpeopled again at *Richard II* 1.2.69 and
  As You Like It 3.2.123, and frequently
  has *people* for *servants*, as, for example, at
  Twelfth Night 2.5.56–7, where Malvolio
  says: 'Seven of my people with an obedi-
  ent start make out for him'.
    The Q reading 'vnpeeled' is almost
  certainly a misprint for a word that
  probably appeared in Shakespeare's
  manuscript as 'vnpeepled'. As Wilson
  notices and *OED* confirms, both 'peple'
  and 'peeple' were not uncommon 16th-
  century spellings of 'people'.

92 **The roof ... court** i.e. the sky

122

KING

Hear me, dear lady. I have sworn an oath—

PRINCESS

Our Lady help my lord! He'll be forsworn.

KING

Not for the world, fair madam, by my will.

PRINCESS

Why, will shall break it; will, and nothing else.

KING

Your ladyship is ignorant what it is.   100

PRINCESS

Were my lord so, his ignorance were wise,

Where now his knowledge must prove ignorance.

I hear your grace hath sworn out housekeeping.

'Tis deadly sin to keep that oath, my lord,

And sin to break it.

But pardon me, I am too sudden bold;

To teach a teacher ill beseemeth me.

Vouchsafe to read the purpose of my coming,

And suddenly resolve me in my suit.

        She gives the King a document

KING

Madam, I will, if suddenly I may.   110

PRINCESS

You will the sooner that I were away,

For you'll prove perjured if you make me stay.

        The King peruses the document

BIRON (*to Rosaline*)

Did not I dance with you in Brabant once?

⌈ROSALINE⌉

Did not I dance with you in Brabant once?

99 it; will,] CAPELL; it will, QF   109.1 *She . . . document*] *not in* QF   112.1 *The . . . document*] *not in* QF   114–25 ROSALINE] F (*Rosa.*); Kath⟨erine⟩. Q

98 **by my will** willingly

99 **will** desire

102 **Where** whereas (Abbott 134)

   prove turn out to be

103 **sworn out housekeeping** renounced hospitality (*OED, housekeeping,* 2). Complaints about the decay of housekeeping, the kind of hospitality practised by Chaucer's Franklin, were common in Shakespeare's day.

106 **sudden** rashly, inconsiderately

109 **suddenly** immediately

   resolve me in give me your answer to (*OED, v.* 11)

111 **You . . . away** i.e. you will do it the more readily in order to have me go

113–26 **Did not I dance . . . be gone** See Introduction, pp. 60–3.

BIRON

  I know you did.

⌈ROSALINE⌉   How needless was it then

  To ask the question!

BIRON   You must not be so quick.

⌈ROSALINE⌉

  'Tis long of you that spur me with such questions.

BIRON

  Your wit's too hot, it speeds too fast, 'twill tire.

⌈ROSALINE⌉

  Not till it leave the rider in the mire.

BIRON

  What time o'day?   120

⌈ROSALINE⌉

  The hour that fools should ask.

BIRON

  Now fair befall your mask.

⌈ROSALINE⌉

  Fair fall the face it covers.

BIRON

  And send you many lovers.

⌈ROSALINE⌉

  Amen, so you be none.

BIRON

  Nay, then will I be gone.

      ⌈*He leaves her*⌉

KING (*to the Princess*)

  Madam, your father here doth intimate

  The payment of a hundred thousand crowns,

  Being but the one half of an entire sum

  Disbursèd by my father in his wars.   130

126.1 *He leaves her*] not in QF   127 KING] F (*Kin.*); *Ferd.* Q   129 of] F; of, of Q

<table>
<tr><td>116 quick (a) impatient (OED, a. 22) (b) sharp, caustic (18b)</td><td>120 What time o' day? Biron asks a silly question in order to change the topic.</td></tr>
<tr><td>117–19 'Tis … mire Proverbial—'Do not spur a willing horse', 'A free horse will soon tire', and 'To leave in the mire' (Dent H638, H642, M989).</td><td>122 fair befall i.e. good luck to (OED, befall, v. 4e)</td></tr>
<tr><td>117 long of owing to, because of (OED, a.²).</td><td>123 Fair fall may good befall (OED, fall, v. 46d)</td></tr>
<tr><td>spur (a) urge on (b) interrogate (OED, speer, v.¹, of which spur was a variant spelling)</td><td>125 so provided that, so long as</td></tr>
<tr><td></td><td>127 intimate notify us of, refer to</td></tr>
<tr><td></td><td>129 entire (stressed on the first syllable)</td></tr>
<tr><td></td><td>130 his i.e. the King of France's</td></tr>
</table>

But say that he, or we—as neither have—
Received that sum, yet there remains unpaid
A hundred thousand more, in surety of the which
One part of Aquitaine is bound to us,
Although not valued to the money's worth.
If then the King your father will restore
But that one half which is unsatisfied,
We will give up our right in Aquitaine,
And hold fair friendship with his majesty.
But that, it seems, he little purposeth,   140
For here he doth demand to have repaid
A hundred thousand crowns, and not demands,
On payment of a hundred thousand crowns,
To have his title live in Aquitaine,
Which we much rather had depart withal,
And have the money by our father lent,
Than Aquitaine, so gelded as it is.
Dear Princess, were not his requests so far
From reason's yielding, your fair self should make
A yielding 'gainst some reason in my breast,   150
And go well satisfied to France again.

PRINCESS

You do the King my father too much wrong,
And wrong the reputation of your name,
In so unseeming to confess receipt
Of that which hath so faithfully been paid.

KING

I do protest I never heard of it;
And if you prove it, I'll repay it back
Or yield up Aquitaine.

PRINCESS   We arrest your word.

---

139 friendship] Q (faiendship), F   141 demand] Q (pemaund), F   repaid] Q (repaide); repaie F
142 A] Q; An F   143 On] THEOBALD; One QF

131 **he** i.e. my father
   as neither have which neither of us has.
   For Shakespeare's use of *as* as a relative in
   parenthetical clauses, and of *neither* as a
   plural pronoun, see Abbott 111 and 12.
133 **surety** guarantee (*OED, sb.* 5)
134 **bound** mortgaged, secured
135 **valued ... worth** i.e. really worth the
   money it is supposed to secure
136 **restore** repay, give back to the true

owner
137 **unsatisfied** unpaid
142 **and not demands** i.e. does not demand
   as in equity he might
145 **had depart withal** would part with
147 **gelded** i.e. deprived of an essential part
   (*OED, v.*¹ 2)
154 **unseeming** not seeming (to be willing
   to) (Onions)
158 **arrest your word** seize your promise as

125

Boyet, you can produce acquittances
For such a sum from special officers   160
Of Charles, his father.

KING   Satisfy me so.

BOYET

So please your grace, the packet is not come
Where that and other specialties are bound.
Tomorrow you shall have a sight of them.

KING

It shall suffice me; at which interview
All liberal reason I will yield unto.
Meantime receive such welcome at my hand
As honour, without breach of honour, may
Make tender of to thy true worthiness.
You may not come, fair Princess, within my gates,   170
But here without you shall be so received
As you shall deem yourself lodged in my heart,
Though so denied fair harbour in my house.
Your own good thoughts excuse me, and farewell.
Tomorrow shall we visit you again.

PRINCESS

Sweet health and fair desires consort your grace.

KING

Thy own wish wish I thee in every place.

                    Exeunt the King, Longueville, and Dumaine

BIRON Lady, I will commend you to mine own heart.

ROSALINE Pray you, do my commendations; I would be
    glad to see it.   180

166 I will] Q; would I F   168 may ∧] F; ~, Q   170 within] Q; in F   177 KING] F
(*Kin.*); *Na.* Q   177.1 *Exeunt ... Dumaine*] CAPELL (*subs.*); *Exit.* QF   178–91 BIRON] Q (*Ber.*,
with '*Bar.*' at l. 185); *Boy⟨et⟩.* F   178 mine own] Q (my none); my owne F

security. Compare *Measure for Measure*
2.4.134: 'I do arrest your words.' *OED* (*v.*
12) cites no other instances of *arrest* in
this figurative sense; but, as David points
out, Shakespeare had been anticipated by
Sir Philip Sidney in his *Arcadia*, where
Artesia 'took the advantage one day
upon Phalantus' unconscionable prais-
ings of her ... to arrest his word as soon
as it was out of his mouth' (i. 99).

163 **specialties** special legal contracts under
    seal (*OED*, 7). Compare *Shrew* 2.1.126–7:

'Let specialties be therefore drawn be-
tween us, | That covenants may be kept
on either hand.'
166 **All liberal reason** 'any civilized argu-
    ment' (Kerrigan)
169 **Make tender of** offer
172 **As that** (Abbott 109)
173 **harbour** quarters, lodgings (*OED*, *sb.*[1]
    2)
176 **consort** accompany, go with
178 **commend** (a) commit (b) remember
179 **do my commendations** i.e. give it my
    greetings

BIRON I would you heard it groan.

ROSALINE Is the fool sick?

BIRON Sick at the heart.

ROSALINE

   Alack, let it blood.

BIRON

   Would that do it good?

ROSALINE

   My physic says ay.

BIRON

   Will you prick't with your eye?

ROSALINE

   Non point, with my knife.

BIRON

   Now God save thy life.

ROSALINE

   And yours—from long living.   190

BIRON

   I cannot stay thanksgiving.   *Exit*
         Enter Dumaine

DUMAINE (*to Boyet*)

   Sir, I pray you a word. What lady is that same?

BOYET

   The heir of Alençon, Katherine her name.

DUMAINE

   A gallant lady! Monsieur, fare you well.   *Exit*
         Enter Longueville

LONGUEVILLE (*to Boyet*)

   I beseech you a word. What is she in the white?

BOYET

   A woman sometimes, an you saw her in the light.

LONGUEVILLE

   Perchance light in the light. I desire her name.

---

182 fool] Q (foole); soule F   188 *Non point*] KERRIGAN; *No poynt* QF   191 *Exit*] QF; *retiring*
CAPELL   193 Katherine] SINGER (*conj.* Capell); *Rosalin* QF   194 *Exit*] Q; *not in* F   194.1 *Enter
Longueville*] F2; *not in* QF   196 an] Q (and); if F   197 name.] F; ~? Q

182 **fool** poor thing (*OED, sb.*¹ c)   the primacy of the French meaning. See
184 **let it blood** bleed it   Wells, *Re-Editing*, p. 26.
186 **physic** medical knowledge   191 **stay thanksgiving** take the time to
188 *Non point* (a) not a bit, not at all (*OED,*   thank you properly
     *point, sb.*¹ 6b) (b) it's blunt. Both Q and F   197 **light in the light** i.e. wanton when seen
     italicize *No poynt*, as they have it, to stress   for what she really is

BOYET

She hath but one for herself; to desire that were a
    shame.

LONGUEVILLE

Pray you, sir, whose daughter?

BOYET

Her mother's, I have heard.   200

LONGUEVILLE

God's blessing on your beard!

BOYET

Good sir, be not offended.

She is an heir of Falconbridge.

LONGUEVILLE

Nay, my choler is ended.

She is a most sweet lady.

BOYET

Not unlike, sir, that may be.   *Exit Longueville*
    Enter Biron

BIRON

What's her name in the cap?

BOYET

Rosaline, by good hap.

BIRON

Is she wedded or no?

BOYET

To her will, sir, or so.   210

BIRON

You are welcome, sir. Adieu.

BOYET

Farewell to me, sir, and welcome to you.   *Exit Biron*

---

201 on] Q; a F   206 *Exit Longueville*] Q; *after l. 205* F   208 Rosaline] SINGER; *Katherin* Q;
Katherine F   211 You] F; O you Q   212 *Exit Biron*] Q (*Exit Bero.*); *Exit* F

201 **God's ... beard** 'may'st thou have some
    sense and seriousness more proportion-
    ate to thy beard, the length of which suits
    ill with such idle catches of wit' (John-
    son).

206 **unlike** unlikely

209–10 **Is she ... so** 'To be wedded to one's
    will' was proverbial (Tilley W392).

211 **You are welcome** at your service
    (Schmidt). This is the reading of F. Q
    begins the line with an intrusive 'O',
    probably caught from the last letter of the
    speech-prefix '*Bero⟨wne⟩*.'

212 **welcome to you** you are welcome to
    go—proverbial (Tilley W259)

MARIA

That last is Biron, the merry madcap lord.

Not a word with him but a jest.

BOYET   And every jest but a word.

PRINCESS

It was well done of you to take him at his word.

BOYET

I was as willing to grapple as he was to board.

⌈ROSALINE⌉

Two hot sheeps, marry!

BOYET   And wherefore not 'ships'?

No sheep, sweet lamb, unless we feed on your lips.

⌈ROSALINE⌉

You sheep, and I pasture. Shall that finish the jest?

BOYET

So you grant pasture for me.

        ⌈*He tries to kiss her*⌉

⌈ROSALINE⌉   Not so, gentle beast.   220

My lips are no common, though several they be.

BOYET

Belonging to whom?

⌈ROSALINE⌉   To my fortunes and me.

PRINCESS

Good wits will be jangling; but, gentles, agree:

217 ROSALINE] This edition; *Lady Ka.* Q; *La. Ma.* F   sheeps, marry!] THEOBALD (*subs.*);
Sheepes marie. Q; Sheepes marie: F   BOYET And ... 'ships'?] Q; *continued to Rosaline* F
219, 221, 222 ROSALINE] This edition; *La⟨dy⟩.* QF   220 *He ... her*] CAPELL; *not in* QF
223 but, gentles,] THEOBALD; but ∧ gentles ∧ QF

213 **madcap** entertainingly wild and eccentric

215 **take him at his word** take him on at his own word-games

216 **grapple ... board** The language is that of a naval battle.

217 **hot sheeps** fiery, ardent sheep—almost a contradiction in terms in view of the sheep's reputed meekness and timidity. Katherine takes a poor view of the verbal battle between the two men.
sheeps ... 'ships' In his early comedies Shakespeare found this pun irresistible—compare *Two Gentlemen* 1.1.72–9 and *Comedy of Errors* 4.1.93–4—but then, mercifully, abandoned it.

219 **pasture** probably quibbling on 'pastor', meaning 'shepherd'

220 **So** provided

221 **My lips ... be** i.e. my lips are no common (pasture on which all the farmers of the village have the right to graze their stock) although they are, admittedly, pasture (but enclosed pasture in private ownership). See *OED, several*, sb. 2, and compare Sonnets 137.9–10: 'Why should my heart think that a several plot | Which my heart knows the wide world's common place?'
several (a) privately owned enclosed land (b) more than one (c) parted

223 **jangling** disputing, wrangling
gentles gentlefolk (*OED, sb.* 1c). Shakespeare and other playwrights of the time often addressed their audiences as 'gentles'. See, for instance, *Henry V* Pro.8.

This civil war of wits were much better used
On Navarre and his book-men, for here 'tis abused.

BOYET

If my observation, which very seldom lies
By the heart's still rhetoric disclosèd wi'th' eyes,
Deceive me not now, Navarre is infected.

PRINCESS With what?

BOYET

With that which we lovers entitle 'affected'.   230

PRINCESS Your reason?

BOYET

Why, all his behaviours did make their retire
To the court of his eye, peeping thorough desire.
His heart, like an agate with your print impressed,
Proud with his form, in his eye pride expressed.
His tongue, all impatient to speak and not see,
Did stumble with haste in his eyesight to be.
All senses to that sense did make their repair,
To feel only looking on fairest of fair.
Methought all his senses were locked in his eye,   240
As jewels in crystal for some prince to buy;
Who, tend'ring their own worth from where they were
    glassed,
Did point you to buy them along as you passed.

226–7 observation, which ... eyes,] F (obseruation (which ... eyes); obseruation (which ...
eyes. Q   226 lies] Q (*corr.*), F; lyes? Q (*uncorr.*)   227 wi'th'] This edition; with QF
231 reason?] ROWE; ∼. QF   232 did] Q; doe F   242 where] Q; whence F   243 point
you] Q; point out F

225 **book-men** scholars. Shakespeare's only
other use of this word is at 4.2.33.
    abused put to a wrong use, misapplied
226–7 **lies | By** conveys a false impression
about, is mistaken about. For *by* in the
sense of 'about', 'concerning', see Abbott
145, and compare *Merchant* 1.2.52–3:
'How say you by the French lord, Monsieur Le Bon?'
227 **still rhetoric** dumb eloquence
    wi'th' by the (Abbott 193). Compare
K. John 2.1.567–8: 'rounded in the ear |
With that same purpose-changer'.
230 **affected** being in love
232–3 **Why ... desire** 'all his powers of
expression were concentrated in his eye,
and shared in the longing look he gave
you' (David)
232 **retire** repair, withdrawal

233 **thorough** through
234 **with your print impressed** i.e. with a
representation of you engraved on it
235 **Proud with his form** made proud by the
form—the Princess's image—stamped
on it
236 **impatient ... see** frustrated because of
being limited to speaking and so unable
to see
239 **looking** through looking
241 **crystal** crystal glass
242 **Who** and they (Abbott 259)
    tend'ring offering, proffering for accep-
tance
    glassed enclosed in glass (*OED, v.* 2;
earliest example of this sense, not used
elsewhere by Shakespeare)
243 **point** direct (Onions)

His face's own margin did quote such amazes
That all eyes saw his eyes enchanted with gazes.
I'll give you Aquitaine, and all that is his
An you give him for my sake but one loving kiss.

PRINCESS

Come, to our pavilion. Boyet is disposed.

BOYET

But to speak that in words which his eye hath
        disclosed.
I only have made a mouth of his eye   250
By adding a tongue which I know will not lie.

⌈MARIA⌉

Thou art an old love-monger, and speakest skilfully.

⌈KATHERINE⌉

He is Cupid's grandfather, and learns news of him.

⌈ROSALINE⌉

Then was Venus like her mother, for her father is but
        grim.

BOYET

Do you hear, my mad wenches?

⌈MARIA⌉   No.

BOYET   What then, do you see?

⌈MARIA⌉

Our way to be gone.   You are too hard for me.   *Exeunt*

BOYET

249 BOYET] Q (*Bo.*); *Bro.* F   252 MARIA] CAPELL; *Lad.* Q; *Lad. Ro.* F   253 KATHERINE]
CAPELL; *Lad. 2.* Q; *Lad. Ma.* F   254 ROSALINE] ROWE; *Lad. 3.* Q; *Lad. 2.* F   255 MARIA]
ROWE; *Lad.* Q; *La.* I. F   256 MARIA Our] This edition (*conj.* Wilson); *Lad.* I, our Q; *Lad. 2.* I,
our F

244 **His ... amazes** The idea of the face as a
  book is common in Shakespeare; compare *Macbeth* 1.5.61–2: 'Your face, my
  thane, is as a book where men | May read
  strange matters.' The *margin* frequently
  contained notes summarizing the contents of a paragraph or drawing the
  reader's attention to something of special
  interest, while to *quote* could mean to
  indicate by means of a pointing index
  finger in the *margin*.
  amazes extremes of admiration. Since
  amaze derives from *maze* (*sb.*), it probably
  suggested the word *enchanted* in the next
  line.
248 **disposed** inclined to be merry, in a

jocund mood (*OED, ppl. a.* 4b)
252 MARIA For the attribution of the ladies'
  speeches see Introduction, p. 61.
  love-monger dealer in love affairs (not
  used elsewhere in Shakespeare)
  skilfully expertly
255 **Do you hear** A formula for gaining
  attention, equivalent to the modern 'Listen'.
  mad wenches high-spirited girls. 'Mad
  wenches' was something of a stock
  phrase (Dent W274.1).
256 MARIA Q reads '*Lad.*'; F '*Lad.* 2.' Following Wilson's suggestion, this edition assumes that Shakespeare wrote '*Lad.* 1.'
  which the compositor misread as '*Lad.* l.'

3.1   *Enter Armado and Moth*

ARMADO Warble, child, make passionate my sense of
    hearing.

MOTH ⌈*sings the song*⌉ 'Concolinel'.

ARMADO Sweet air! Go, tenderness of years, take this key,
    give enlargement to the swain, bring him festinately
    hither. I must employ him in a letter to my love.

MOTH Master, will you win your love with a French
    brawl?

ARMADO How meanest thou? Brawling in French?

MOTH No, my complete master; but to jig off a tune at the   10
    tongue's end, canary to it with your feet, humour it
    with turning up your eyelids, sigh a note and sing a
    note, sometime through the throat as if you swallowed
    love with singing love, sometime through the nose as if
    you snuffed up love by smelling love, with your hat
    penthouse-like o'er the shop of your eyes, with your

3.1.0.1 *Enter Armado and Moth*] ROWE; Enter *Braggart* and his *Boy*. Q; *Enter Braggart and Boy*. | Song. F   1–63 ARMADO] ROWE; *Bra⟨ggart⟩*. QF   3–62 MOTH] ROWE; *Boy*. QF   3 *sings the song*] THEOBALD (*subs.*); *not in* QF   7 Master, will] Q; Will F   11 with your] Q; with the F   12 eyelids] Q (eylids); eie F   13 throat as if] THEOBALD (*subs.*); throate, if Q; throate: if F   14 singing love,] THEOBALD; singing loue ∧ Q; singing, loue ∧ F   through the nose] F2; through: nose QF   15 love, with] F2; loue ∧ with QF

3.1.1 **make passionate ... hearing** i.e. assure
    that my sense of hearing is deeply affected
    by the passion of love (*OED, passionate, a.*
    4)

3 **Concolinel** The likeliest explanation of
    this strange word is that it is the title of
    Moth's song. If it is, it could well be a
    corruption of the Irish lyric '*Can cailin
    gheal*', pronounced 'Con colleen yal' and
    meaning 'Sing, fair maiden'. Compare
    Pistol's reference to another Irish song,
    '*Calin o custure me*', at *Henry V* 4.4.4.
    Alternatively, it might be the opening of
    some lost French song beginning '*Quand
    Colinelle*'.

5 **give enlargement to** free
    festinately immediately (only example
    cited by *OED*)

7–8 **French brawl** a kind of French dance
    resembling a cotillon (*OED, brawl, sb.*¹ 2).
    A dance in which 'the dancers move
    sideways and not forward', a *brawl* is
    staged in John Marston's *The Malcontent*
    (4.2.1–14).

10 **jig off a tune** sing a tune in the style of a

jig (earliest example of *jig* as a verb in
OED)

10–11 **at the tongue's end** proverbial (Tilley
T413)

11 **canary** i.e. dance as if you were dancing
the *canaries*. So called because it seems to
have originated in the Canary Islands,
the *canaries* was a quick and lively dance.
OED cites this as its earliest instance of
canary as a verb.

    humour it adapt yourself to it (*OED, v.* 2;
earliest example of this meaning)

15–19 **with your hat ... painting** See the
picture of the melancholy lover Inamo-
rato in the frontispiece to Robert Burton's
The Anatomy of Melancholy (1621).

16 **penthouse-like o'er the shop** Many Elizabethan shops had a stall, or *bulk*, as it was
called, at their fronts for the display of
wares. This stall was protected from the
weather by a wooden *penthouse*, a kind of
awning that could be raised during the
day to provide a sloping roof and lowered
at night.

arms crossed on your thin-belly doublet like a rabbit on
a spit, or your hands in your pocket like a man after the
old painting; and keep not too long in one tune, but a
snip and away. These are compliments, these are hu-   20
mours, these betray nice wenches that would be betrayed without these; and make them men of note—do
you note me?—that most are affected to these.

ARMADO How hast thou purchased this experience?

MOTH By my penny of observation.

ARMADO But O—but O—

MOTH 'The hobby-horse is forgot.'

ARMADO Call'st thou my love 'hobby-horse'?

MOTH No, master. The hobby-horse is but a colt, and your
love perhaps a hackney. But have you forgot your love?   30

ARMADO Almost I had.

MOTH Negligent student! Learn her by heart.

ARMADO By heart and in heart, boy.

17 thin-belly] F (thinbellie); thinbellies Q   22–3 note—do you note me?—that] HANMER
(*subs.*); note: do you note men that Q F; note—do you note? *men*—that OXFORD   25 penny]
HANMER; penne QF   29 and] Q; and | and F

17 **arms crossed** Folded arms were regarded
as infallible signs of disappointed love. See
Two Gentlemen 2.1.17–19: 'you have
learned, like Sir Proteus, to wreath your
arms, like a malcontent'.
  your thin-belly doublet doublet cut to
emphasize the thinness of your belly

18 **after** in the manner of

18–19 **the old painting** It seems unlikely
that Moth has any particular painting in
mind. He appears, as Kerrigan points out,
to be thinking about the kind of painting
Borachio describes in his account of the
effect fashion can have on young men:
'sometimes fashioning them like Phar-
aoh's soldiers in the reechy painting,
sometime like god Bel's priests in the old
church window, sometime like the
shaven Hercules in the smirched, worm-
eaten tapestry' (*Much Ado* 3.3.128–32).

19–20 **a snip and away** a snatch and then
on to another. 'A snatch and away' was
proverbial (Tilley S587).

20 **compliments** gentlemanly accomplishments

20–1 **humours** fashionable affectations
(*OED*, *sb*. 6)

21 **betray** seduce (Schmidt)
  nice wanton (*OED*, *a*. 2a)

22 **of note** of eminence, of distinction

22–3 **do you note me?** are you paying
attention to me? Q, followed by F, reads
'do you note men', which yields no ready
sense.

23 **affected** inclined, given

24 **purchased** acquired (*OED*, *v*. 4). Moth
takes the word to mean 'bought'.

25 **penny** pennyworth (*OED*, 7). Q and F
read 'penne', but the connection with
'purchase' validates the emendation to
'penny'. Compare the title of Robert
Greene's pamphlet of 1592, *Greene's
Groatsworth of Wit bought with a million of
repentance*.

27 **The hobby-horse is forgot** Moth derisively
interprets Armado's sighs as part of the
line given in full in *Hamlet* 3.2.129, 'For
O, for O, the hobby-horse is forgot.' These
words seem to have been the refrain of a
popular ballad which has not survived.
The hobby-horse, a dancer got up to look
like a horse, was a very popular figure in
May-games and similar festivities.

28 **hobby-horse** Elizabethan slang for 'prostitute' (*OED*, 3b).

29 **colt** (a) young horse (b) lascivious man
(*OED*, 2c)

30 **hackney** (a) horse kept for hire (*OED*, *sb*.
2) (b) slang for 'whore' (*OED*, *sb*. 4)

MOTH And out of heart, master. All those three I will prove.

ARMADO What wilt thou prove?

MOTH A man, if I live; and this 'by', 'in', and 'without' upon the instant. 'By' heart you love her because your heart cannot come by her. 'In' heart you love her because your heart is in love with her. And 'out' of   40
heart you love her, being out of heart that you cannot enjoy her.

ARMADO I am all these three.

MOTH And three times as much more—(*aside*) and yet nothing at all.

ARMADO Fetch hither the swain. He must carry me a letter.

MOTH A message well sympathized—a horse to be ambassador for an ass.

ARMADO Ha, ha, what sayest thou?   50

MOTH Marry, sir, you must send the ass upon the horse, for he is very slow-gaited. But I go.

ARMADO The way is but short. Away!

MOTH As swift as lead, sir.

ARMADO Thy meaning, pretty ingenious?
Is not lead a metal heavy, dull, and slow?

MOTH
Minime, honest master, or rather, master, no.

---

37 and this] Q (*corr.*); (and this) F; and (this) Q (*uncorr.*)   55 Thy] F; The Q   57 *Minime*] Q (Minnime); F (*Minnime*)

35–6 **prove** (a) demonstrate (b) turn out to be

44–5 **And ... all** Continuing the lesson in arithmetic which he began at 1.2.39, Moth now observes that three noughts are nought, and so Armado is still the *cipher* that he was then.

48 **well sympathized** i.e. whose parts are in perfect harmony with one another (*OED*, v. 3c)

48–52 **a horse ... slow-gaited** The precise point of these exchanges is obscure. The ass was, of course, regarded as the type of stupidity, and so in some contexts was the horse—compare *1 Henry IV*

2.5.194–6: 'I tell thee what, Hal, if I tell thee a lie, spit in my face, call me horse.' So Moth may well be saying that one stupid creature (Costard) is the right messenger (*ambassador*) for another (Armado). *Slow-gaited* could, perhaps, mean 'slow in the uptake'.

54 **As swift as lead**. Moth's paradox is made up of two conventional similes: 'As heavy as lead' (Tilley L134) and 'As swift as a bullet' (Dent B719.1).

55 **ingenious** Shakespeare often uses adjectives as nouns. See Abbott 5.

57 *Minime* Latin for 'certainly not'

ARMADO

I say lead is slow.

MOTH   You are too swift, sir, to say so.

Is that lead slow which is fired from a gun?

ARMADO Sweet smoke of rhetoric!   60

He reputes me a cannon; and the bullet, that's he.

I shoot thee at the swain.

MOTH   Thump then, and I flee. *Exit*

ARMADO

A most acute juvenal, voluble and free of grace!

By thy favour, sweet welkin, I must sigh in thy face.

Most rude melancholy, valour gives thee place.

My herald is returned.

> *Enter Moth with Costard*

MOTH

A wonder, master! Here's a costard broken in a shin.

ARMADO

Some enigma, some riddle. Come, thy *l'envoi*—begin.

COSTARD No egma, no riddle, no *l'envoi*, no salve in the

mail, sir! O, sir, plantain, a plain plantain! No *l'envoi*,   70

no *l'envoi*, no salve, sir, but a plantain!

62 *Exit*] F2; *not in* QF   63 voluble] F; volable Q   66.1 *Enter Moth with Costard*] ROWE (*subs.*); Enter *Page* and *Clowne.* QF   67–95 MOTH] ROWE; *Pag.* QF   69–140 COSTARD] ROWE; *Clow⟨ne⟩.* QF   69–70 salve in the mail] MALONE (*after* Johnson; the F2); salue, in thee male QF   70 O] Q; Or F   plain] Q (pline), F

- 60 **smoke** mist. Shakespeare, on several occasions, uses *smoke* to describe the insubstantial nature of words. Compare, for instance, *Lucrece* 1027: 'This helpless smoke of words doth me no right.'
- 62 **Thump** i.e. make a noise like a gun going off
- 63 **acute** This is the earliest example cited by *OED* (*a.* 7) of *acute* applied to the intellectual powers.
- 65 **gives thee place** yields its place to you
- 67 **Here's ... shin** here's a head with a graze on its shin. 'To break one's shins' was a common expression (Dent S342.1). David, taking up a suggestion of John Crow's, gives some good reasons for thinking that the phrase could mean 'to suffer a disappointment in love'.
- 68 **enigma** Shakespeare's only other use of this word is at *Coriolanus* 2.3.90. *l'envoi* The *envoi* was the concluding part of a literary composition, the author's parting words to it before sending it on its

way into the world. Armado, however, as he tells us at lines 78–9, regards it as a summary or explanation of what has gone before.

- 69 **No egma ... l'envoi** Costard evidently thinks Armado is ordering some outlandish remedies for his broken shin, and is very alarmed at the prospect. Kerrigan tentatively suggests that 'he confuses *enigma* or *egma* with "enema", and thinks that *l'envoi* has something to do with the verb "to lenify" (that is "to purge gently")'. Unfortunately *OED* has no instance of 'enema' prior to 1681. It therefore seems more likely that Costard takes *enigma* to be some nostrum made from eggs, and mishears *riddle* as 'ruddle', a variety of red ochre used for marking sheep.
- 69–70 **salve in the mail** ointment or plaster in the bag (carried by a quacksalver)
- 70 **plantain** The leaves of the plantain were considered a good old remedy for bruises,

ARMADO By virtue, thou enforcest laughter; thy silly
thought my spleen; the heaving of my lungs provokes
me to ridiculous smiling. O, pardon me, my stars! Doth
the inconsiderate take *salve* for *l'envoi* and the word
'*l'envoi*' for a *salve*?

MOTH Do the wise think them other? Is not *l'envoi* a *salve*?

ARMADO

No, page. It is an epilogue or discourse to make plain
Some obscure precedence that hath tofore been sain.
I will example it: 80
    The fox, the ape, and the humble-bee
    Were still at odds, being but three.
There's the moral. Now the *l'envoi*.

MOTH I will add the *l'envoi*. Say the moral again.

ARMADO

    The fox, the ape, and the humble-bee
    Were still at odds, being but three.

MOTH

Until the goose came out of door,
And stayed the odds by adding four.

80–81 I ... four] Q; *not in* F

grazes, and the like. Compare *Romeo*
1.2.50–2: 'Your plantain leaf is excellent
for that. | —For what, I pray thee?—For
your broken shin.'

72 **silly** simple-minded, naïve

73 **spleen** i.e. uncontrollable mirth. The
spleen, it was thought, was the source of
both anger and merriment.

74 **ridiculous** derisive

74–6 **Doth ...** *salve*? As David succinctly
remarks, the answer to this question is
'yes'. Armado misinterprets Costard's
salve (*OED*, *sb.*¹) as *salve* (*OED*, *sb.*⁵),
meaning 'a greeting or salutation on
meeting' and derived from the Latin *salve*
i.e. 'hail!', 'greetings!', the exact opposite
of *l'envoi*.

75 **inconsiderate** thoughtless person (*OED*,
sb.)

79 **precedence** something, as Armado re-
dundantly explains, said before (*OED*,
2)—earliest example of the word in this
sense. Compare *Antony* 2.5.50–1: 'I do
not like "But yet"; it does allay | The
good precedence.'
sain said. This form of the past participle
was popular with poets of the 16th and

17th centuries because, perhaps, of the
readiness with which it lent itself, as
here, to rhyming.

80 **example** provide an example of (*OED*, *v.*
1)

81–94 **The fox ... four** There has been much
throwing about of brains—and of
names—in the many attempts that have
been made to extract topical significance
out of these lines. None, however, of the
'solutions' proposed has proved really
convincing. It seems far better therefore
to take the four lines of doggerel for what
they so obviously are, a miniature beast
fable, which, like the beast fable at large,
deals with the general rather than the
particular and with the self-evident
rather than the arcane.

82 **still** always
at odds (a) quarrelling (b) an odd number

83 **moral** The meaning of *moral* here, not
adequately covered by *OED*, appears to
be, as Schmidt glosses it, 'a truth proposed', or, in other words, 'a glimpse into
the obvious'. Compare *Dream* 5.1.120–1:
'A good moral, my lord: it is not enough
to speak, but to speak true.'

88 **stayed the odds** (a) settled the quarrel

Now will I begin your moral, and do you follow with
my *l'envoi*.   90
    The fox, the ape, and the humble-bee
    Were still at odds, being but three.
ARMADO
    Until the goose came out of door,
    Staying the odds by adding four.
MOTH A good *l'envoi*, ending in the goose. Would you
desire more?
COSTARD
    The boy hath sold him a bargain, a goose, that's flat.
    Sir, your pennyworth is good, an your goose be fat.
    To sell a bargain well is as cunning as fast and loose.
    Let me see: a fat *l'envoi*—ay, that's a fat goose.   100
ARMADO
    Come hither, come hither. How did this argument
        begin?
MOTH
    By saying that a costard was broken in a shin.
    Then called you for the *l'envoi*.
COSTARD True, and I for a plantain—thus came your
    argument in. Then the boy's fat *l'envoi*, the goose that
    you bought; and he ended the market.
ARMADO But tell me, how was there a costard broken in a
    shin?
MOTH I will tell you sensibly.
COSTARD Thou hast no feeling of it, Moth. I will speak that   110
l'envoi.

101 ARMADO (Come ... argument] Q (*corr.*), F (*Ar.* Come ... argument); *Arm.* Come ... argumet
Q (*uncorr.*)   110 it, Moth. I] ROWE (*subs.*);   it, *Moth*, I QF

(*OED, v.*[1] 28) (b) made the odd number
even
88 **adding** making the arithmetical sum add
up to

95 ***l'envoi*, ending in the goose** Moth's point
is that *l'envoi* ends in *oie*, the French for
'goose'.
97 **sold him a bargain, a goose** i.e. made a
complete fool of him. 'To sell one a goose
for a bargain', a saying that appears to
have originated in this passage, became
proverbial (Dent B80). Compare the mod-

ern slang expression 'To sell someone a
pup'.
99 **fast and loose** See note to 1.2.149.
101 **argument** discussion
106 **ended the market** An allusion to the
proverb 'Three women and a goose make
a market' (Tilley W690).
107 **how** in what possible sense
109 **sensibly** (a) in a way that is easily
understandable (*OED, adv.* 3) (b) with
real feeling—the sense in which Costard
takes it

I, Costard, running out, that was safely within,
Fell over the threshold, and broke my shin.

ARMADO We will talk no more of this matter.

COSTARD Till there be more matter in the shin.

ARMADO Sirrah Costard, I will enfranchise thee.

COSTARD O, marry me to one Frances! I smell some *l'envoi*,
some goose in this.

ARMADO By my sweet soul, I mean setting thee at liberty,
enfreedoming thy person. Thou wert immured, re-   120
strained, captivated, bound.

COSTARD True, true, and now you will be my purgation
and let me loose.

ARMADO I give thee thy liberty, set thee from durance, and
in lieu thereof impose on thee nothing but this: (*he gives
Costard a letter*) bear this significant to the country maid
Jaquenetta. (*He gives him a coin.*) There is remuneration;
for the best ward of mine honour is rewarding my
dependants. Moth, follow.   *Exit*

MOTH

Like the sequel, I. Signor Costard, adieu.   *Exit*   130

COSTARD

My sweet ounce of man's flesh, my incony Jew!
Now will I look to his remuneration. 'Remuneration'!

125-6 *he ... letter*] COLLIER (*subs.*); *not in* QF   127 *He ... coin*] STEEVENS (*subs.*); *not in* QF
128 honour] Q; honours F   129 *Exit*] F2; *not in* QF   130 Signor] OXFORD; Signeur QF
131 ounce] Q (ouce), F

115 **matter** pus
116 **enfranchise** release
117 **Frances** This name appears, like Doll, to
have been used as a typical name for a
prostitute. The whore whom the poet
visits in Thomas Nashe's *The Choice of
Valentines* is called Francis (Nashe, iii.
406). Francis and Frances were indiffer-
ent spellings of the same name in
Shakespeare's England.
117-18 **I smell ... this** Costard suspects, or
pretends to suspect, that Armado is seeking to inveigle him into marrying a cast-
off mistress of Armado's.
122 **be my purgation** (a) clear me of the
imputation of guilt (b) quibbling on *bound*
(l. 121) which could mean 'constipated'
126 **significant** Literally something which
conveys a meaning, here a letter.
Shakespeare seems to have been the first

writer to use *significant* as a noun.
128 **ward** guard, protection
130 **sequel** that which follows in a story or a
book
131 **incony** The precise meaning of this
word, first found in Marlowe's *The Jew of
Malta* (1589-90), is not known. Combining admiration with affection, it has been
variously glossed as *darling, rare, fine,
delicate*, etc. It occurs again at 4.1.141.
Jew Almost as puzzling as the *incony* that
qualifies it, *Jew* is used as a term of
affection in *Dream* 3.1.89, where Flute,
playing Thisby, describes Pyramus as
'Most [brisky juvenal], and eke most
lovely Jew'. This led Wilson to hazard the
view, which may be right, that it is
intended as a diminutive of *Juvenal*.
Another suggestion is that it represents a
shortened version of *jewel*.

O, that's the Latin word for three farthings. Three farthings—remuneration. 'What's the price of this inkle?' 'One penny.' 'No, I'll give you a remuneration.' Why, it carries it! 'Remuneration'! Why, it is a fairer name than French crown. I will never buy and sell out of this word.

Enter Biron

BIRON O, my good knave Costard, exceedingly well met.

COSTARD Pray you, sir, how much carnation ribbon may a   140
man buy for a remuneration?

BIRON What is a remuneration?

COSTARD Marry, sir, halfpenny-farthing.

BIRON Why then, three-farthing-worth of silk.

COSTARD I thank your worship. God be wi' you.

BIRON Stay, slave. I must employ thee.

As thou wilt win my favour, good my knave,
Do one thing for me that I shall entreat.

COSTARD When would you have it done, sir?

BIRON This afternoon.   150

COSTARD Well, I will do it, sir. Fare you well.

BIRON Thou knowest not what it is.

COSTARD I shall know, sir, when I have done it.

BIRON Why, villain, thou must know first.

COSTARD I will come to your worship tomorrow morning.

134 remuneration] Q2; remuration QF   135 One penny] CAMBRIDGE; i.d. QF   136 Why, ... it! 'Remuneration'!] THEOBALD (*subs.*); Why? ... it remuneration QF   137 than French] Q; then a French F   139 O, my] QF (O my); My CAMBRIDGE   142 What] F; O what Q   144, 146, 150, 152, 167 Why, | Stay, | This, | Thou, | And] CAMBRIDGE; O, why, | O stay, | O this, | O thou, | O and QF

133 **three farthings** A coin of this value was issued at various dates between 1561 and 1581.

135 **inkle** a kind of tape made of linen. Along with ribbons, cambrics, and so forth, it is sold by Autolycus (*Winter's Tale* 4.4.208).

136 **it carries it** it's a winner, it takes the prize

137 **French crown** (a) the *écu*, a French gold coin (b) the bald head caused by the 'French disease', i.e. syphilis

137–8 **out of** without using

139, 142, 144, 148, 150, 156, 167 Q, followed by F except at 142, begins each of these lines with the word 'O'. The exclamation seems natural enough at

139, where Biron suddenly meets Costard whom he is looking for, but not in the other six cases. 'O' could, of course, be a kind of verbal tic, but it seems far more likely that the compositor misread the speech-prefix '*Bero.*' as '*Ber. O*'—speech-prefix plus text.

140 **carnation** flesh-coloured

145 **God be wi' you** good-bye (which derives from it)

146 **slave** rogue (in a jestingly familiar sense) (*OED*, *sb.* 1c). Compare *Titus* 4.2.119–20: 'Look how the black slave smiles upon the father, | As who should say "Old lad, I am thine own."'

154 **villain** (used in the same way as *slave* is at line 146)

BIRON

It must be done this afternoon.
Hark, slave, it is but this:
The Princess comes to hunt here in the park,
And in her train there is a gentle lady;
When tongues speak sweetly, then they name her
     name,   160
And Rosaline they call her. Ask for her,
And to her white hand see thou do commend
This sealed-up counsel.
     He gives Costard a letter
                           There's thy guerdon; go.
     He gives Costard a shilling
COSTARD Gardon, O sweet gardon! Better than remunera-
tion, eleven-pence-farthing better. Most sweet gardon! I
will do it, sir, in print. Gardon! Remuneration!   *Exit*
BIRON

And I, forsooth, in love! I, that have been love's whip,
A very beadle to a humorous sigh,
A critic, nay, a night-watch constable,
A domineering pedant o'er the boy,   170
Than whom no mortal so magnificent!
This wimpled, whining, purblind, wayward boy,
This Signor Junior, giant dwarf, Dan Cupid,

163.1 *He ... letter*] *not in* QF   163.2 *He ... shilling*] JOHNSON; *not in* QF   164–6 Gardon] QF;
Guerdon F2   169 critic] Q (Crietick), F   173 Signor] OXFORD; signior QF; Senior HANMER
Junior] HART; *Iunios* QF   Dan] Q (dan); don F

163 **counsel** private communication (*OED*,
     sb. 5b)
     guerdon reward (pronounced by Biron,
     Kerrigan suggests, as in French)
164 **Gardon** Another spelling of *guerdon*
     showing the way the word was pro-
     nounced in England.
166 **in print** perfectly, exactly to the letter.
     'A man (thing, action) in print' was
     proverbial (Tilley M239). Compare *Two
     Gentlemen* 2.1.159: 'All this I speak in
     print, for in print I found it.'
168 **beadle** parish officer who whipped off-
     enders, especially whores
     humorous melancholy, love-lorn
169 **critic** censurer, adverse critic (earliest
     OED example of *critic* as a noun)
170 **pedant** schoolmaster, tutor
     boy Cupid
171 **Than** as, compared with (*OED*, 5)

magnificent proud (*OED*, *adj.* 1c)
172 **wimpled** blindfolded (not used else-
     where in Shakespeare)
     purblind completely blind
173 **Signor Junior** i.e. senior junior—al-
     luding to the idea that Eros (Cupid) was
     the oldest of the classical deities, since it
     was love that brought order out of chaos,
     and simultaneously the youngest of
     them, a mere boy
     Dan lord, sir. A variant form of *don*,
     which is a contracted version of the Latin
     dominus, meaning 'master', *dan* was used
     as a title for Cupid by Chaucer, who calls
     him 'daun Cupido' in *The Hous of Fame*
     (l. 137). Spenser refers to 'Dan Cupid' in
     The Faerie Queene III. xi. 46 in the course
     of a very full account of his power over
     the other gods.

Regent of love-rhymes, lord of folded arms,
Th'anointed sovereign of sighs and groans,
Liege of all loiterers and malcontents,
Dread prince of plackets, king of codpieces,
Sole imperator and great general
Of trotting paritors—O my little heart!—
And I to be a corporal of his field,   180
And wear his colours like a tumbler's hoop!
What? I love, I sue, I seek a wife?—
A woman that is like a German clock,
Still a-repairing, ever out of frame,
And never going aright, being a watch,
But being watched that it may still go right!
Nay, to be perjured, which is worst of all;
And among three to love the worst of all,
A whitely wanton with a velvet brow,

182 What? I] QF; What I? I MALONE   183 clock] F2 (Clocke); Cloake QF   189 whitely] F3;
whitly QF

174 **Regent** ruler, governor (*OED*, *sb.* 1b).
Nashe in his *Pierce Penniless* (1592) addresses Satan as 'Lord high Regent of
Lymbo' in a list of mock titles which could
well have been in Shakespeare's mind
when he wrote lines 172 to 179 (Nashe i.
165).

177 **plackets** A *placket* could be a petticoat, a
slit in a petticoat, the pocket to which
that slit gave access, and so by extension
a woman or the female genitalia. Compare *Tragedy of Lear* 3.4.90: 'Keep thy
foot out of brothels, thy hand out of
plackets'. *OED* does not cite this example
from *LLL* which is, in fact, earlier than
any of those it does cite.

codpieces bagged appendages to the front
of the close-fitting hose or breeches worn
by men from the 15th to the 17th
century; often conspicuous and orna-
mented (*OED*). Concealing and, at the
same time, displaying the male sexual
organs, the *codpiece* came to be identified
with them and was used as slang for
'penis'. Compare *Measure* 3.1.378–9:
'Why, what a ruthless thing is this in
him, for the rebellion of a codpiece to take
away the life of a man!'

178 **imperator** emperor, absolute ruler

179 **paritors** A shortened form of *apparitors*,
officers who served writs summoning
men to appear before the ecclesiastical

courts which tried sexual offenders.

180 **corporal of his field** i.e. field officer to
Cupid the *general*. *OED* defines *corporal of
the field* as 'a superior officer of the army
in the 16th and 17th centuries, who
acted as an assistant or a kind of aide-de-
camp to the sergeant-major' (*sb.* 2).

181 **his colours** i.e. the colours denoting his
regiment (*OED*, *sb.* 7b)
like a tumbler's hoop flauntingly (Wilson). A *tumbler's hoop* was a hoop decorated with ribbons with which the tumbler did his tricks and which he wore
across his body like a corporal's scarf
(Wilson).

183–4 **A woman ... a-repairing** Originating
in this passage, this simile was taken up
by one dramatist after another (Tilley
W658).

183 **German clock** A German clock in
Shakespeare's day was elaborately con-
structed, often containing automatic
figures of persons or animals (*OED*,
German, *a.²* 4), and therefore very liable
to go wrong.

184 **frame** order

185 **watch** time-piece

186 **being** i.e. needing to be

189 **whitely** pale, whitish
velvet brow forehead as smooth and soft
as velvet

With two pitch-balls stuck in her face for eyes;   190
Ay, and, by heaven, one that will do the deed
Though Argus were her eunuch and her guard.
And I to sigh for her, to watch for her,
To pray for her! Go to! It is a plague
That Cupid will impose for my neglect
Of his almighty dreadful little might.
Well, I will love, write, sigh, pray, sue, and groan.
Some men must love my lady, and some Joan.   *Exit*

4.1   *Enter the Princess, Maria, Katherine, Rosaline, Boyet,*
         two more Lords, and a Forester

PRINCESS

Was that the King that spurred his horse so hard
Against the steep-up rising of the hill?

⌈BOYET⌉

I know not, but I think it was not he.

PRINCESS

Whoe'er a was, a showed a mounting mind.
Well, lords, today we shall have our dispatch.
On Saturday we will return to France.
Then, forester, my friend, where is the bush
That we must stand and play the murderer in?

FORESTER

Hereby, upon the edge of yonder coppice,
A stand where you may make the fairest shoot.   10

197 sue, and groan] F2; shue, grone QF   198 *Exit*] ROWE; *not in* QF
   4.1.0.1–2 *Enter . . . Forester*] ROWE (*subs.*); *Enter the Princesse, a Forrester, her Ladyes, and her
   Lordes.* QF   1 (*and throughout the scene*) PRINCESS] F2; *Quee*⟨n⟩. QF   2 steep-up rising]
   HART; steepe vp rising Q; steepe vprising F   3 BOYET] F (*Boy.*); *Forr*⟨ester⟩. Q   6 On] F;
   Ore Q; Ere OXFORD

190 **pitch-balls** 'As black as pitch' was and is
   proverbial (Tilley P357).
191 **do the deed** engage in sexual intercourse
192 **Argus** A monster with a hundred eyes,
   all of which he never closed at the same
   time, Argus was set by Juno to keep
   watch over Io and ensure that Jupiter did
   not make love to her. Jupiter, however,
   employed Mercury to kill Argus, who
   was then transformed into a peacock.
   eunuch bedchamber attendant in a
   harem, who, to be 'safe', had to be
   castrated (Partridge).
193 **watch** stay awake all night

198 **Joan** 'Joan is as good as my lady in the
   dark' was proverbial (Tilley J57). In
   Shakespeare's day *Joan* was regarded as a
   lower-class name.
4.1.2 **steep-up** abrupt, precipitous. Compare
   Sonnets 7.5: 'And having climbed the
   steep-up heavenly hill'.
   4 **mounting mind** (a) readiness to climb (b)
   aspiring mind
   5 **dispatch** i.e. official dismissal or leave to
   go, given to an ambassador after comple-
   tion of his errand (*OED, sb.* 2)
  10 **stand** standing place or station from
   which the archer could shoot deer
   fairest most favourable, best. The Prin-

PRINCESS

I thank my beauty, I am fair that shoot,

And thereupon thou speak'st 'the fairest shoot'.

FORESTER

Pardon me, madam, for I meant not so.

PRINCESS

What, what? First praise me, and again say no?

O short-lived pride! Not fair? Alack for woe!

FORESTER

Yes, madam, fair.

PRINCESS   Nay, never paint me now.

Where fair is not, praise cannot mend the brow.

Here, good my glass, take this for telling true;

    She gives him some money

Fair payment for foul words is more than due.

FORESTER

Nothing but fair is that which you inherit.   20

PRINCESS

See, see, my beauty will be saved by merit!

O heresy in fair, fit for these days!

A giving hand, though foul, shall have fair praise.

But come, the bow. Now mercy goes to kill,

And shooting well is then accounted ill.

Thus will I save my credit in the shoot:

Not wounding, pity would not let me do't;

If wounding, then it was to show my skill,

That more for praise than purpose meant to kill.

And out of question so it is sometimes,   30

Glory grows guilty of detested crimes,

14 and again] Q; & then again F   18.1 *She ... money*] JOHNSON; *not in* QF   27 do't] Q (doote), F

cess deliberately takes it in the sense of 'most beautiful'.

16 **paint** flatter (*OED*, *v.*¹ 6b)

17 **fair** beauty. Compare *Errors* 2.1.97–8: 'My decayèd fair | A sunny look of his would soon repair.'

18 **good my glass** my reliable mirror

20 **you inherit** you own, is naturally yours

21 **by merit** (a) by its own intrinsic worth (b) because I give rewards (c) by good works, the way to salvation for Roman Catholics but not for Protestants, who held that

only faith could save the soul and that justification by works was *heresy*

22 **in fair** i.e. where beauty is concerned

23 **A giving ... praise** Referring perhaps to the proverb 'The giving hand is fair' (Dent H68.1).

31 **Glory** the disposition to gain honour for oneself (*OED*, *sb.* 1)

detested detestable, abominable. On Shakespeare's tendency to use the ending *-ed* where modern English would use *-able* see Abbott 375.

When, for fame's sake, for praise, an outward part,
We bend to that the working of the heart;
As I for praise alone now seek to spill
The poor deer's blood, that my heart means no ill.
BOYET
Do not curst wives hold that self sovereignty
Only for praise' sake when they strive to be
Lords o'er their lords?
PRINCESS
Only for praise—and praise we may afford
To any lady that subdues a lord.   40
    Enter Costard
BOYET Here comes a member of the commonwealth.
COSTARD God dig-you-den all! Pray you, which is the head
lady?
PRINCESS Thou shalt know her, fellow, by the rest that
have no heads.
COSTARD Which is the greatest lady, the highest?
PRINCESS The thickest and the tallest.
COSTARD
The thickest and the tallest. It is so; truth is truth.
An your waist, mistress, were as slender as my wit,
One o' these maids' girdles for your waist should be fit.   50
Are not you the chief woman? You are the thickest
    here.
PRINCESS What's your will, sir? What's your will?
COSTARD
I have a letter from Monsieur Biron to one Lady
    Rosaline.

40.1 *Enter Costard*] ROWE; *Enter Clowne.* QF   42 (*and throughout the scene*) COSTARD]
ROWE; *Clo⟨wne⟩.* QF   49 mistress] Q (Mistrs), F   50 fit] Q (*corr.*), F; fir Q (*uncorr.*)
51 here.] Q; ～? F

36 **curst** shrewish
   self same
41 **member of the commonwealth** 'Here, I
   believe, is a kind of jest intended; a
   member of the *common*-wealth is put for
   one of the *common* people, one of the
   meanest' (Johnson). Shakespeare uses
   this expression again at 4.2.75 and in
   Merchant 3.5.31–4: 'he says you are no

good member of the commonwealth, for
in converting Jews to Christians you raise
the price of pork'. For other examples of
the phrase see Dent M868.1.
42 **God dig-you-den** An abbreviated colloquial form of 'God give you good even', a
greeting used at any time of the day after
noon.
48 **truth is truth** proverbial (Tilley T581)

PRINCESS

O, thy letter, thy letter! He's a good friend of mine.
> *She takes the letter*

Stand aside, good bearer. Boyet, you can carve.

Break up this capon.

BOYET   I am bound to serve.
> *He looks at the letter*

This letter is mistook; it importeth none here.

It is writ to Jaquenetta.

PRINCESS   We will read it, I swear.

Break the neck of the wax, and everyone give ear.

BOYET *(reads)* 'By heaven, that thou art fair is most   60
infallible; true that thou art beauteous; truth itself that
thou art lovely. More fairer than fair, beautiful than
beauteous, truer than truth itself, have commiseration
on thy heroical vassal. The magnanimous and most
illustrate King Cophetua set eye upon the penurious and
indubitate beggar Zenelophon, and he it was that might
rightly say, "*Veni, vidi, vici*", which to annothanize in

54.1 *She ... letter] not in* QF   55 Boyet,] F; ~ ∧ Q   56.1 *He ... letter] not in* QF   60 BOYET
(reads) Q (*Boyet reedes.*), F (*reades*)   62 beautiful] QF; more beautiful TYRWHITT   65 set] Q
(corr.), F; sets Q (*uncorr.*); set's OXFORD   penurious] WILSON; pernicious QF   66 was] Q
(corr.), F; is was Q (*uncorr.*)   67 annothanize] QF; anatomize F2

---

56 **Break up** A technical term in carving
meaning 'cut open', 'cut up'.
capon (a) fowl (b) love-letter (*OED, sb.* 4).
Compare the French *poulet* signifying
both *fowl* and *billet-doux*.

57 **is mistook** i.e. has been delivered to the
wrong person
importeth concerns (*OED, v.* 7)

59 **Break ... wax** 'Still alluding to the "capon"' (Johnson).

65 **illustrate** illustrious
King Cophetua ... Zenelophon See
1.2.104–5 and note.
penurious The justification for this emendation is that 'pernicious', the reading of
both Q and F, makes no sense in this
context. The beggarmaid of the ballad is
neither 'wicked' nor 'destructive', nor,
for that matter, is Jaquenetta. The beggarmaid is, however, 'indubitably penurious', 'penurious and indubitate' being a
typically Shakespearian hendiadys. *Penurious*, especially if spelled *pennurious*,
could easily be read as *pernicious*.

67 *Veni, vidi, vici* The original source of

these famous words is Plutarch, who
writes (in North's translation): 'Caesar
... fought a great battle with King Phar-
naces by the city of Zela, where he slew
his army, and drove him out of all the
realm of Ponte. And because he would
advertise [inform] one of his friends of the
suddenness of this victory he only wrote
three words unto Anitius at Rome: *Veni,
Vidi, Vici*: to wit, I came, I saw, I overcame. These three words, ending all with
the like sound and letters in the Latin,
have a certain short grace, more pleasant
to the ear than can be well expressed in
any other tongue' (Bullough, v. 75).
annothanize give an analytical explanation (of those words). This gloss rests on
the assumption that 'annothanize',
found in both Q and F, is a Shakespearian
coinage combining the senses of *anatomize* (often spelled 'anathomize' in the 16th
century, and meaning 'analyse') and
annote (meaning 'provide with explanatory notes') in one word.

145

the vulgar—O base and obscure vulgar!—*videlicet*: he
came, see, and overcame. He came, one; see, two;
overcame, three. Who came? The King. Why did he   70
come? To see. Why did he see? To overcome. To whom
came he? To the beggar. What saw he? The beggar.
Who overcame he? The beggar. The conclusion is
victory. On whose side? The King's. The captive is
enriched. On whose side? The beggar's. The catastrophe
is a nuptial. On whose side? The King's. No, on both in
one, or one in both. I am the King, for so stands the
comparison; thou the beggar, for so witnesseth thy
lowliness. Shall I command thy love? I may. Shall I
enforce thy love? I could. Shall I entreat thy love? I will.   80
What shalt thou exchange for rags? Robes. For tittles?
Titles. For thyself? Me. Thus, expecting thy reply, I
profane my lips on thy foot, my eyes on thy picture, and
my heart on thy every part.

   Thine in the dearest design of industry,
      Don Adriano de Armado.
Thus dost thou hear the Nemean lion roar
'Gainst thee, thou lamb, that standest as his prey.

---

69 see] QF (See); Saw F2 see, two] QF; saw, two ROWE 70 overcame] F3; couercame
QF, F2 74 King's] Q2 (Kinges); King QF 81 What ∧] F4; ∼ , QF 83 picture] Q (*corr.*),
F; pictture Q (*uncorr.*) 86 Adriano] Q2; Adriana QF Armado] F2; Armatho QF

---

68 **vulgar** vernacular
 obscure humble, of lowly origin
69 **see ... see** saw ... saw. Armado is using
 an archaic form, still acceptable in Elizabethan English, of the past tense of the
 verb 'to see'. Compare *2 Henry IV*
 3.2.28–30, where Shallow says of Falstaff in his youth: 'I see him break
 Scoggin's head at the court gate when a
 was a crack, not thus high.' Shakespeare
 employs the more familiar translation of
 the Latin, 'I came, saw, and overcome',
 which had become proverbial (Tilley
 C540), on the other occasions when he
 has recourse to it—*2 Henry IV* 4.2.41, *As
 You Like It* 5.2.30–1, and *Cymbeline*
 3.1.24.
75 **catastrophe** dénouement
81 **exchange** receive in exchange (*OED, v.*
 1c)
 tittles the merest nothings. *Tittle* was 'a
 name for the (usually) three dots follow-

ing the letters and contractions, in the
alphabet or horn-book' (*OED, sb.* 1c).
82 **expecting** awaiting
82–3 **I profane ... foot** These words come
 close to being a parody of *Romeo* 1.5.92–
 5: 'If I profane with my unworthiest hand |
 This holy shrine, the gentler sin is this: |
 My lips, two blushing pilgrims, ready
 stand | To smooth that rough touch with
 a tender kiss.'
 thy picture i.e. my mental image of you
85 **in ... industry** i.e. with the most heartfelt
 determination to be a model of amorous
 gallantry—Armado's version of 'most
 sincerely'
87–90 **Thus ... play** A prolix and bombastic
 rendering of the proverb 'The lion spares
 the suppliant' (Tilley L316).
87 **the Nemean lion** The killing of the Nemean lion, referred to again at *Hamlet*
 1.4.60, was the first of the twelve labours
 of Hercules.

Submissive fall his princely feet before,
   And he from forage will incline to play.   90
But if thou strive, poor soul, what art thou then?
Food for his rage, repasture for his den.'

PRINCESS

What plume of feathers is he that indited this letter?
What vane? What weathercock? Did you ever hear
   better?

BOYET

I am much deceived but I remember the style.

PRINCESS

Else your memory is bad, going o'er it erewhile.

BOYET

This Armado is a Spaniard that keeps here in court,
A phantasime, a Monarcho, and one that makes sport
To the Prince and his book-mates.

PRINCESS (*to Costard*)   Thou, fellow, a word.
   Who gave thee this letter?

COSTARD   I told you: my lord.   100

PRINCESS

   To whom shouldst thou give it?

COSTARD   From my lord to my lady.

PRINCESS

   From which lord to which lady?

COSTARD

   From my Lord Biron, a good master of mine,
   To a lady of France that he called Rosaline.

---

100 you: my] THEOBALD (*subs.*); you, my QF

90 **from forage ... play** will abandon his
destructive raging in favour of acting
playfully
92 **repasture** food (that which provides a
repast). Apparently a coinage of
Shakespeare's, this word is not found
elsewhere in his writings.
93 **plume of feathers** ostentatious fool (*OED*,
feather, *sb.* 8b)
94 **vane** constantly changing person, giddy-
minded man (*OED*, 1b)
95 **but I** if I do not (Abbott 126)
96 **going o'er** since you read, since you
climbed over (with the same quibble on
stile as at 1.1.97)

96 **erewhile** recently, such a short time ago
97 **keeps** lodges, lives
98 **phantasime** fantastic being, creature full
of fantasies. Presumably the same word
as the *phantasimes* of 5.1.18, this coinage
is to be found in these two places only.
Monarcho The title assumed by an in-
sane Italian who hung about Elizabeth's
court and imagined himself to be emperor
of the world; hence applied to one who is
the object of ridicule for his absurd pretensions.
99 **To** for. Compare *Henry V* 4.3.35: 'he
which hath no stomach to this fight'.

PRINCESS

Thou hast mistaken his letter. Come, lords, away.

(*To Rosaline*) Here, sweet, put up this; 'twill be thine
  another day.

　　　　　Exeunt all but Boyet, Rosaline, Maria, and Costard

BOYET

Who is the shooter? Who is the shooter?

ROSALINE　　　　　　　　　　　Shall I teach you to know?

BOYET

Ay, my continent of beauty.

ROSALINE　　　　　　　　　Why, she that bears the bow.

Finely put off!

BOYET

My lady goes to kill horns, but if thou marry,　　　　　　110

Hang me by the neck if horns that year miscarry.

Finely put on!

ROSALINE

Well then, I am the shooter.

BOYET　　　　　　　　　　And who is your deer?

ROSALINE

If we choose by the horns, yourself come not near.

Finely put on indeed!

MARIA

You still wrangle with her, Boyet, and she strikes at
  the brow.

BOYET

But she herself is hit lower. Have I hit her now?

---

106 *Exeunt ... Costard*] WILSON; *Exeunt* F; *not in* Q　　107 *shooter*] QF; *suitor* JOHNSON and
STEEVENS 1785 (*conj.* Farmer)

105 **mistaken his letter** taken his letter to the
　wrong person
106 **put up** put away, keep
　'twill be thine another day your turn will
　come one day. 'Let him mend his man-
　ners, it will be his own another day' was
　proverbial (Tilley M628).
107 **shooter ... shooter** It seems right to
　preserve this spelling, common to Q and
　F, because it establishes the quibble *shoot-*
　er / suitor, both pronounced *shooter*, on
　which the ensuing dialogue rests.
　Furthermore, this dialogue is a kind of
　shooting match in which the participants
　try to score points against one another.
108 **continent** container, treasury

109 **put off** evaded, turned aside (*OED*, *v.*¹
　45g)
110 **horns** horned creatures, deer
111 **horns that year miscarry** there is a
　shortage of cuckolds that year
112 **put on** applied, laid on
113 **deer** punning on *dear*
114 **by the horns** according to the finest
　spread of cuckold's horns
116 **strikes at the brow** (a) takes good aim
　(b) accuses you of being a cuckold
117 **hit lower** i.e. wounded in a lower part of
　the body. Boyet is talking 'greasily'; the
　sexual innuendo is obvious.
　hit her hit upon her meaning

ROSALINE Shall I come upon thee with an old saying, that
     was a man when King Pépin of France was a little boy,
     as touching the hit it?   120
BOYET So I may answer thee with one as old, that was a
     woman when Queen Guinevere of Britain was a little
     wench, as touching the hit it.
ROSALINE (*sings*)
     Thou canst not hit it, hit it, hit it,
          Thou canst not hit it, my good man.
BOYET (*sings*)
     An I cannot, cannot, cannot,
          An I cannot, another can.   *Exit Rosaline*
COSTARD
     By my troth, most pleasant! How both did fit it!
MARIA
     A mark marvellous well shot, for they both did hit it.
BOYET
     A mark! O, mark but that mark! A mark, says my
          lady.   130
     Let the mark have a prick in't, to mete at, if it may be.
MARIA
     Wide o' the bow hand. I'faith, your hand is out.
COSTARD
     Indeed, a must shoot nearer, or he'll ne'er hit the
          clout.

119 France] Q (Frannce), F   120 touching] Q (touchiug), F   126 An I] Q (And I); I F
127 *Exit Rosaline*] ROWE; *Exit (after l. 125)* Q; *after l. 127* F   129 did hit it] F4; did hit Q
(*corr.*), F; hid hit Q (*uncorr.*)   132 o'] Q (*corr.*), F (a'); a Q (*uncorr.*)   133 a] Q (*corr.*), F (a');
a Q (*uncorr.*)

118 **come upon thee** advance against thee,
     i.e. retort
119 **King Pépin** The father of Charlemagne,
     he died in 768. Shakespeare seems to
     have regarded him as the emblem of
     bygone days; see *All's Well* 2.1.75 and
     All is True 1.3.10.
120 **the hit it** A popular song and dance. See
     Appendix C.
122 **Queen Guinevere** King Arthur's queen,
     supposed to have lived long before Pépin,
     was notorious for her infidelity.
126–7 **An … can** proverbial in the form 'If
     one will not another will' (Tilley O62)
128 **did fit it** were in perfect harmony. For
     the superfluous 'it' see Abbott 226.
129 **mark** target

129 **well shot** most accurately hit. Costard's
     use of this exclamation antedates *OED*,
     shoot, v. 22c by about forty-five years.
130 **mark but** only note
131 **mark** (a) target (b) female genitals
     prick (a) bull's eye (b) penis
     mete aim (*OED, v.*¹ 2b)
132 **Wide o' the bow hand** wide of the mark.
     This expression, which became prover-
     bial (Tilley B567), seems to have origin-
     ated here, or at least have been first
     recorded here.
     out (a) inaccurate (b) out of practice
133 **clout** 'The target was fixed by a pin or
     clout (French *clou*), the head of which
     was painted white and marked the
     centre' (David).

BOYET

An if my hand be out, then belike your hand is in.

COSTARD

Then will she get the upshoot by cleaving the pin.

MARIA

Come, come, you talk greasily, your lips grow foul.

COSTARD

She's too hard for you at pricks, sir. Challenge her to
    bowl.

BOYET

I fear too much rubbing. Good night, my good owl.

Exeunt Boyet and Maria

COSTARD

By my soul, a swain, a most simple clown!

Lord, Lord, how the ladies and I have put him down!   140

O' my troth, most sweet jests, most incony vulgar wit,

When it comes so smoothly off, so obscenely, as it
    were, so fit.

Armado o'th' t'other side—O a most dainty man!

To see him walk before a lady, and to bear her fan!

To see him kiss his hand, and how most sweetly a will
    swear!

135 pin] F2; is in QF   138 *Exeunt... Maria*] THEOBALD (*subs.*); *not in* QF   143 Armado o'th'
t'other] KEIGHTLEY (o'th't'other); *Armatho* ath toothen Q; *Armathor* ath to the F; to th'one
WILSON

134 **An ... in** i.e. if I'm out of practice where
  sex is concerned, then it's all too likely
  you are not
135 **upshoot** (a) best shot of the match (b)
  ejaculation
  cleaving the pin splitting the *pin* in the
  centre of the target—proverbial (Tilley
  P336). Compare *Romeo* 2.3.14–15: 'the
  very pin of his heart cleft with the blind
  bow-boy's butt-shaft'.
136 **greasily** smuttily, indecently. The earliest citation in *OED*, not used elsewhere in
  Shakespeare.
137 **pricks** archery (with the inevitable
  quibble)
  bowl play at bowls (pronounced like 'owl'
  and 'foul')
138 **rubbing** In the game of bowls the bowl is
  said to 'rub' when it meets some impedi-
  ment which retards or diverts its course
  (*OED*, *rub*, *v*.¹ 14b), in this case Maria's
  sharp tongue. Partridge gives the word

the bawdy sense of 'a fricative sexual
caress'.
owl Schmidt regards this as 'a term of
contempt', but 'term of condescending
raillery' would seem nearer the mark.
141 **incony** See note to 3.1.131.
142 **obscenely** It is not clear what word
  Costard has in mind, any more than it is
  clear what Bottom is thinking of when he
  says: 'there we may rehearse most obscenely and courageously' (*Dream*
  1.2.100–1); but *obscene* is certainly the
  right word for the preceding passage.
143 **o'th' t'other side** on the other hand
  (*OED*, *side*, *sb*.¹ 17b). Q reads 'ath toothen
  side'; F 'ath to the side'. Costard is
  contrasting Armado, very much to the
  Spaniard's advantage, with Boyet. See
  Wells, *Re-Editing*, pp. 54–5.
  dainty man man of most elegant manners

And his page o' t'other side, that handful of wit!
Ah, heavens, it is a most pathetical nit!
  Shout within
Sola, sola!   *Exit*

4.2   *Enter Dull, Holofernes, and Nathaniel*
NATHANIEL Very reverend sport, truly, and done in the
  testimony of a good conscience.
HOLOFERNES The deer was, as you know, in blood, *sanguis*,
  ripe as the pomewater, who now hangeth like a jewel in
  the ear of *caelum*, the sky, the welkin, the heaven, and
  anon falleth like a crab on the face of *terra*, the soil, the
  land, the earth.

146 o' t'other] ROWE 1714; atother QF   147 a] F2; *not in* QF   147.1 *Shout within*] F2
(Showt within); Shoot within Q (*in roman and after l. 148*); Shoote within F (*in roman and on
separate line*); *arranged as here* CAPELL   148 *Exit*] CAPELL; *Exeunt* QF (*before 'Shoot within'*)
    4.2.0.1 *Enter ... Nathaniel*] ROWE; Enter *Dull, Holofernes, the Pedant and Nathaniel* Q, F
(*subs.*)   1–62 NATHANIEL] QF (*Nat⟨haniel⟩., with 'Curat. Nath.' at l. 8*)   3 HOLOFERNES]
ROWE; *Ped⟨ant⟩.* QF   in blood, *sanguis*] This edition; sanguis in blood QF; *sanguis*—in blood
OXFORD   4 the] Q; a F   5 *caelum*] DYCE; *Celo* QF

147 **pathetical nit** appealing little thing. A
  nit could be a gnat, or small fly (*OED, sb.*
  1b).
147.1 ***Shout within*** Q reads 'Shoot within'
  and F 'Shoote within'. Both treat the
  words as part of the text, and place them
  after the stage direction '*Exeunt*.', which
  follows Costard's 'Sola, sola!' This exclamation, found again at *Merchant* 5.1.39,
  appears to be a hunting cry; and, since it
  needs something to provoke it, it seems
  reasonable to read 'Shoot' as 'Shout' of
  which it was a variant spelling. The
  twang of a bow-string *within* would not,
  one imagines, be heard in the auditorium
  of an Elizabethan theatre.
4.2.0.1 *Holofernes* Shakespeare could have
  taken this name from Rabelais who gives
  it to Gargantua's tutor (I. xiv), but it
  seems far more likely that he was thinking of the biblical Holofernes, the tyrant
  slaughtered by Judith in the apocryphal
  Book of Judith. Interludes dealing with
  his fate were performed in 1556 and
  1564 (Schoenbaum, 34 and 38), and
  probably on many other occasions.
  1 **reverend** worthy of respect (on account
  of the rank of those engaged in it)
1–2 **in the testimony** with the warrant.
  Nathaniel alludes to 2 Corinthians 1 : 12:
  'For our rejoicing is this, the testimony of
  our conscience'.

3 **in blood** in prime condition. Compare *1*
  Henry VI 4.2.48–50: 'If we be English
  deer, be then in blood, | Not rascal-like to
  fall down with a pinch, | But rather,
  moody-mad and desperate stags'.
  in blood, *sanguis* Q and F read 'sanguis in
  blood', which is meaningless. The emendation made here rests on the fact that
  the Q compositors were prone to transpose words as well as letters (see Introduction, pp. 74–5). Holofernes, it is true,
  usually gives the Latin first and then the
  English, but not invariably. See line 22:
  'Twice-sod simplicity, *bis coctus*!'
4 **pomewater** A large juicy kind of apple no
  longer cultivated.
4–5 **hangeth ...** *caelum* Compare *Romeo*
  1.5.44–5: 'It seems she hangs upon the
  cheek of night | As a rich jewel in an
  Ethiope's ear'.
5 *caelum* For Kerrigan's justification of
  caelum as the correct reading—the word
  appears as '*Celo*' in Q and F—see Introduction, p. 75. Subsequent emendations
  of errors in Holofernes' Latin are based on
  the assumption (see pp. 74–5) that those
  errors are far more likely to be compositorial than the result of ignorance on their
  speaker's part.
6 **anon** a moment later
  crab crab-apple

NATHANIEL Truly, Master Holofernes, the epithets are sweetly varied, like a scholar at the least. But, sir, I assure ye it was a buck of the first head.   10

HOLOFERNES Sir Nathaniel, *haud credo*.

DULL 'Twas not a 'auld grey doe', 'twas a pricket.

HOLOFERNES Most barbarous intimation! Yet a kind of insinuation, as it were, *in via*, in way, of explication, *facere*, as it were, replication, or rather *ostentare*, to show, as it were, his inclination, after his undressed, unpolished, uneducated, unpruned, untrained, or rather unlettered, or ratherest unconfirmed fashion, to insert again my *haud credo* for a deer.

DULL I said the deer was not a 'auld grey doe', 'twas a   20
pricket.

HOLOFERNES Twice-sod simplicity, *bis coctus*!
O thou monster Ignorance, how deformed dost thou
    look!

NATHANIEL
Sir, he hath never fed of the dainties that are bred in a
    book.

8 epithets] POPE; epythithes QF   11–54 HOLOFERNES] QF (*Holo⟨fernes⟩*.)   12, 20 a 'auld grey doe'] OXFORD (*conj.* Rowse); an awd grey doe KERRIGAN; a *haud credo* QF   14 explication, *facere*] THEOBALD (*subs.*); explication ∧ *facere* QF   22 *bis coctus*] F; bis coctus Q

9 **at the least** i.e. to go no further

10 **of the first head** in its fifth year (the age at which a buck grows its first full set of antlers)

11 ***haud credo*** I don't believe it, you are quite wrong

12, 20 **'auld grey doe'** This is Oxford's and, substantially, Kerrigan's emendation of the '*haud credo*' found in Q and F. Originally proposed by A. L. Rowse in 1952, and strongly supported by Stanley Wells (*Re-Editing*, p. 53), it is adopted here because it has the virtues of making sense and raising a laugh. It also has to be said, however, that it is out of line with what appears to be Shakespeare's usual practice when making fun of misapprehensions of foreign words and phrases, which is to spell them out himself rather than leave that task to the actor or reader. For instance, when Titus asks the Clown 'What says Jupiter?', the Clown replies 'Ho, the gibbet-maker?' (*Titus Andronicus* 4.3.79–80). Even more to the point is Parson Evans's examination of William in *Merry Wives* 4.1.23–6. Asked

by Evans 'What is "fair", William?', the boy answers '*Pulcher*', whereupon Mistress Quickly interjects 'Polecats? There are fairer things than polecats, sure.'

12 **pricket** buck in its second year

13 **intimation** intrusive suggestion—not elsewhere in Shakespeare

14 **insinuation** subtle introduction
   explication explanation—not elsewhere in Shakespeare

15 ***facere*** Latin for 'to make'
   replication reply

16 **after** according to, in keeping with
   undressed shapeless

18 **unconfirmed** uninstructed, ignorant (*OED*, 2b). Compare *Much Ado* 3.3.112–13: 'I wonder at it.—That shows thou art unconfirmed.' These are the only instances of 'unconfirmed' in this sense cited by *OED*.

19 **insert again** intrusively substitute

22 **Twice-sod simplicity** i.e. stupidity upon stupidity. 'Twice-sod' meant 'twice boiled' (*bis coctus* in Latin). 'Cabbage twice sodden' was proverbial (Tilley C511).

He hath not eat paper, as it were, he hath not drunk
    ink.
His intellect is not replenished. He is only an animal,
    only sensible in the duller parts.
And such barren plants are set before us that we
    thankful should be—
Which we of taste and feeling are—for those parts that
    do fructify in us more than he.
For as it would ill become me to be vain, indiscreet, or
    a fool,
So were there a patch set on learning, to see him in a
    school.   30
But *omne bene*, say I, being of an old father's mind:
Many can brook the weather that love not the wind.

DULL

You two are book-men; can you tell me by your wit
What was a month old at Cain's birth that's not five
    weeks old as yet?

HOLOFERNES *Dictynna*, Goodman Dull. *Dictynna*, Goodman
Dull.

DULL What is *Dictima*?

NATHANIEL A title to Phoebe, to *Luna*, to the moon.

28 of] TYRWHITT; *not in* QF   29 indiscreet] Q (indistreell), F   33 me] Q; *not in* F
35 *Dictynna ... Dictynna*] ROWE; *Dictisima ... dictisima* QF   37 *Dictima*] QF (*dictima*);
Dictinna F2

25 **eat** eaten
26 **replenished** i.e. properly furnished with the things it needs to make it complete (*OED, replenish, v.* 1b). Compare *Richard III* 4.3.18–19, where the Princes in the Tower are referred to as 'The most replenishèd sweet work of nature, | That from the prime creation e'er she framed.'
    sensible capable of feeling, sensitive
28 **Which** as (*OED,* 10 and Abbott 272)
    fructify bear fruit—not elsewhere in Shakespeare
    he him (Abbott 206)
30 **So ... learning** (a) it would be putting a fool to his lessons (b) a disgrace to the cause of learning. It is not clear which of these two senses Nathaniel has in mind.
    patch As well as having its normal sense, *patch* could denote a fool because domestic fools wore patched or parti-coloured clothes.

31 *omne bene* all's well
    being ... mind i.e. holding the same opinion as a wise old man long ago
32 **Many ... wind** i.e. 'What can't be cured must be endured'. This line in *LLL* seems to have become proverbial in the form of 'There is no weather ill when the wind is still' (Tilley W220).
35 *Dictynna* goddess of the moon (as Nathaniel explains). This name for Diana is not very common in Latin; but Holofernes' preference for the rare word is not confined to the English words he uses.
    Goodman title used when addressing someone under the rank of gentleman (*OED,* 3b). Compare *Much Ado* 3.5.9: 'Goodman Verges'.
37 *Dictima* The Q spelling is retained here because the mistake could well be Dull's rather than the compositor's.

HOLOFERNES

The moon was a month old when Adam was no more,

And raught not to five weeks when he came to

 fivescore.   40

Th'allusion holds in the exchange.

DULL 'Tis true, indeed; the collusion holds in the exchange.

HOLOFERNES God comfort thy capacity! I say th'allusion
holds in the exchange.

DULL And I say the pollution holds in the exchange, for
the moon is never but a month old. And I say beside
that 'twas a pricket that the Princess killed.

HOLOFERNES Sir Nathaniel, will you hear an extemporal
epitaph on the death of the deer? And, to humour the   50
ignorant, call I the deer the Princess killed a pricket.

NATHANIEL *Perge*, good Master Holofernes, *perge*, so it
shall please you to abrogate scurrility.

HOLOFERNES I will something affect the letter, for it argues
facility.

The preyful Princess pierced and pricked a pretty

 pleasing pricket;

 Some say a sore, but not a sore till now made sore

  with shooting.

40 raught] HANMER (*after* Q; rought); wrought F   48 'twas] Q (*corr.*), F; was Q (*uncorr.*)   49 HOLOFERNES Sir] Q ('*Holo.* Sir' *text*); Sir Q (*c.w.*)   51 ignorant] Q (ignorault), F
call I] CAMBRIDGE; cald Q; call'd F; I have called ROWE   deer ∧] ROWE; ∼ : Q; ∼ , F
53 scurrility] F (scurilitie); squirilitie Q

40 **raught** reached
41 **Th'allusion ... exchange** i.e. 'the riddle is
as good when I use the name of Adam, as
when you use the name of Cain' (Warburton).
 allusion word-play, pun, jest (*OED*, 2)
42 **collusion** trick or ambiguity in words or
reasoning. Dull has, for once, the right
word. He recognizes that the two learned
men are trying to make a fool of him.
44 **comfort** help (*OED, v.* 6)
 capacity ability to comprehend
46 **pollution** (a) mistakenly for *allusion* (b)
your perversion of what I said
52 *Perge* carry on (disyllabic)
53 **abrogate** avoid, have nothing to do with.
Nathaniel seems to fear that Holofernes
may exploit the bawdy possibilities of
pricket.

54 **something affect the letter** i.e. make some
use of alliteration
54–5 **argues facility** shows an easy command (of the language)
56 **preyful** i.e. bent on hunting. The suffix
-ful carries here the sense of 'apt to',
'accustomed to' (*OED*, 1) rather than 'full
of'. Defined by *OED* as meaning 'killing
much prey or quarry; prone to prey',
which does not fit this context, *preyful*
appears to have originated here and
never 'caught on'. *OED* has but one other
citation, and that from George Chapman,
writing in 1624.
57 **Some say a sore** i.e. some say the deer was
a *sore* (namely a buck in its fourth year)
but ... shooting but it was not a *sore* until
being shot made it sore

The dogs did yell; put 'L' to sore, then sorel jumps
    from thicket,
  Or pricket sore, or else sorel; the people fall a-
    hooting.
If sore be sore, then 'L' to sore makes fifty sores o'
    sorel: 60
Of one sore I an hundred make by adding but one more
    'L'.

NATHANIEL A rare talent!

DULL If a talent be a claw, look how he claws him with a
talent.

HOLOFERNES This is a gift that I have, simple, simple, a
foolish extravagant spirit, full of forms, figures, shapes,
objects, ideas, apprehensions, motions, revolutions.
These are begot in the ventricle of memory, nourished
in the womb of *pia mater*, and delivered upon the
mellowing of occasion. But the gift is good in those in   70
whom it is acute, and I am thankful for it.

NATHANIEL Sir, I praise the Lord for you, and so may my
parishioners, for their sons are well tutored by you, and

65–102 HOLOFERNES] ROWE 1714; *Nath.* QF   69 *pia mater*] ROWE; primater QF   70–1 in
whom] F; whom Q   72–144 NATHANIEL] ROWE 1714; *Hol⟨ofernes⟩.* QF

58 **yell; put 'L' to sore, then sorel** The word
yell and the letter *L* are sufficiently alike
in pronunciation to allow the one to be
interpreted as the other; and the addition
of *L* to *sore* gives *sorel*, the name for a buck
in its third year.

59 **Or ... sorel** i.e. no matter whether it is a
wounded pricket or a sorel

60 **If sore be sore** if the deer is hurt
    fifty sores (because *L* is the Roman
numeral for *fifty*)

61 **Of ... 'L'.** The line is a fitting ending for
Holofernes' laborious exercise in what
John Cleveland might have called 'vena-
tious arithmetic'.
    more 'L' perhaps quibbling on 'moral'

63 **If a talent be a claw** In Shakespeare's day
a *talent* often was a *claw*, since *talent* was
a common spelling of *talon*. In fact, *talon*
appears as *talent* not only here but also in
the earliest quartos of the other four plays
in which it is used: *1 Henry IV* (2.5.333);
The First Part of the Contention (3.2.196);
Richard Duke of York (1.4.42); and *Pericles* (17.49).
    claws him (a) scratches his back (in an

ingratiating manner) (b) flatters him,
curries favour with him

65 HOLOFERNES Both Q and F attribute this
speech to '*Nath.*', thus beginning a confusion of names that continues to line 144.
See Introduction pp. 63–4.

65–70 **This ... occasion** This speech comes
remarkably close to being an anticipation
of Falstaff's praise of sack (*2 Henry IV*
4.2.93–121).

67 **motions** impulses (*OED*, *sb.* 9)
    revolutions reflections (*OED*, *sb.* 5b)

68 **ventricle** belly (*OED*, 3c) used figura-
tively. *Ventricles* are divisions of the
brain; and the *memory* was thought to be
seated in the hindmost of them.

69 *pia mater* the membrane surrounding
the brain. *OED* quotes Thomas Vicary's
Anatomy (1548) to the following effect:
'It is called Piamater ... for because it is so
soft and tender over the brain that it
nourisheth the brain and feedeth it, as
doth a loving mother unto her tender
child.'

69–70 **delivered ... occasion** i.e. born when
the time is ripe for it

their daughters profit very greatly under you. You are a
good member of the commonwealth.

HOLOFERNES *Mehercle*, if their sons be ingenious, they shall
want no instruction; if their daughters be capable, I will
put it to them. But *vir sapit qui pauca loquitur*. A soul
feminine saluteth us.

Enter Jaquenetta with a letter, and Costard

JAQUENETTA God give you good morrow, Master Person.   80

HOLOFERNES Master Person, *quasi* 'pierce one'? An if one
should be pierced, which is the one?

COSTARD Marry, Master Schoolmaster, he that is likeliest
to a hogshead.

HOLOFERNES 'Of piercing a hogshead'—a good lustre of
conceit in a turf of earth, fire enough for a flint, pearl
enough for a swine. 'Tis pretty, it is well.

JAQUENETTA Good Master Parson, be so good as read me

---

76 *Mehercle*] F (*Me hercle*); Me hercle (*in roman*) Q   ingenious] CAPELL; ingenous Q; ingen-
nous F   78 *sapit*] Q2; *sapis* QF   79.1 *Enter... Costard*] ROWE (*subs.*); *Enter laquenetta and the
Clowne* QF   80, 83, 88 Master] QF (M.)   80, 81 Person] QF; Parson F2   81 'pierce one']
HALLIWELL (pierce-one); Person QF   82 pierced] QF (perst)   83 COSTARD] ROWE; *Clo⟨wne⟩.* QF
likeliest] WILSON; liklest Q; likest F

---

74 **profit** (a) make progress (b) increase in
size (by becoming pregnant). The innuendo, unconscious on Nathaniel's part, is
reinforced by 'under you'.

76 **Mehercle** by Hercules
ingenious intelligent (*OED*, *a*. 2)

77 **want** lack, go short of
capable capable of (a) learning (b) sexual
intercourse

78 **put it** (a bawdy quibble). Compare *Winter's Tale* 1.2.278–80: 'My wife's a
hobby-horse, deserves a name | As rank
as any flax-wench that puts to | Before
her troth-plight.'
vir... loquitur he's a wise man who says
little. The saying was proverbial (Tilley
W799).

80 **Person** parson. *Person* and *parson* were
originally the same word, both coming
from the Latin *persona*, and in
Shakespeare's day each of them could
still be spelled in either way. *Person* is
preferred here because it seems to represent Jaquenetta's pronunciation to
which Holofernes objects as incorrect.

81 **quasi** as if it were
pierce-one Halliwell's emendation of
'Person', the reading of Q and F, has been
adopted here, as in most modern editions,
because it best fits the context. The
pronunciation of 'pierce' is attested to by
1 Henry IV 5.3.56: 'Well, if Percy be
alive, I'll pierce him' and by the title of
Nashe's pamphlet *Pierce Penniless his
Supplication to the Devil* (1592) with its
pun on *Pierce* and *Purse*. As for 'one', it
was often written 'on' and pronounced
'on' or 'un'.

83–4 **likeliest to** most like

84 **hogshead** large cask for wine or the like

85 **piercing** broaching. 'To pierce a hogshead' was probably proverbial (Dent
H504.1).

85–6 **lustre of conceit** spark of imagination
(Riverside)

86 **turf** clod (Onions)

86–7 **fire ... swine** Holofernes brings two
proverbs together: 'In the coldest flint
there is hot fire' and 'Cast not pearls
before swine' (Tilley F371 and P165).

this letter. It was given me by Costard, and sent me from
Don Armado. I beseech you, read it.   90
            Sir Nathaniel takes the letter and peruses it while
            Holofernes ruminates
HOLOFERNES

  Fauste, precor gelida quando pecus omne sub umbra
  Ruminat—
and so forth. Ah, good old Mantuan, I may speak of thee
as the traveller doth of Venice:
  Venetia, Venetia,
  Chi non ti vede, non ti pretia.
Old Mantuan, old Mantuan, who understandeth thee
not, loves thee not. (*He sings*) Ut, re, sol, la, mi, fa.—
Under pardon, sir, what are the contents? Or rather, as
Horace says in his—What, my soul, verses?   100
NATHANIEL Ay, sir, and very learned.
HOLOFERNES Let me hear a staff, a stanza, a verse. *Lege,*
domine.

90.1–2 *Sir ... ruminates*] not in QF   91–2 *Fauste ... Ruminat*] F2 ; *Facile precor gellida, quando*
pecas omnia sub vmbra ruminat QF   95–6 *Venetia ... pretia*] CAMBRIDGE; *vemchie, vencha, que*
non te vnde, que non te perreche QF; *Venezia, Venezia, | Chi non ti vede, chi non ti prezia* OXFORD
98 loves thee not] Q; *not in* F   *He sings*] not in QF   100 his—] HANMER; ~, QF
102 stanza] Q (stauze), F

91–2 *Fauste ... Ruminat* 'Faustus, since all
    your flock are chewing the cud in the cool
    shade, I pray you—.' This is the begin-
    ning of Mantuan's first eclogue in his
    Eclogues of 1498, a work that rapidly
    became extremely popular all over Eur-
    ope. These opening words were so well
    known that the errors Q and F make in
    their rendering of them seem far more
    likely to be the compositor's than
    Shakespeare's or the Pedant's, a view
    evidently shared by the compilers of the
    Second Folio. Binns, who thinks, as
    many have done, that the playwright
    deliberately makes Holofernes blunder in
    his Latin in order to hold him up to
    ridicule, also points out that 'the Latinate
    members of the audience would have
    been able to deduce a kind of sense from
    most of the line: "Easily, I pray, since you
    are getting everything into a mess under
    the cool shade" (the verb *pecco* is used

transitively by Cicero)' (p. 124).
93 **Mantuan** Johannes Baptista Spagnolo of
    Mantua (1448–1516), known as Man-
    tuanus, whose Latin eclogues, imitations
    of Virgil's, were much used in the schools
    of Tudor England.
95–6 *Venetia ... pretia* An Italian proverb
    that passed into English as 'Venice, he
    that does not see thee does not esteem
    thee' (Tilley V26).
98 **Ut ... fa** *Ut* corresponds to the modern
    'doh', and *sol* to the modern 'soh'; but it
    is not clear whether Holofernes is trying
    to sing a scale and getting it wrong, or
    whether he is humming a bit of a tune.
    Compare *Tragedy of Lear* 1.2.134–5: 'Fa,
    sol, la, mi.'
102 **staff ... stanza ... verse** All three words
    mean the same thing—a *stanza* (*OED*,
    staff, *sb.*[1] 19c).
102–3 *Lege, domine* read, master

NATHANIEL (*reads*)

'If love make me forsworn, how shall I swear to love?
  Ah, never faith could hold, if not to beauty vowed!
Though to myself forsworn, to thee I'll faithful prove;
  Those thoughts to me were oaks, to thee like osiers
    bowed.
Study his bias leaves, and makes his book thine eyes,
  Where all those pleasures live that art would
    comprehend.
If knowledge be the mark, to know thee shall suffice;   110
  Well learnèd is that tongue that well can thee
    commend,
All ignorant that soul that sees thee without wonder;
  Which is to me some praise, that I thy parts admire.
Thy eye Jove's lightning bears, thy voice his dreadful
    thunder,
  Which, not to anger bent, is music and sweet fire.
Celestial as thou art, O, pardon love this wrong,
That sings heaven's praise with such an earthly
    tongue.'

HOLOFERNES You find not the apostrophus, and so miss the

104 NATHANIEL] ROWE 1714; *continued to Nathaniel (for Holofernes)* QF   *reads*] CAPELL (*subs.*); *not in* QF   105 Ah] QF; O *Pilgrim*   107 were] QF; like *Pilgrim*   bowed.] F; ~ ∧ Q   108 eyes,] *Pilgrim*; ~. QF   109 would] QF; can *Pilgrim*   114 Thy ... bears] QF; Thine ... seems *Pilgrim*   116 pardon love this] QF; do not loue that *Pilgrim*   wrong] Q (*corr.*), F; woug Q (*uncorr.*)   117 That sings heaven's] QF; To sing heauens *Pilgrim*; That singeth heauen's MARSHALL   118 HOLOFERNES] ROWE; *Ped⟨ant⟩.* QF   apostrophus] HART (*conj. OED*); apostraphas QF

104–17 **If ... tongue** This sonnet, along with the poems of Longueville (4.3.58–71) and Dumaine (4.3.99–118), was taken over by William Jaggard, and printed in his collection *The Passionate Pilgrim* (1599). Although the title-page of the collection describes it as being 'By W. Shakespeare', the volume also has poems by a number of other authors, including Marlowe.

107 **thoughts to me were oaks** i.e. thoughts which were to me oaks (in their strength) **osiers** well known and valued for their pliability

108 **Study ... eyes** i.e. the student abandons the subject he preferred to all others and makes your eyes his book

109 **art** scholarship, learning (*OED*, *sb.* 3b)

113 **that** because (Abbott 284)
  parts could mean either or both physical

and or mental endowments

116 **love** i.e. my love for you

117 **That** i.e. that it

118 **apostrophus** A recognized variant spelling of *apostrophe*², i.e. the sign (') used to indicate the omission of a letter or letters in a word. Q and F read 'apostrophas', which could, Onions thinks, perhaps be the plural of 'apostropha', a word used by Florio in his *First Fruits* (1578). There is, however, so far as one can see, no word in the sonnet that needs to be elided in order to preserve the right emphasis ('accent'). David suggests—and it is an attractive suggestion—that Holofernes is trying 'to blind Nathaniel with science' as a means of asserting his own superiority, and so employs a bit of technical jargon that sounds impressive but means nothing.

accent. Let me supervise the canzonet. (*He takes the
letter*) Sir Nathaniel, here are only numbers ratified, but   120
for the elegancy, facility, and golden cadence of poesy,
caret. Ovidius Naso was the man. And why indeed
'Naso' but for smelling out the odoriferous flowers of
fancy, the jerks of invention? *Imitari* is nothing. So doth
the hound his master, the ape his keeper, the tired horse
his rider.—But, *domicella*—virgin—was this directed to
you?

JAQUENETTA Ay, sir.

HOLOFERNES I will overglance the superscript. (*He reads*)
'To the snow-white hand of the most beauteous Lady   130
Rosaline.' I will look again on the intellect of the letter
for the nomination of the party writing to the person

119 canzonet] cangenct Q; cangenet F   120 Sir Nathaniel, here] This edition; *Nath.* Here
QF; *continued to Holofernes* THEOBALD   124 fancy,] CAPELL; fancy? F; fancie? Q   invention?] THEOBALD; in-uention ∧ QF   *Imitari*] THEOBALD; imitarie QF   126 *domicella*—virgin]
OXFORD; *Damosella virgin* QF   128 Ay, sir.] OXFORD; I sir from one mounsier *Berowne*, one of
the strange Queenes Lordes QF   129 HOLOFERNES] THEOBALD; *Nath.* QF   *He reads*] not in QF
132 writing] ROWE; written QF

119 **supervise** look over, peruse (*OED, v.* 1;
   earliest citation)
   canzonet little poem
120–7 **here are ... to you?** Q and F assign
   these lines to '*Nath.*', which is patently
   wrong, since they are a continuation of
   Holofernes' speech. The likeliest explanation of the error is that Shakespeare
   wrote 'Sir Nathaniel, here are' and the
   compositor took 'Sir Nathaniel' for a
   speech heading which he then abbreviated to '*Nath.*'
120 **numbers ratified** i.e. lines that are
   metrically correct
121 **for** as for (Abbott 149)
   elegancy elegance (*OED*, 2)
   facility fluency (*OED*, 3b)
   cadence rhythmical flow—not elsewhere
   in Shakespeare
122 *caret* it is missing
   Naso The cognomen (family name) of
   Ovid, meaning 'big-nosed'.
124 **jerks** flashes, sallies (*OED, sb.*¹ 3; earliest *OED* citation of this sense; not elsewhere in Shakespeare)
   Imitari to imitate
125 **tired** attired, decked out with trappings
   (Onions)
126 *domicella* Medieval Latin for 'maiden'.
   Q and F read '*Damosella*'. The emendation

brings the word into line with Holofernes'
characteristic manner—a bit of Latin
followed by its English equivalent. See
Wells, *Re-Editing*, p. 53.
128 **Ay, sir** Q and F read: 'I sir from one
   mounsier *Berowne*, one of the strange
   Queenes Lordes.' Only the first two words
   here make sense. For the rest, Biron is not
   in attendance on the Princess, and Jaquenetta has already said of the letter: 'It
   was given me by Costard, and sent me
   from Don Armado.' The nonsense is
   therefore ignored in this edition.
129 **overglance** cast an eye over. Apparently
   a Shakespearian coinage, it occurs again
   at *Henry V* 5.2.78.
   superscript superscription, address (*OED,
   sb.* A; no other example of this sense
   cited)
130 **snow-white** a time-honoured epithet
   (Dent S591.1)
131 **intellect** *OED*, referring to this context,
   defines *intellect* as 'meaning, significa-
   tion, purport' (*sb.* 5). Schmidt, on the
   other hand, following a suggestion by
   Baynes quoted in Furness, thinks it could
   mean 'sign, signature'. In the light of
   what follows *signature* appears to be
   right.
132 **nomination** name (*OED*, 4)

written unto: 'Your ladyship's in all desired employment, Biron.' Sir Nathaniel, this Biron is one of the
votaries with the King, and here he hath framed a letter
to a sequent of the stranger Queen's, which acciden-
tally, or by the way of progression, hath miscarried. (*To
Jaquenetta*) Trip and go, my sweet, deliver this paper into
the royal hand of the King. It may concern much. Stay
not thy compliment. I forgive thy duty. Adieu.   140

JAQUENETTA Good Costard, go with me. Sir, God save your
life.

COSTARD Have with thee, my girl.

Exeunt Costard and Jaquenetta

NATHANIEL Sir, you have done this in the fear of God, very
religiously; and as a certain father saith—

HOLOFERNES Sir, tell not me of the father, I do fear
colourable colours. But to return to the verses: did they
please you, Sir Nathaniel?

NATHANIEL Marvellous well for the pen.

HOLOFERNES I do dine today at the father's of a certain   150
pupil of mine, where, if before repast it shall please you
to gratify the table with a grace, I will, on my privilege I
have with the parents of the foresaid child or pupil,
undertake your *ben venuto*, where I will prove those

134 Sir] *continued to Holofernes* THEOBALD; *assigned to* Ped⟨ant⟩. Q, *and to* Per⟨son⟩. F
Nathaniel] CAPELL; *Holofernes* QF   139 royal] Q; *not in* F   140 forgive] Q (forgine), F
141 JAQUENETTA] ROWE; *Mayd.* Q; *Maid.* F   143 *Exeunt ... Jaquenetta*] ROWE; *Exit* QF
144 NATHANIEL] ROWE; *Holo⟨fernes⟩.* QF   145 saith—] F2; ~ ∧ QF   146, 150 HOLO-
FERNES] ROWE 1714; *Ped⟨ant⟩.* QF   151 before] Q; *being* F   154 *ben venuto*] ROWE
1714; *bien venuto* Q; *bien vonuto* F; *bien venu* too CAMBRIDGE *conj.*

133–4 **all desired employment** i.e. any use
  you care to make of me
136 **sequent** follower (*OED, sb.* 1; the only
  instance of *sequent* in this sense)
137 **by ... progression** i.e. as a consequence
  of the route it has taken
138 **Trip and go** a common phrase, frequently used in the songs that accompanied morris dances. See, for instance,
  Summer's Last Will and Testament
  212–19 (Nashe, iii. 240).
139 **concern much** be of great importance
  (*OED, v.* 4b)
139–40 **Stay ... compliment** i.e. don't waste
  time on a polite farewell
140 **I forgive thy duty** i.e. I excuse you from
  making a curtsy

143 **Have with thee** I'll go along with you
147 **colourable colours** plausible pretexts
  (*OED, colour, sb.* 12). Holofernes is
  quibbling on the proverbial assertion 'I
  fear no colours' (Tilley C520), where
  colours means 'hostile flags or standards'.
  A staunch Protestant, he will have nothing to do with the sayings of the Fathers
  of the Church.
149 **for the pen** as far as the calligraphy is
  concerned
151 **repast** the meal
152 **gratify** (a) please (b) grace
154 **undertake your *ben venuto*** guarantee
  your welcome. Compare *Shrew* 1.2.282
  for a similar use of the Italian phrase.

verses to be very unlearned, neither savouring of
poetry, wit, nor invention. I beseech your society.

NATHANIEL And thank you too, for society, saith the text,
is the happiness of life.

HOLOFERNES And, certes, the text most infallibly concludes
it. *(To Dull)* Sir, I do invite you too; you shall not say me   160
nay. *Pauca verba*. Away, the gentles are at their game,
and we will to our recreation.   *Exeunt*

4.3   *Enter Biron with a paper in his hand, alone*

BIRON The King he is hunting the deer; I am coursing
myself. They have pitched a toil; I am toiling in a
pitch—pitch that defiles—defile! a foul word. Well, set
thee down, sorrow; for so they say the fool said, and so
say I, and I the fool. Well proved, wit! By the Lord, this
love is as mad as Ajax. It kills sheep, it kills me—I a
sheep. Well proved again o' my side! I will not love. If I
do, hang me. I'faith, I will not. O, but her eye! By this
light, but for her eye I would not love her. Yes, for her
two eyes. Well, I do nothing in the world but lie, and lie   10
in my throat. By heaven, I do love, and it hath taught
me to rhyme and to be melancholy; *(showing his paper)*
and here is part of my rhyme, *(pressing his hand to his
breast)* and here my melancholy. Well, she hath one o'

4.3.8 do,] F2; ∼ ∧ QF   12, 14 melancholy] ROWE; mallicholie QF   12 *showing his paper*]
OXFORD *(subs.)*; *not in* QF   13–14 *pressing ... breast*] OXFORD *(subs.)*; *not in* QF

157 **the text** The authority Nathaniel is
thinking of has not been identified. Kerrigan suggests Ecclesiastes 4: 8–12; but
the parallel is not convincing.

159 **certes** certainly

161 *Pauca verba* few words—referring to
the tag 'Few words are best' (Dent W798)
gentles gentlefolk
game (a) sport (b) quarry

162 **recreation** (a) refreshment (*OED, sb.* 1)
(b) amusement, pleasant diversion

4.3.1 **coursing** (a) hunting, chasing (b) beating, inflicting blows on (*OED, v.* 4),
tormenting

2 **pitched a toil** set up a net, enclosure, or
snare. Compare *Hamlet* 3.2.334–5: 'why
do you go about to recover the wind of me
as if you would drive me into a toil?'
Having been driven into the *toil* (*OED,
sb.²* 1), the deer were then killed with

crossbows.

2–3 **toiling in a pitch** i.e. striving to escape
from the feelings engendered by Rosaline's eyes, the 'two pitch-balls' of
3.1.190.

3 **pitch that defiles** 'He that touches pitch
shall be defiled' was proverbial (Tilley
P358).

3–4 **set thee down, sorrow** See 1.1.301–2,
and note.

6 **as mad as Ajax. It kills sheep** Disappointed because Agamemnon awarded
the armour of Achilles to Odysseus rather
than to him, Ajax went mad and attacked
flocks of sheep thinking they were the
enemy. 'As mad as Ajax' became
proverbial (Dent A95).

10–11 **lie in my throat** lie outrageously—a
very common expression (Dent T268)

my sonnets already. The clown bore it, the fool sent it,
and the lady hath it. Sweet clown, sweeter fool, sweetest
lady! By the world, I would not care a pin if the other
three were in. Here comes one with a paper. God give
him grace to groan.

    He stands aside.
    Enter the King ⌈with a paper⌉

KING Ay me!   20
BIRON (*aside*) Shot, by heaven! Proceed, sweet Cupid. Thou
    hast thumped him with thy bird-bolt under the left pap.
    In faith, secrets.
KING (*reads*)

    'So sweet a kiss the golden sun gives not
      To those fresh morning drops upon the rose
    As thy eye-beams when their fresh rays have smote
      The night of dew that on my cheeks down flows.
    Nor shines the silver moon one half so bright
      Through the transparent bosom of the deep
    As doth thy face through tears of mine give light.   30
      Thou shin'st in every tear that I do weep.
    No drop but as a coach doth carry thee,
      So ridest thou triumphing in my woe.
    Do but behold the tears that swell in me,
      And they thy glory through my grief will show.
    But do not love thyself, then thou wilt keep
      My tears for glasses, and still make me weep.
    O Queen of queens, how far dost thou excel,
      No thought can think nor tongue of mortal tell.'
How shall she know my griefs? I'll drop the paper.   40
Sweet leaves, shade folly. Who is he comes here?

    Enter Longueville with papers. The King steps aside
What, Longueville, and reading! Listen, ear!

19.2 *Enter ... King*] QF (*The King entreth*)   *with a paper*] *not in* QF   24 (*reads*)] *not in* QF
26 rays] QF (rayse)   smote ∧] ROWE; smot. QF   36 wilt] F; will Q   40 paper] Q (*corr.*), F;
pa d er Q (*uncorr.*)   41 leaves,] THEOBALD; ~ ∧ QF   41.1 *Enter ... aside*] Q (*Enter Longauill.
The King steps a side*), F

17 **I ... pin** proverbial (Tilley P333)
18 **in** (a) in the same predicament (b) in love
22 **bird-bolt** blunt-headed arrow for shoot-
    ing birds
    under the left pap i.e. in the heart.
    Compare *Dream* 5.1.293–4: 'that left

    pap | Where heart doth hop.'
27 **night of dew** nightly dew (tears that flow
    every night)
37 **glasses** mirrors
41 **shade** hide (*OED v.*¹ 3)

BIRON (*aside*)

Now, in thy likeness, one more fool appear!

LONGUEVILLE

Ay me! I am forsworn.

BIRON (*aside*) Why, he comes in like a perjure, wearing
papers.

KING (*aside*)

In love, I hope. Sweet fellowship in shame.

BIRON (*aside*)

One drunkard loves another of the name.

LONGUEVILLE

Am I the first that have been perjured so?

BIRON (*aside*)

I could put thee in comfort—not by two that I know.   50

Thou makest the triumviry, the corner-cap of society,

The shape of Love's Tyburn that hangs up simplicity.

LONGUEVILLE

I fear these stubborn lines lack power to move.

O sweet Maria, empress of my love,

These numbers will I tear, and write in prose.

BIRON (*aside*)

O rhymes are guards on wanton Cupid's hose;

Disfigure not his shop.

LONGUEVILLE   This same shall go.

He reads his sonnet

---

47 KING] ROWE 1714; *Long⟨auill⟩.* QF   51 triumviry] ROWE 1714; triumpherie Q;
triumphery F   57 shop] QF; slop POPE 1728   57.1 *his*] *the* QF

43 **in thy likeness** This is ambiguous. It can
mean either 'looking like the king' or 'in
your own shape'. Compare *Romeo*
2.1.17–21: 'I conjure thee ... That in
thy likeness thou appear to us.'

45 **perjure** perjurer

45–6 **wearing papers** Part of the punishment for perjury was to wear a placard
stating the nature of the offence. It looks
as though Longueville should come in
with a sonnet or two tucked into his
hatband.

49–50 **Am I ... know** 'I am not the first
(and shall not be the last)' was proverbial
(Dent F295).

51 **triumviry** triumvirate
corner-cap cap with four (or three) cor-
ners, worn by divines and members of the
Universities in the 16th and 17th centu-

ries (*OED*)—much like the modern *mor-
tar-board*

52 **The shape ... Tyburn** Tyburn was the
regular place of execution for the county
of Middlesex. The gallows there, like
gallows in general, were triangular in
shape, being made of three pieces of
timber.
simplicity folly, silliness

53 **stubborn** rough, unpolished

55 **numbers** verses

56 **guards** (a) ornamental borders or trim-
mings (b) defences

57 **his shop** i.e. the place where Cupid
houses and displays his wares. The reference is obviously to the *hose*, complete
with *codpiece*. This garment concealed
and protected the male genitals while, at
the same time, calling attention to them

'Did not the heavenly rhetoric of thine eye,
  'Gainst whom the world cannot hold argument,
Persuade my heart to this false perjury?   60
  Vows for thee broke deserve not punishment.
A woman I forswore, but I will prove,
  Thou being a goddess, I forswore not thee.
My vow was earthly, thou a heavenly love;
  Thy grace, being gained, cures all disgrace in me.
Vows are but breath, and breath a vapour is.
  Then thou, fair sun, which on my earth dost shine,
Exhal'st this vapour-vow, in thee it is.
  If broken then, it is no fault of mine:
If by me broke, what fool is not so wise   70
  To lose an oath to win a paradise?'

BIRON *(aside)*

This is the liver vein, which makes flesh a deity,
A green goose a goddess. Pure, pure idolatry.
God amend us, God amend! We are much out o'th' way.

LONGUEVILLE *(aside)*

By whom shall I send this?
                    Enter Dumaine with a paper
                                        Company? Stay.
                    He stands aside

BIRON *(aside)*

All hid, all hid, an old infant play.

58 heavenly] Q (heanenly), F   59 cannot] QF; could not *Pilgrim*   66 Vows are but] QF;
My vow was *Pilgrim*   67 which on my] QF; that on this *Pilgrim*   68 Exhal'st] Q (Exhalst);
Exhalest F   69 broken then,] QF; broken, then *Pilgrim*   70 wise ∧] *Pilgrim*; ~ , QF
71 lose] QF (loose); breake *Pilgrim*   72 deity,] DYCE; ~ . QF   73 idolatry] F; ydotarie Q
75.1 *Enter ... paper*] CAPELL; *Enter Dumaine.* QF (*after l. 74*)   75.2 *He ... aside*] JOHNSON
(*subs.*); *not in* QF

by its use of costly and elaborate materials.

58–71 **Did not ... paradise** See note at
4.2.104–17.
59 **whom** which. Compare *Tempest* 3.3.61–
2: 'The elements | Of whom your swords
are tempered'.
65 **grace** favour
66 **Vows ... vapour is** proverbial: 'Words
are but wind' (Tilley W833)
68 **Exhal'st** It was thought that the sun
exhaled (drew up) vapours from the earth,
and thus produced meteors. Compare
Romeo 3.5.12–13: 'Yon light is not day-

light; I know it, I, | It is some meteor that
the sun exhaled'.
70–1 **what ... paradise** Compare 'To bring
one into a fool's paradise' (Dent F523).
71 **To** as to
72 **liver vein** style of a man in love. The liver
was regarded as the source of sexual
desire.
73 **green goose** giddy young girl. See note to
1.1.97.
74 **are ... way** i.e. have gone badly astray
(from the purpose with which we began)
76 **All hid** A cry used by children when
playing at hide-and-seek or blindman's
buff. Biron sees himself as the supervisor

Like a demigod here sit I in the sky,

And wretched fools' secrets heedfully o'er-eye.

More sacks to the mill! O heavens, I have my wish!

Dumaine transformed! Four woodcocks in a dish!   80

DUMAINE O most divine Kate!

BIRON (*aside*) O most profane coxcomb!

DUMAINE

By heaven, the wonder in a mortal eye!

BIRON (*aside*)

By earth, she is not, corporal. There you lie.

DUMAINE

Her amber hairs for foul hath amber quoted.

BIRON (*aside*)

An amber-coloured raven was well noted.

DUMAINE

As upright as the cedar.

BIRON (*aside*)   Stoop, I say.

Her shoulder is with child.

DUMAINE   As fair as day.

---

80 transformed] F (transform'd); transformed Q   83 in] Q; of F   84 corporal] Q (*corr.*) F;
croporall Q (*uncorr.*)

---

of the game, watching it from a superior
position, since he knows more about
what is going on than does anyone else.
Exactly how the scene was staged is not
clear. Biron, it would seem, is somewhere
above, 'Like a demi god ... in the sky',
while the King and Longueville are concealed somewhere on the main stage,
probably each behind one of the two
pillars that supported the 'shadow or
cover over the stage'. Property trees
which could be climbed were not unknown in the Elizabethan theatre. John
Marston calls for one in 5.1 of his *The
Fawn* (1605), where the initial stage
direction includes the words: 'Tiberio
climbs the tree, and is received above by
Dulcimel'.

79 **More sacks to the mill** proverbial (Tilley
S12)

80 **woodcocks** fools. Because of the ease
with which it allowed itself to be caught,
the *woodcock* was looked on as the emblem of stupidity. Compare *Shrew*
1.2.158: 'O this woodcock, what an ass

it is!'

84 **corporal** Biron sees Dumaine as an officer
in Cupid's army, exactly as he saw himself in the same role at 3.1.180. But he
also insists that Katherine is 'corporal',
i.e. flesh and blood (*OED, a.* 2). Compare
Macbeth 1.3.79–80: 'and what seemed
corporal | Melted as breath into the wind'.

85 **Her amber ... quoted** i.e. her amber-
coloured hair has made amber itself look
ugly when compared with it
quoted regarded as

86 **An ... noted** Twisting Dumaine's *foul* to
fowl, Biron ironically remarks that anyone who could describe Katherine's *raven*
locks as amber-coloured must have been
an accurate observer indeed.

87 **As ... cedar** a very conventional simile
(Tilley C207)
Stoop (a) bent, bowed (b) come down to
earth, 'come off it'. Both glosses have to
be deduced from the context; support for
them is lacking.

88 **with child** humped, bulging (like a pregnant woman: *OED, child, sb.* 17b)
As fair as day a stock simile (Dent D56.1)

BIRON (*aside*)

Ay, as some days—but then no sun must shine.

DUMAINE

O that I had my wish!

LONGUEVILLE (*aside*)   And I had mine!   90

KING (*aside*)

And I mine too, good Lord!

BIRON (*aside*)

Amen, so I had mine! Is not that a good word?

DUMAINE

I would forget her, but a fever she

Reigns in my blood, and will remembered be.

BIRON (*aside*)

A fever in your blood? Why then incision

Would let her out in saucers. Sweet misprision!

DUMAINE

Once more I'll read the ode that I have writ.

BIRON (*aside*)

Once more I'll mark how love can vary wit.

DUMAINE (*reads his sonnet*)

    'On a day—alack the day!—

    Love, whose month is ever May,   100

    Spied a blossom passing fair

    Playing in the wanton air.

    Through the velvet leaves the wind,

    All unseen, can passage find;

    That the lover, sick to death,

    Wished himself the heavens' breath.

    "Air", quoth he, "thy cheeks may blow;

91 I] JOHNSON; *not in* QF   96 misprision] Q (misprison), F   97 ode] Q (Odo), F   99 *reads his sonnet*] QF (*Dumaine reades his Sonnet.*)   100 is ever] Q; is euery F; was euer *Pilgrim, Helicon*   103 velvet ∧] F4; ~ , QF   104 can] QF; gan *Pilgrim, Helicon*   106 Wished] *Pilgrim* (Wisht), *Helicon* (Wish'd)   Wish QF

92 **Is not ... word?** (a) is not that kind of me? (b) is not *Amen* a good word?

95 **incision** cutting for the purpose of letting blood; regarded as the right treatment for a fever

96 **in saucers** (a) into the saucers used to catch the blood (b) by the saucerful **misprision** substitution of one meaning for another

98 **vary wit** i.e. make an intelligent man unlike himself (Schmidt). Compare 'It is

impossible to love and be wise' (Tilley L558).

99–118 **On a day ... thy love** As well as being printed in *The Passionate Pilgrim* (1599), this poem was also included in another anthology, *England's Helicon* (1600). Both collections omit lines 113 and 114 which link the lyric to the play.

101 **passing** exceedingly, surpassingly

104 **can** did (*OED, v.² 2*)

105 **That** so that (Abbott 283)

Air, would I might triumph so!
But, alack, my hand is sworn
Ne'er to pluck thee from thy thorn.   110
Vow, alack, for youth unmeet,
Youth so apt to pluck a sweet.
Do not call it sin in me,
That I am forsworn for thee;
Thou for whom Jove would swear
Juno but an Ethiop were,
And deny himself for Jove,
Turning mortal for thy love." '
This will I send, and something else more plain,
That shall express my true love's fasting pain.   120
O, would the King, Biron, and Longueville
Were lovers too! Ill, to example ill,
Would from my forehead wipe a perjured note,
For none offend where all alike do dote.

LONGUEVILLE (*coming forward*)
Dumaine, thy love is far from charity,
That in love's grief desir'st society.
You may look pale, but I should blush, I know,
To be o'erheard and taken napping so.

KING (*coming forward*)
Come, sir, you blush. As his your case is such.
You chide at him, offending twice as much.   130
You do not love Maria? Longueville
Did never sonnet for her sake compile,
Nor never lay his wreathèd arms athwart

108 Air] QF (Ayre); Ah! JOHNSON *conj.*   109 alack] QF; alas *Pilgrim, Helicon*   is] QF; hath
Pilgrim, Helicon   110 thorn] *Helicon* (thorne); throne QF, *Pilgrim*   113–14 Do ... thee] QF;
not in Pilgrim, Helicon   115 whom Jove] QF, *Pilgrim, Helicon*; whom great Jove COLLIER 1853;
whom ev'n Jove ROWE 1714   119 plain,] ROWE; ~. QF   120 true love's] ROWE;
trueloues Q; true-loues F   125 *coming forward*]ROWE; *not in* QF

116 **Ethiop** blackamoor (thought of as unat-
tractive)
117 **deny himself for** disown the name of
120 **fasting pain** pain caused by abstinence
122 **example** provide a precedent for
123 **perjured note** See notes on *perjure* and
wearing papers at lines 45 and 46 above.
125 **charity** Christian love (*caritas*) as opposed to profane love (*amor*).
126 **That** you who

126 **in love's ... society** Probably referring
to the saying 'It is good to have company
in trouble' from the Latin *Solamen miseris
socios habuisse doloris* (Tilley C571).
128 **taken napping** taken unawares, caught
in the act
129–30 **As his ... much** Compare the much
used saying 'He finds fault with others
and does worse himself' (Tilley F107).
133 **wreathèd arms** See note on 3.1.16–18.

His loving bosom to keep down his heart?
I have been closely shrouded in this bush,
And marked you both, and for you both did blush.
I heard your guilty rhymes, observed your fashion,
Saw sighs reek from you, noted well your passion.
'Ay me!' says one; 'O Jove!' the other cries.
One, her hairs were gold; crystal the other's eyes.   140
(*To Longueville*) You would for paradise break faith and
          troth;
(*To Dumaine*) And Jove, for your love, would infringe
          an oath.
What will Biron say when that he shall hear
Faith so infringèd, which such zeal did swear?
How will he scorn, how will he spend his wit!
How will he triumph, leap, and laugh at it!
For all the wealth that ever I did see,
I would not have him know so much by me.
BIRON (*coming forward*)
Now step I forth to whip hypocrisy.
Ah, good my liege, I pray thee pardon me.   150
Good heart, what grace hast thou, thus to reprove
These worms for loving, that art most in love?
Your eyes do make no coaches; in your tears
There is no certain princess that appears;
You'll not be perjured, 'tis a hateful thing;
Tush, none but minstrels like of sonneting!

140 One] Q, F (On); One that TAYLOR *conj., in* OXFORD   141 *To Longueville*] JOHNSON; *not in* QF
142 *To Dumaine*] JOHNSON; *not in* QF   144 Faith so] GLOBE (*conj.* W. S. Walker); Fayth Q, F
(Faith); Our faith OXFORD *conj.*   149 *coming forward*] ROWE; *not in* QF   153 coaches] ROWE
1714; couches QF   coaches; in your tears ∧] HANMER; couches in your tears. QF

135 **closely shrouded** secretly hidden (*OED*,
     shroud, v. 4)
137 **fashion** behaviour (*OED, sb.* 6)
138 **reek** smoke, emanate. Compare *Romeo*
     1.1.187: 'Love is a smoke made with the
     fume of sighs'.
143 **when that** when (Abbott 287)
146 **leap, and laugh** proverbial (Dent
     L92a.1)
148 **by** about
149 **Now ... whip hypocrisy** Biron consci-
     ously adopts the role of the satirist, whose
     task was, it was thought, to *whip* the
     vices and the follies of the time.

152 **worms** wretches (*OED, sb.* 10)
156 **minstrels** i.e. hired entertainers, includ-
     ing jugglers and the like as well as
     singers. The word *minstrel* had none of
     the romantic overtones it was to acquire
     later. Mercutio, accused by Tybalt of
     consorting with Romeo, retorts: '"Con-
     sort"! What, dost thou make us min-
     strels? An thou make minstrels of us,
     look to hear nothing but discords' (*Romeo*
     3.1.44–7).
     like of derive pleasure from (*OED, v.*¹ 5)
     sonneting composing sonnets—earliest
     citation by *OED*

But are you not ashamed? Nay, are you not,
All three of you, to be thus much o'ershot?
You found his mote, the King your mote did see,
But I a beam do find in each of three.   160
O, what a scene of fool'ry have I seen,
Of sighs, of groans, of sorrow, and of teen!
O me, with what strict patience have I sat,
To see a king transformèd to a gnat!
To see great Hercules whipping a gig,
And profound Solomon to tune a jig,
And Nestor play at push-pin with the boys,
And critic Timon laugh at idle toys!
Where lies thy grief? O, tell me, good Dumaine.
And, gentle Longueville, where lies thy pain?   170
And where my liege's? All about the breast.
A caudle, ho!
KING   Too bitter is thy jest.
Are we betrayed thus to thy over-view?
BIRON
Not you to me, but I betrayed by you.
I that am honest, I that hold it sin
To break the vow I am engagèd in,
I am betrayed by keeping company
With men like you, men of inconstancy.

157 ashamed] Q (a shamed), F   159 mote ... mote] QF (Moth ... Moth)   166 to tune] Q;
tuning F   172 caudle] Q (Caudle); Candle F   174 to ... by] CAPELL; by ... to QF
178 men like you] DYCE (*conj.* W. S. Walker); men like Q; men, like F; moon-like MASON

158 **o'ershot** outshot. Compare *Henry V*
   3.7.121 and Dent O91.1.
159–60 **You found ... three** There is plainly
   an allusion here to the figure of the *mote*
   and the *beam* used by Christ in his attack
   on *hypocrisy* (Matthew 7: 3–5 and Luke
   6: 41–2), and referred to by writers
   innumerable (Tilley M1191).
162 **teen** grief, vexation
164 **gnat** i.e. something quite insignificant
165 **gig** top
166 **tune a jig** sing a lively popular song; or,
   possibly, play the accompaniment to a
   popular dance
167 **Nestor** The oldest and wisest of the
   Greeks who fought at Troy.
   push-pin A children's game in which each
   player pushes his pin with the object of
   crossing that of another player (Onions).

168 **critic** censorious (*OED, a.* 2)
   Timon The notorious misanthrope of
   classical antiquity whom Shakespeare
   would later make the hero of his *Timon of
   Athens*.
   idle toys empty nothings, pointless trifles
172 **caudle** A warm drink consisting of thin
   gruel, mixed with wine or ale, sweetened
   or spiced, given chiefly to sick people,
   especially women in childbed (*OED*).
173 **betrayed** given up or exposed (*OED, v.*
   1b). Compare *Errors* 5.1.91: 'She did
   betray me to my own reproof.'
   over-view overlooking, inspection—
   earliest *OED* citation
175 **honest** true in word and deed
176 **am engagèd in** i.e. have sworn to keep
178 **men like you, men** Q reads 'men like
   men' which F alters to 'men, like men'.

When shall you see me write a thing in rhyme?
Or groan for Joan? Or spend a minute's time   180
In pruning me? When shall you hear that I
Will praise a hand, a foot, a face, an eye,
A gait, a state, a brow, a breast, a waist,
A leg, a limb—
KING   Soft! Whither away so fast?
A true man, or a thief, that gallops so?
BIRON

I post from love. Good lover, let me go.
            Enter Jaquenetta with a letter, and Costard
JAQUENETTA

God bless the King!
KING   What present hast thou there?
COSTARD

Some certain treason.
KING   What makes treason here?
COSTARD

Nay, it makes nothing, sir.
KING   If it mar nothing neither,
The treason and you go in peace away together.   190
JAQUENETTA

I beseech your grace let this letter be read.
Our person misdoubts it; 'twas treason, he said.

180 Joan] Q (*corr.*: Ione), F (*loane*); Loue Q (*uncorr.*)   181 me?] F3; ~ ∧ Q; ~, F
184 limb—] DELIUS; limme. QF   186.1 *Enter ... Costard*] ROWE (*subs.*); *Enter Iaquenetta and
Clowne.* Q (*after 'God bless the King'*); *placed as here* F   188, 189 COSTARD] ROWE; *Clow⟨ne⟩.* QF
192 'twas] Q (twas); it was F

Neither reading makes sense, and both
are metrically defective. Various attempts
have been made to put things right,
including 'moon-like men, men', but the
emendation adopted here has the virtue
of simplicity—it assumes only that the
compositor omitted the word 'you'—and
it fits the context with its stress on the
contrast between 'I' and 'you'.

180 **Joan** See note to 3.1.198.
181 **pruning me** titivating myself, preening
myself
183 **state** posture, bearing, mode of standing
(Schmidt)
184 **Soft!** Steady! Be careful!
Whither away so fast i.e. why are you in
such a hurry—proverbial (Dent W316.1)
185 **true** honest

186 **post from** ride fast to get away from
187 **present** (a) gift (b) writing (*OED sb.*[1] 2b).
The singular in the latter sense is most
unusual, since the normal form was
presents, as in Rosalind's comment:
'With bills on their necks: "Be it known
unto all men by these presents"' (*As You
Like It* 1.2.114–15).
188 **makes treason** is treason doing
189 **Nay ... neither** An adaptation of the
common saying 'To make or mar' (Tilley
M48).
192 **person** See note to 4.2.81.
misdoubts is suspicious of, has misgivings
about. In fact, it was Holofernes, not
Nathaniel, who expressed the idea that
the letter might 'concern much'; but
neither mentioned the word *treason*.

KING

Biron, read it over.

  He gives the letter to Biron, who peruses it

(*To Jaquenetta*) Where hadst thou it?

JAQUENETTA Of Costard.

KING (*to Costard*) Where hadst thou it?

COSTARD Of Dun Adramadio, Dun Adramadio.

  Biron tears the letter

KING

How now, what is in you? Why dost thou tear it?

BIRON

A toy, my liege, a toy. Your grace needs not fear it.

LONGUEVILLE

It did move him to passion, and therefore let's hear it.

DUMAINE (*picking up the pieces*)

It is Biron's writing, and here is his name.   200

BIRON (*to Costard*)

Ah, you whoreson loggerhead, you were born to do

  me shame.

Guilty, my lord, guilty! I confess, I confess.

KING What?

BIRON

That you three fools lacked me fool to make up the mess.

He, he, and you—and you, my liege—and I

Are pick-purses in love, and we deserve to die.

O, dismiss this audience, and I shall tell you more.

DUMAINE

Now the number is even.

193.1 *He ... it*] CAPELL (*subs.*); *He reades the letter.* QF 193 Where] F2; *King.* Where QF
196.1 *Biron ... letter*] CAPELL (*subs.*); *not in* QF 200 *picking up the pieces*] CAPELL (*subs.*);
not in QF 205 —and you,] QF (and you ∧); even you, DYCE 1866; e'en you, OXFORD

201 **whoreson** (used as a term of abuse)
 loggerhead blockhead, thick-headed fool.
 If the play belongs to 1595, this is one of
 the two earliest citations in *OED*.
204 **mess** group of four people eating together at the same table and from the
 same dishes, a common arrangement at
 great banquets, the universities, and the
 Inns of Court. 'Four make up a mess' was
 proverbial (Tilley F621).
205 **and you, my liege** i.e. yes, I mean you,
 my liege

206 **pick-purses** thieves (because they are
 trying to steal *love*)
 deserve to die The punishment for picking
 purses was hanging. Compare Ben Jonson's *Bartholmew Fair* 3.5.79–80:
 'Youth, youth, thou hadst better been
 starved by thy nurse, | Than live to be
 hangèd for cutting a purse.'
208 **the number is even** i.e. we are revenged,
 because the score is now level (*OED, even,*
 a. 10c)

BIRON   True, true, we are four.

  Will these turtles be gone?

KING   Hence, sirs, away!

COSTARD

  Walk aside the true folk, and let the traitors stay.   210

                              Exeunt Costard and Jaquenetta

BIRON

  Sweet lords, sweet lovers, O, let us embrace!

    As true we are as flesh and blood can be.

  The sea will ebb and flow, heaven show his face;

    Young blood doth not obey an old decree.

  We cannot cross the cause why we were born,

  Therefore of all hands must we be forsworn.

KING

  What, did these rent lines show some love of thine?

BIRON

  'Did they?' quoth you. Who sees the heavenly Rosaline,

  That, like a rude and savage man of Ind

    At the first op'ning of the gorgeous east,   220

  Bows not his vassal head, and strucken blind,

    Kisses the base ground with obedient breast?

  What peremptory eagle-sighted eye

    Dares look upon the heaven of her brow

  That is not blinded by her majesty?

KING

  What zeal, what fury, hath inspired thee now?

---

210 COSTARD] ROWE; *Clo⟨wne⟩*. QF   210.1 *Exeunt ... Jaquenetta*] THEOBALD; *not in* QF
213 show] Q (shew); will shew F   215 were] Q; are F   220 op'ning] Q (opning);
opening F   223 peremptory] Q (peromptorie), F

209 **turtles** turtledoves, i.e. lovers
  sirs *Sir* as a polite form of address could be
  used when speaking to a woman. Com-
  pare *Antony* 4.16.86–7: 'Ah, women,
  women! Look, | Our lamp is spent, it's
  out. Good sirs, take heart'.
212 **as flesh ... be** 'To be flesh and blood as
  other men are' is proverbial (Dent F367).
213 **The sea ... flow** proverbial (Dent
  S182.1)
214 **Young ... decree** proverbial (Dent
  Y44.1)
215 **cross** thwart, oppose
216 **of all hands** in any case (*OED, hand, sb.*
  30b)

218 **Who** is there any man who (Abbott
  257)
219 **rude** ignorant
  savage uncivilized
  Ind India. Compare *Tempest* 2.2.58: 'savages and men of Ind'.
223 **peremptory** overbearing (Onions)
  eagle-sighted The eagle was credited with
  the unique capacity of being able to stare
  at the sun with no impairment of its
  vision (Dent E7.1). Compare *Richard Duke
  of York* 2.1.91–2: 'Nay, if thou be that
  princely eagle's bird, | Show thy descent
  by gazing 'gainst the sun'.
226 **fury** frenzy of poetic inspiration (*OED*, 4)

My love, her mistress, is a gracious moon,
  She, an attending star, scarce seen a light.
BIRON
My eyes are then no eyes, nor I Biron.
  O, but for my love, day would turn to night.   230
Of all complexions the culled sovereignty
  Do meet as at a fair in her fair cheek,
Where several worthies make one dignity,
  Where nothing wants that want itself doth seek.
Lend me the flourish of all gentle tongues—
  Fie, painted rhetoric! O, she needs it not.
To things of sale a seller's praise belongs.
  She passes praise, then praise too short doth blot.
A withered hermit, fivescore winters worn,
  Might shake off fifty, looking in her eye.   240
Beauty doth varnish age, as if new-born,
  And gives the crutch the cradle's infancy.
O, 'tis the sun that maketh all things shine.
KING
By heaven, thy love is black as ebony.
BIRON
Is ebony like her? O word divine!
  A wife of such wood were felicity.
O, who can give an oath? Where is a book,
  That I may swear beauty doth beauty lack,

245 word] QF; wood THEOBALD

227–8 **a gracious … star** 'To be like the moon to the stars' was proverbial (Dent S826.2).
  scarce seen a light i.e. only with great difficulty to be perceived as a light
231 **the culled sovereignty** those picked out as supreme
233 **several worthies** i.e. several different kinds of excellence
  dignity i.e. perfect beauty
234 **wants** is missing
  want the desire for perfection
235 **Lend me** endow me with
  flourish embellishment (*OED*, *sb.* 3)
  gentle noble
236 **painted rhetoric** i.e. rhetoric with its artificial colours. Compare 'Truth has no

  need of rhetoric' (Dent T575).
237 **To … belongs** proverbial in the form 'He praises who wishes to sell' (Tilley P546)
  of sale for sale
238 **She … blot** i.e. she is beyond all praise, and, consequently, any attempt to praise her is bound to be inadequate and harmful
  blot stain, sully
241 **Beauty … age** i.e. the sight of a beautiful woman makes an old man feel young
242 **gives … infancy** i.e. endows old age with the youth of a child in the cradle
244 **black as ebony** proverbial (Dent E56a)
245 **word** See Wells, *Re-Editing*, p. 44.
247 **book** Bible

If that she learn not of her eye to look?
  No face is fair that is not full so black.   250
KING

O paradox! Black is the badge of hell,
  The hue of dungeons, and the school of night;
And beauty's crest becomes the heavens well.
BIRON

Devils soonest tempt, resembling spirits of light.
O, if in black my lady's brows be decked,
  It mourns that painting and usurping hair
Should ravish doters with a false aspect;
  And therefore is she born to make black fair.
Her favour turns the fashion of the days,
  For native blood is counted painting now;   260
And therefore red, that would avoid dispraise,
  Paints itself black to imitate her brow.

DUMAINE

To look like her are chimney-sweepers black.
LONGUEVILLE

And since her time are colliers counted bright.

252 school] QF (Schoole); scowl THEOBALD; stole HANMER; style OXFORD (*conj.* Shapiro)
253 And] QF; A WILSON 1962   256 and] F4; *not in* QF   257 doters] F; dooters Q

249 **If ... look** if she (beauty) does not learn
how to look from studying her (Rosal-
ine's) eye

250 **fair** beautiful

251 **badge** symbol, token. 'As black as hell'
was, and remains, proverbial (Tilley
H397).

251–2 **Black is ... the school of night** The
simplest and most satisfactory way of
dealing with this much debated, much
emended, and much exploited passage is
that proposed by Sisson (*New Readings*, i.
115–16): to let the words stand as they
are in the control text and gloss them as
'night is the scholar or pupil of blackness', or, to put it another way, 'black is
the school where night learns to be really
black'. A striking parallel with *Lucrece*
endorses this explanation. Pleading with
Tarquin before the rape takes place,
Lucrece tells him: 'princes are the glass,
the school, the book | Where subjects'
eyes do learn, do read, do look. | And wilt
thou be the school where lust shall
learn?' (615–17). Just as Tarquin's lust-
fulness outdoes lust itself and so has

something to teach it, so black, the
quintessence of blackness, outdoes the
darkness of night and so has something
to teach night. Compare also 4.3.298,
where Biron calls the ladies 'beauty's
tutors'.

253 **beauty's crest** i.e. brightness which is
the badge of beauty (Schmidt)

254 **Devils ... light** proverbial (Tilley D231).
Compare *Hamlet* 2.2.600–1: 'the devil
hath power | T'assume a pleasing shape',
and 2 Corinthians 11 : 14: 'Satan himself
is transformed into an angel of light'.
resembling when they resemble

256 **usurping hair** wigs, hair that has no
right to be where it is

257 **aspect** appearance

259 **favour** countenance
turns ... days i.e. completely changes the
idea of what is fashionable

260 **native blood** a complexion that is naturally pink
counted regarded as, taken to be

261 **red** a healthy red

264 **colliers** traders in charcoal or pit-coal

KING

And Ethiops of their sweet complexion crack.

DUMAINE

Dark needs no candles now, for dark is light.

BIRON

Your mistresses dare never come in rain,
For fear their colours should be washed away.

KING

'Twere good yours did; for, sir, to tell you plain,
I'll find a fairer face not washed today.   270

BIRON

I'll prove her fair, or talk till doomsday here.

KING

No devil will fright thee then so much as she.

DUMAINE

I never knew man hold vile stuff so dear.

LONGUEVILLE (*showing his shoe*)

Look, here's thy love; my foot and her face see.

BIRON

O, if the streets were pavèd with thine eyes,
Her feet were much too dainty for such tread.

DUMAINE

O, vile! Then, as she goes, what upward lies
The street should see as she walked overhead.

KING

But what of this? Are we not all in love?

BIRON

Nothing so sure, and thereby all forsworn.   280

KING

Then leave this chat; and, good Biron, now prove
Our loving lawful and our faith not torn.

DUMAINE

Ay marry, there; some flattery for this evil.

274 *showing his shoe*] JOHNSON; *not in* QF   277 lies ∧] ROWE 1714; lyes? QF   280 Nothing]
F2; O nothing QF

265 **crack** boast (*OED, v.* 6)
267 **in** into contact with (Abbott 159)
272 **then** i.e. on doomsday
273 **vile** cheap, wretched
276 **tread** a path (*OED, sb.* 3), a surface

277 **goes** walks
280 **so** as (Abbott 275)
283 **there** that's the point, that's it
     flattery ... evil i.e. nice verbal trickery to
     make our wickedness look better

LONGUEVILLE
      O, some authority how to proceed—
   Some tricks, some quillets, how to cheat the devil.
DUMAINE
      Some salve for perjury.
BIRON   O, 'tis more than need.
   Have at you then, affection's men-at-arms.
   Consider what you first did swear unto:
   To fast, to study, and to see no woman—
   Flat treason 'gainst the kingly state of youth.   290
   Say, can you fast? Your stomachs are too young,
   And abstinence engenders maladies.
   O, we have made a vow to study, lords,
   And in that vow we have forsworn our books.
   For when would you, my liege, or you, or you,
   In leaden contemplation have found out
   Such fiery numbers as the prompting eyes
   Of beauty's tutors have enriched you with?
   Other slow arts entirely keep the brain,
   And therefore, finding barren practisers,   300
   Scarce show a harvest of their heavy toil;
   But love, first learnèd in a lady's eyes,
   Lives not alone immurèd in the brain,
   But with the motion of all elements
   Courses as swift as thought in every power,

286 O] QF; *omitted* CAMBRIDGE   290 'gainst] Q (gainst); against F   293] *At this point* Q, *followed by* F, *prints the lines given in Appendix A (i).*

285 **quillets** verbal niceties, subtle distinctions. *OED* cites this as its first instance of the word; but Shakespeare had already used it in *1 Henry VI* 2.4.17–18: 'in these nice sharp quillets of the law, | Good faith, I am no wiser than a daw.'
   how to cheat the devil proverbial in the form 'This is the way to catch the old one' (Dent W149)
287 **Have at you** here goes
   affection's men-at-arms love's soldiers (a reversal of 1.1.8–10)
290 **state** status, rank (*OED*, *sb.* 15)
291 **young** unpractised, immature
292 After this line Q and F print what is obviously, and generally recognized to be, a first draft of lines 293–340. The original lines are to be found in Appendix A, and are of peculiar interest, since they

offer the most extended evidence we have of what the poet came to regard as unsatisfactory, and, when they are compared with the final version, of how he went about the task of revision.
296 **leaden** dull, heavy
297 **fiery numbers** Biron now praises his fellows' poems which earlier he held up to ridicule.
299 **Other ... brain** i.e. other kinds of learning, being lethargic (by comparison with the art of love), occupy, confine themselves to, the brain alone
301 **of their** i.e. from those practisers'
303 **immurèd** walled up
304 **motion of all elements** i.e. celerity of winds and storms (*OED*, *element*, *sb.* 11)
305 **as swift as thought** proverbial (Dent T240)

And gives to every power a double power,
Above their functions and their offices.
It adds a precious seeing to the eye:
A lover's eye will gaze an eagle blind.
A lover's ear will hear the lowest sound,   310
When the suspicious head of theft is stopped.
Love's feeling is more soft and sensible
Than are the tender horns of cockled snails.
Love's tongue proves dainty Bacchus gross in taste.
For valour, is not Love a Hercules,
Still climbing trees in the Hesperides?
Subtle as Sphinx, as sweet and musical
As bright Apollo's lute, strung with his hair,
And when Love speaks, the voice of all the gods
Make heaven drowsy with the harmony.   320
Never durst poet touch a pen to write
Until his ink were tempered with Love's sighs.
O then his lines would ravish savage ears
And plant in tyrants mild humility.
From women's eyes this doctrine I derive.
They sparkle still the right Promethean fire;

310 sound,] ROWE; ~. QF   311 head] QF; heed WILSON   314 dainty ∧] F2; ~, QF
315–16 Hercules, ... Hesperides?] THEOBALD 1740; *Hercules? ... Hesperides.* QF   317 Subtle]
Q (Subtit), F   320 Make] QF; Makes HANMER

306 **every power a double power** a double
  strength to every faculty
307 **Above ... offices** over and above their
  allotted functions (a sort of hendiadys)
309 **gaze an eagle blind** blind an eagle that
  gazes at it (thus showing itself stronger
  than the sun). See note to line 223.
311 **the suspicious ... stopped** i.e. the ears of
  the thief, apprehensive of the slightest
  noise, can hear nothing. Shakespeare
  frequently uses the abstract for the con-
  crete. Schmidt (pages 1421–3) provides
  a list of examples.
312–13 **more soft ... snails** Compare *Venus*
  1033–4: 'Or as the snail, whose tender
  horns being hit | Shrinks backward in his
  shelly cave with pain'.
312 **sensible** sensitive
313 **cockled** equipped with a shell. *OED* cites
  no other example of this sense.
316 **the Hesperides** The last of the twelve
  labours of Hercules was to obtain the
  golden apples from a tree growing in a

garden that was watched over by the
Hesperides, the daughters of Hesperus,
and guarded by a dragon. Shakespeare,
however, like many other writers of the
time, thought of the *Hesperides* as the
name of the garden itself.
317 **Sphinx** The monster, supposed to have
  the head of a woman and the body of a
  lion, that proposed the riddle which was
  eventually solved by Oedipus.
319 **voice** voices (responding to, or joining
  in with, Love's voice). For Shakespeare's
  tendency to drop the final *s* in the plural
  of words ending in *ce* and the like, see
  Abbott 471.
324 **humility** 'a gentleness of the mind, or a
  gentle patience without all anger or
  wrath' (Richard Huloet, *Abcedarium*,
  1552, as quoted by Furness)
326 **Promethean fire** i.e. the fire Prometheus
  stole from heaven and gave to men. See
  note to Appendix A(i).9.

They are the books, the arts, the academes,
That show, contain, and nourish all the world,
Else none at all in aught proves excellent.
Then fools you were these women to forswear,   330
Or, keeping what is sworn, you will prove fools.
For wisdom's sake, a word that all men love,
Or for love's sake, a word that loves all men,
Or for men's sake, the authors of these women,
Or women's sake, by whom we men are men,
Let us once lose our oaths to find ourselves,
Or else we lose ourselves to keep our oaths.
It is religion to be thus forsworn,
For charity itself fulfils the law,
And who can sever love from charity?   340

KING

Saint Cupid, then! And, soldiers, to the field!

BIRON

Advance your standards, and upon them, lords!
Pell-mell, down with them! But be first advised
In conflict that you get the sun of them.

LONGUEVILLE

Now to plain dealing. Lay these glozes by.
Shall we resolve to woo these girls of France?

KING

And win them too! Therefore let us devise
Some entertainment for them in their tents.

BIRON

First, from the park let us conduct them thither.
Then homeward every man attach the hand   350
Of his fair mistress. In the afternoon

---

334 authors] CAPELL; authour Q; author F   336 Let us] F2; Lets vs Q; Let's F
342 standards] F; standars Q

---

329 **Else ... excellent** without their help, no
   man can become excellent at anything
333 **loves** makes love to, woos
339 **charity ... law** Alluding to Romans 13:
   8: 'he that loveth another hath fulfilled
   the law'.
342–3 **Advance ... with them** Biron is indulging in bawdy quibbles.
343 **be first advised** i.e. take the initial
   precaution

344 **get the sun of them** ensure that they
   have the sun in their eyes (*OED, sun, sb.*
   1e(c))—possibly proverbial (Dent S987)
345 **glozes** clever comments, specious bits of
   word-play
346–7 **woo ... too** Compare the saying
   'Woo, wed (win), and bed (wear) her'
   (Tilley W731).
350 **attach** seize, grasp (*OED, v.* 3b). The
   word was originally a legal one.

We will with some strange pastime solace them,
Such as the shortness of the time can shape;
For revels, dances, masques, and merry hours
Forerun fair Love, strewing her way with flowers.

KING

Away, away! No time shall be omitted
That will be time, and may by us be fitted.

BIRON

Allons, allons!

⎡*Exeunt the King, Longueville, and Dumaine*⎤
Sowed cockle reaped no corn,
And justice always whirls in equal measure:
Light wenches may prove plagues to men forsworn;   360
If so, our copper buys no better treasure.   *Exit*

5.1 *Enter Holofernes, Nathaniel, and Dull*

HOLOFERNES *Satis quod sufficit.*

NATHANIEL I praise God for you, sir. Your reasons at

356 omitted ∧] CAMBRIDGE; ~ , QF   357 be time] QF; betime ROWE 1714   be fitted]
F; befitted Q   358 *Allons, allons*] THEOBALD; Alone alone Q; Alone, alone F   *Exeunt ...
Dumaine*] KERRIGAN (*subs.*); *not in* QF   360 forsworn] Q (forsorne), F   361 *Exit*] KERRIGAN;
Exeunt F; *not in* Q

5.1.0.1 *Enter ... Dull*] ROWE; *Enter the Pedant, the Curat, and Dull*, Q, F (*subs.*)   1 (*and
throughout the scene*) HOLOFERNES] ROWE; *Pedant. (variously abbreviated)* QF   *quod*] ROWE; *quid* QF
2 (*and throughout the scene*) NATHANIEL] ROWE; *Curat.* QF

352 **strange** novel, highly original

357 **time** time enough (for our purpose) (*OED, sb.* 8)

  fitted used in a fitting manner

358 *Allons, allons!* Q reads 'Alone alone'; F 'Alone, alone'. There can be little doubt, however, that the French for 'let us go' is what the author intended. Exactly the same mistake, presumably compositorial, occurs at 5.1.139, and also in the 1602 Quarto of *Merry Wives*, where the final words in Act 2 are: '*Host*. Let us wag then. *Doc*. Alon, alon, alon' (sig. D2). Compare 'Alloune, alloune, *let us march*' (Nashe, iii. 110. 12) and John Marston's 'aloune' and 'aloun, aloun' in his *What You Will* (1601) (Harvey Wood, ii. 252 and 266).

358.1 *Exeunt ... Dumaine* Q has no direction for getting the men off the stage, while F has merely '*Exeunt*' at the end of the scene. Biron's ominous and accurate forecast of what is about to happen appears, however, to be meant for the audience in the theatre, rather than for his fellow-students now turned ardent lovers. Hence the present arrangement.

358 **Sowed ... corn** i.e. the man who sowed weed-seed reaped no grain. There may be an allusion here to the parable of the tares and the wheat (Matthew 13: 24–30).

359 **whirls ... measure** i.e. is even-handed. Compare *Richard III* 4.4.105: 'Thus hath the course of justice whirled about' and the proverbial 'As they sow so let them reap' (Tilley S687).

360 **Light** frivolous, wanton

361 **copper** coins of small value

5.1.1 *Satis quod sufficit* This should be '*Satis est quod sufficit*', the Latin for 'Enough is enough' (Dent E159), with a glance at 'Enough is as good as a feast' (Tilley E158). They have just come from dinner, which in Shakespeare's day was eaten about 11 a.m. or shortly thereafter.

2 **reasons** disquisitions (*OED, sb.* 3)

179

dinner have been sharp and sententious, pleasant without scurrility, witty without affection, audacious without impudency, learned without opinion, and strange
without heresy. I did converse this *quondam* day with a
companion of the King's, who is intituled, nominated,
or called Don Adriano de Armado.

HOLOFERNES *Novi hominem tanquam te.* His humour is lofty,
his discourse peremptory, his tongue filed, his eye   10
ambitious, his gait majestical, and his general behaviour vain, ridiculous, and thrasonical. He is too picked,
too spruce, too affected, too odd, as it were, too peregrinate, as I may call it.

NATHANIEL A most singular and choice epithet.

He draws out his table-book

HOLOFERNES He draweth out the thread of his verbosity
finer than the staple of his argument. I abhor such
fanatical phantasimes, such insociable and point-device
companions, such rackers of orthography, as to speak

4 affection] QF; affectation F2   9 *hominem*] F3; *hominum* QF   15.1 *He ... table-book*] Q
(*Draw-out his Table-booke.*), F (*subs.*)

3 **sharp** pointed, acute
sententious pithy, full of meaning (*OED*,
  1)
  pleasant amusing
4 **affection** affectation (*OED*, *sb.* 13)
  audacious spirited, confident
5 **impudency** immodesty, indelicacy
  opinion arrogance, dogmatism (*OED*, *sb.*
  5c). Compare *1 Henry IV* 3.1.181: 'Pride,
  haughtiness, opinion, and disdain'.
  strange fresh, original
6 **this *quondam* day** the other day
9 *Novi ... te* I know him as well as I know
  you—a phrase culled from William Lily's
  Brevissima Institutio (1549), the Latin
  Grammar used in English schools. The
  mistake of *hominum* for *hominem* in Q and
  F is almost certainly compositorial.
  humour disposition
10 **peremptory** dogmatic, overbearing
  filed smooth. Compare Sonnets 85.4:
  'precious phrase by all the muses filed',
  and Dent T400.2.
12 **thrasonical** boastful, bragging. *Thraso* is
  the name of the braggart soldier in Ter-
  ence's *Eunuchus*.
  picked finical, fastidious (*OED*, *ppl. a.* 2).
  Compare *K. John* 1.1.193.
13 **spruce** over-elegant
  odd eccentric, peculiar in behaviour

(*OED*, *a.* 9b; earliest citation of the word
  in this sense)
13–14 **peregrinate** outlandish, having the
  air of one who has travelled abroad—a
  Shakespearian coinage
15 **singular** unparalleled, excellent (*OED*, *a.*
  11)
15.1 ***table-book*** notebook, memorandum
  book
16–17 **He ... argument** The figure is from
  spinning, the *staple* being the fibre of
  which a thread is composed. Holofernes
  of all people accuses Armado of 'spinning
  out' his discourse by using more words
  than his subject-matter warrants. *OED*
  cites no earlier example of *staple* in this
  figurative sense.
18 **fanatical** extravagant (*OED*, *a.* 2b; no
  other example cited)
  phantasimes See note to 4.1.98.
  insociable unfit for social intercourse.
  OED (*a.* 2) has no earlier instance.
  point-device pedantically precise
19 **companions** fellows (used as a term of
  contempt). Compare *Coriolanus*
  4.5.11–13: 'Has the porter his eyes in his
  head, that he gives entrance to such
  companions?'
  rackers of orthography torturers of spelling

'dout', *sine* 'b', when he should say 'doubt'; 'det', when   20
he should pronounce 'debt'—'d, e, b, t', not 'd, e, t'. He
clepeth a calf 'cauf'; half 'hauf'; neighbour *vocatur*
'nebour', 'neigh' abbreviated 'ne'. This is abhominable,
which he would call 'abominable'. It insinuateth me of
insanire. Ne intelligis, domine? To make frantic, lunatic.

NATHANIEL *Laus Deo, bone intelligo.*

HOLOFERNES *Bone? 'Bone'* for *'bene'*! Priscian a little
scratched; 'twill serve.

      Enter Armado, Moth, and Costard

NATHANIEL *Videsne quis venit?*

HOLOFERNES *Video et gaudeo.*   30

20 *sine* 'b'] RIDLEY; fine QF   21 'd, e, t'] POPE; det QF   24 'abominable'] Q (abbominable);
abhominable F   25 *insanire*] SINGER; infamie QF; insanie THEOBALD (*conj.* Warburton);
insania COLLIER 1858   26 *bone*] THEOBALD; *bene* QF   27 *Bone?* ... Priscian] THEOBALD;
Bome boon for boon prescian QF ; *Bon, bon, fort bon,* Priscian CAMBRIDGE   28.1 *Enter* ... *Costard*]
ROWE; *Enter Bragart, Boy* QF   29 *Videsne*] POPE 1728 ; *Vides ne* QF   30 *gaudeo*] F2 ; *gaudio* QF

20 **sine 'b'** without pronouncing the letter
'b', omitting the letter 'b'. Q and F both
read 'fine', which can be defended if
glossed as 'mincingly', but the Latin '*sine*'
is in the true Holofernes vein.

22 **clepeth** calls (archaic)
   vocatur is called

23–4 **abhominable ... 'abominable'** As the
result of a mistaken etymology deriving
abominable from *ab homine*, i.e. 'away
from man', 'inhuman', the word was
written 'abhominable' from the 14th to
the 17th century and invariably takes
this form in the First Folio, where it
occurs some eighteen times. The correct
spelling, arising from a recognition that
abominable comes from the Latin *abomina-
bilis*, meaning 'deserving imprecation or
abhorrence', began to prevail around the
middle of the 17th century. In the light of
other Shakespearian uses of the word,
and especially of *Measure* 3.1.292, where
the Duke accuses Pompey the bawd of
making his living 'From their abominable
and beastly touches', it looks as though
the poet accepted the false etymology,
together with the spelling to which it
gave rise; but the present passage also
makes it clear that he knew the *h* was
dropped in normal speech.

24–5 **It ... insanire** It (this way of speaking)
seems to me to be subtly designed to drive
one mad. Q, followed by F, reads 'infamie', which makes no sense in this
context. Most editors have followed Theo-

bald in emending 'infamie' to read 'insanie', a very rare word, but *insanire* fits
better with Holofernes' own gloss 'To
make frantic, lunatic'.

25 **Ne intelligis, domine?** Do you understand, sir?

26–8 **Laus ... serve** This passage (see Introduction, p. 75) is hopelessly corrupt. For
some alternative emendations and comments see Binns, p. 126.

26 **Laus Deo, bone intelligo** Praise be to God,
I understand perfectly. Q and F read '*bene*'
for '*bone*', giving a sentence that is impec-
cable Latin. The ingenious Theobald
changed '*bene*', which is correct, into
'*bone*', which is a solecism, in order to
provide a justification for Holofernes'
reproof.

27 **Bone? 'Bone' for 'bene'!** Theobald's
emendation of the totally unintelligible
'*Bome boon for boon*' of Q and F.

27–8 **Priscian a little scratched** i.e. Latin
that is not quite what it ought to be—
alluding to the expression 'To break
Priscian's head' (Tilley P595), meaning
'To speak bad Latin'. Priscian's works on
Latin grammar, written in the early part
of the 6th century AD, were regarded as
standard by the scholars of the Renaissance.

29 **Videsne quis venit?** Do you see who is
coming?

30 **Video et gaudeo** I do see and I'm delighted. Q and F read '*Video, et gaudio*';
and '*gaudio*', meaning 'with joy', makes

ARMADO Chirrah!

HOLOFERNES *Quare* 'chirrah', not 'sirrah'?

ARMADO Men of peace, well encountered.

HOLOFERNES Most military sir, salutation.

MOTH (*to Costard*) They have been at a great feast of
languages and stolen the scraps.

COSTARD (*to Moth*) O, they have lived long on the alms-
basket of words. I marvel thy master hath not eaten
thee for a word, for thou art not so long by the head as
honorificabilitudinitatibus. Thou art easier swallowed   40
than a flap-dragon.

MOTH Peace, the peal begins.

ARMADO (*to Holofernes*) Monsieur, are you not lettered?

MOTH Yes, yes. He teaches boys the hornbook. What is 'a,
b' spelt backward with the horn on his head?

HOLOFERNES Ba, *pueritia*, with a horn added.

MOTH Ba, most silly sheep with a horn.—You hear his
learning.

HOLOFERNES *Quis, quis*, thou consonant?

MOTH The last of the five vowels, if you repeat them, or   50
the fifth, if I.

31 (*and for the rest of the scene*) ARMADO] ROWE; *Brag⟨gart⟩.* QF   32 *Quare*] F2; *Quari* QF
35 MOTH] ROWE; *Boy.* QF   37 (*and for the rest of the scene*) COSTARD] ROWE; *Clow⟨ne⟩.* QF
38 master] QF (M.)   40 *honorificabilitudinitatibus*] QF (*in roman*)   42 (*and for the rest of the
scene*) MOTH] ROWE; *Page.* QF   46 *pueritia*] QF (*puericia*)

quite good sense, but it does not accord,
as '*gaudeo*' does, with the Curate's love of
parallelism.

31 **Chirrah!** Hail! This explanation is J. A. K.
Thomson's. He takes 'Chirrah' to be
Armado's attempt at '*chaere*' (Greek
χαῖρε), one of the forms of salutation
listed by Erasmus in the first and most elementary part of his *Familiaria Colloquia*, a
work much used in Elizabethan schools
(*Shakespeare and the Classics*, p. 71).

32 *Quare* why

37–8 **alms-basket of words** i.e. words rejected by others. Each parish had an
alms-basket to contain scraps for distri-
bution to the poor.

40 *honorificabilitudinitatibus* Reputed to
be the longest of words, this is the
dative/ablative plural of a medieval Latin
word meaning 'the state of being loaded
with honours'.

41 **flap-dragon** raisin, plum, or the like,

floating in burning brandy. Used in the
game of snap-dragon, it had to be caught
with the mouth and eaten.

42 **peal** peal of bells, i.e. tintinnabulation of
verbiage

43 **lettered** (a) learned (Armado's meaning)
(b) literate (Moth's meaning)

44 **hornbook** 'A leaf of paper containing the
alphabet (often with the addition of the
ten digits, some elements of spelling, and
the Lord's Prayer) protected by a thin
plate of translucent horn, and mounted
on a tablet of wood with a projecting
piece for a handle' (*OED*).

46 *pueritia* child (literally 'childishness')

49 *Quis* who
consonant nothing, nonentity—because
a consonant can only be sounded when
accompanied by a vowel. *OED* does not
record this sense.

50–3 **The last . . . o, u** Moth lures Holofernes
into repeating the five vowels, interrupts
him at *i*, thus making him a sheep, and

HOLOFERNES I will repeat them: a, e, i—

MOTH The sheep. The other two concludes it—o, u.

ARMADO Now by the salt wave of the *Mediterraneum*, a
sweet touch, a quick venue of wit, snip, snap, quick and
home! It rejoiceth my intellect. True wit!

MOTH Offered by a child to an old man—which is wit-old.

HOLOFERNES What is the figure? What is the figure?

MOTH Horns.

HOLOFERNES Thou disputes like an infant. Go whip thy gig.   60

MOTH Lend me your horn to make one, and I will whip
about your infamy *manu cita*. A gig of a cuckold's horn!

COSTARD An I had but one penny in the world, thou
shouldst have it to buy gingerbread. Hold, there is the
very remuneration I had of thy master, thou halfpenny
purse of wit, thou pigeon-egg of discretion. O, an the
heavens were so pleased that thou wert but my bastard,

---

54 salt wave] F (salt waue); sault wane Q   *Mediterraneum*] ROWE; mediteranium QF
55 venue] DYCE; vene we QF   60 disputes] QF; disputes't F2   62 *manu cita*] DAVID; *vnū
cita* Q; *vnum cita* F; *circum circa* THEOBALD   67 wert] F; wart Q

---

then concludes the performance and
wins the game by adding 'o, u (i.e.
ewe / you)' himself.

54 **salt** This word could have the secondary
sense of 'pungent', 'witty'. Compare *Troi-
lus* 1.3.364: 'the pride and salt scorn of
his eyes'.
  Mediterraneum Mediterranean. Armado's preference for the Latin (*mare Mediterraneum*) may not be so affected as it
looks. To judge from the examples cited
by *OED*, *Mediterranean* was just coming
into use about the time when *LLL* was
written.

55 **touch** a hit scored on an opponent in a
fencing-match. Compare *Hamlet* 5.2.239:
'A touch, a touch, I do confess.'
  venue thrusting attack (*OED*, 2b)

56 **home** i.e. hitting the target

57 **wit-old** Moth quibbles on *wittol*, often
written *wittold*, a contented cuckold.

58 **figure** (a) figure of speech (the sense
Holofernes intends) (b) emblem (the
sense Moth gives it)

60 **disputes** Shakespeare often employs this
form of the second person singular, especially for verbs ending in *t* or *te* (Abbott

340). Compare 5.2.208: 'Thou now requests'.

60–1 **gig ... one** According to Halliwell,
quoted by Furness at 4.3.165, there is
some evidence that whipping-tops were
'made of the tip of a horn, hollow, but
with a small ballast at the bottom of the
inside'.

62 **manu cita** with a lively hand. Binns
(p. 125) would accept the QF reading
'*unum cita*' as it stands, taking it to mean
'cite one [example]', and explain the
entire speech thus: 'I will whip about
your Infamy—give me an instance (or
example)—a top made out of a cuckold's
horn.' This, however, sounds rather la-
boured for Moth, whereas '*manu cita*'
looks forward to the comic threat Falstaff's page utters to Mistress Quickly
when he tells her 'I'll tickle your catastrophe' (*2 Henry IV* 2.1.62).

65–6 **halfpenny purse** tiny purse (probably
for holding silver halfpence). Compare
Merry Wives 3.5.134–5, referring to Falstaff: 'He cannot creep into a halfpenny
purse, nor into a pepperbox'.

66 **pigeon-egg** apparently as an instance of
something small

what a joyful father wouldst thou make me! Go to, thou
hast it *ad dunghill*, at the fingers' ends, as they say.
HOLOFERNES O, I smell false Latin, 'dunghill' for '*unguem*'.   70
ARMADO Arts-man, preambulate. We will be singuled
    from the barbarous. Do you not educate youth at the
    charge-house on the top of the mountain?
HOLOFERNES Or *mons*, the hill.
ARMADO At your sweet pleasure, for the mountain.
HOLOFERNES I do, *sans question*.
ARMADO Sir, it is the King's most sweet pleasure and
    affection to congratulate the Princess at her pavilion in
    the posteriors of this day, which the rude multitude call
    the afternoon.   80
HOLOFERNES The posterior of the day, most generous sir, is
    liable, congruent, and measurable for the afternoon.
    The word is well culled, choice, sweet, and apt, I do
    assure you, sir, I do assure.
ARMADO Sir, the King is a noble gentleman, and my
    familiar, I do assure ye, very good friend. For what is

69 *dunghill*] THEOBALD; *dungil* QF   70 dunghill] THEOBALD; *dunghel* QF   71 Arts-man,]
THEOBALD; *Arts-man* ∧] QF   preambulate] CAMBRIDGE; *preambulat* QF; *preambulate* OXFORD
singuled] Q; singled F   83 choice] F2 (choise); chose QF   86 ye,] ROWE; ∼ ∧ QF

69–70 *ad dunghill ... unguem* 'To have
    something at one's fingers' ends' was a
    familiar saying (Tilley F245) stemming
    from the Latin *ad unguem* meaning 'down
    to the fingernail', 'exact in every detail',
    originally used of a piece of sculpture.
71 **Arts-man** i.e. learned sir, man skilled in
    the liberal arts (*OED*, 2). This instance
    antedates *OED*'s earliest example by
    about ten years.
    preambulate walk forward (with me).
    OED cites no instance of this rare word
    prior to 1607 (Schoenbaum's date for
    Every Woman in Her Humour). It is to be
    found, however, in George Chapman's
    An Humorous Day's Mirth (3.53), where
    it has precisely the sense it has here. First
    played in May 1597, Chapman's comedy
    was published in 1599.
    singuled singled out, separated. 'Singled'
    has not the 'singularity' Armado re-
    quires, so he coins his own version of it.
72–6 **Do you ... *sans question*** J. A. K.
    Thomson (pp. 72–3) has provided a most
    attractive solution to this passage which
    baffled earlier commentators. He shows

that it is based on a dialogue between
    Georgius and Livinus near the beginning
    of Erasmus' *Colloquies*. Georgius asks:
    '*Unde prodis?* (Where do you come
    from?)' Livinus replies: '*E collegio Montis
    Acuti* (From the college of the pointed
    Mountain).' Georgius then remarks:
    '*Ergo ades nobis onustus literis* (So you
    must come to us loaded with learning).'
    '*Immo pediculis* (No, with lice),' answers
    Livinus. The college in question is the
    Collège de Montaigu in Paris where Eras-
    mus had been a student in his youth, and
    had suffered.
73 **charge-house** house for the charge of
    youth, boarding-school (*OED*, 1; no
    other instance cited)
78 **congratulate** salute (*OED, v.* 5)
79 **posteriors** buttocks, backside—not the
    happiest of synonyms for 'later part'
81 **generous** nobly born
82 **liable** suitable, apt (*OED, a.* 6)
    measurable fit (*OED, a.* 4)
86 **familiar** intimate. It is not clear whether
    familiar is used as an adjective or as a
    noun.

inward between us, let it pass—I do beseech thee,
remember thy courtesy; I beseech thee apparel thy
head. And among other important and most serious
designs, and of great import indeed, too—but let that   90
pass; for I must tell thee it will please his grace, by the
world, sometime to lean upon my poor shoulder, and,
with his royal finger, thus dally with my excrement,
with my mustachio—but, sweetheart, let that pass. By
the world, I recount no fable! Some certain special
honours it pleaseth his greatness to impart to Armado, a
soldier, a man of travel, that hath seen the world—but
let that pass. The very all of all is—but, sweetheart, I do
implore secrecy—that the King would have me present
the Princess—sweet chuck—with some delightful osten-   100
tation, or show, or pageant, or antic, or firework. Now,
understanding that the curate and your sweet self are
good at such eruptions and sudden breaking-out of
mirth, as it were, I have acquainted you withal, to the
end to crave your assistance.

HOLOFERNES Sir, you shall present before her the Nine
Worthies. Sir Nathaniel, as concerning some entertainment of time, some show in the posterior of this day to
be rendered by our assistance, the King's command,
and this most gallant, illustrate, and learned gentleman   110
before the Princess, I say none so fit as to present the
Nine Worthies.

89 important] COLLIER (*conj.* Capell); importunt Q; importunate F   94 mustachio] F;
mustachie Q   99 secrecy] F (secrecie); secretie Q   107 Nathaniel] CAPELL; *Holofernes* QF
109 rendered] F (rendred); rended Q   assistance] HANMER (*conj.* Theobald); assistants QF
111 as to present] QF; to present as HUDSON (*conj.* Dyce)

87 **inward** confidential, private
88 **remember thy courtesy** be covered, put
  your hat on again (*OED, v.* 1d). Compare
  Hamlet 5.2.105: 'I beseech you, remember'.
93 **excrement** i.e. that which grows out of
  the body, such as the hair and the nails
  (*OED, excrement²,* 1). Compare *Errors*
  2.2.78–9: 'Why is Time such a niggard
  of hair, being, as it is, so plentiful an
  excrement?' There is probably a quibble,
  not intentional on Armado's part, on the
  modern sense of the word.
98 **all of all** sum of it all
100 **chuck** chick (used as a term of endear-

ment or familiarity; earliest citation in
  OED)
100–1 **ostentation** spectacular show or ex-
  hibition (*OED,* 2c). *OED* offers no other
  example of this sense.
101 **antic** grotesque pageant (*OED, sb.* 3;
  earliest example of this sense)
103 **eruptions** *OED*'s first example of the
  word in a figurative sense.
104 **withal** with it
111–18 **the Nine Worthies ... Hercules**
  Traditionally the Nine Worthies (men of
  great renown) were three Gentiles (Hector of Troy, Alexander the Great, and
  Julius Caesar), three Jews (Joshua, David,

NATHANIEL Where will you find men worthy enough to
present them?

HOLOFERNES Joshua, yourself; myself, Judas Maccabeus;
and this gallant gentleman, Hector. This swain, because
of his great limb or joint, shall pass Pompey the Great;
the page, Hercules.

ARMADO Pardon, sir, error! He is not quantity enough for
that Worthy's thumb. He is not so big as the end of his   120
club.

HOLOFERNES Shall I have audience? He shall present Hercules in minority. His enter and exit shall be strangling a
snake; and I will have an apology for that purpose.

MOTH An excellent device! So, if any of the audience hiss,
you may cry 'Well done, Hercules, now thou crushest
the snake!' That is the way to make an offence gracious,
though few have the grace to do it.

ARMADO For the rest of the Worthies?

HOLOFERNES I will play three myself.   130

MOTH Thrice-worthy gentleman!

ARMADO Shall I tell you a thing?

HOLOFERNES We attend.

ARMADO We will have, if this fadge not, an antic. I
beseech you, follow.

115–16 myself ... Hector] OXFORD (*conj.* Proudfoot); my selfe, and this gallant Gentleman
Iudas Machabeus QF

and Judas Maccabeus), and three Christians (King Arthur, Charlemagne, and
Godfrey of Bouillon). They were the subject of pageants from at least the latter
part of the 15th century onwards; but
there is no record of Hercules and Pompey the Great being included among
them prior to their appearance here.

114 **present** represent (*OED, v.* 7b; earliest
instance of this sense). Compare *Merry
Wives* 4.6.19–20: 'Tonight at Herne's
Oak, just 'twixt twelve and one, | Must
my sweet Nan present the Fairy Queen'.

115–16 **Joshua ... Hector** This is the reading of the Oxford Shakespeare suggested
by Richard Proudfoot. Q, followed substantially by F, runs thus: '*Iosua*, your
selfe, my selfe, and this gallant Gentleman *Iudas Machabeus*', which makes no
sense. Proudfoot thinks that either 'and
this gallant Gentleman' or '*Iudas Macha-*

beus' was misplaced by the compositor
and led to the omission of '*Hector*', and he
points out that such misplacement would
be all the more likely if either of these
phrases was interlined or written in the
margin.

117 **pass** pass for, serve to enact the role of (a
sense not recognized by *OED* but tentatively accepted by Onions)

122 **have audience** be given a hearing

123 **in minority** when a child
enter entrance. This is the most recent
example of *enter* as a noun cited by *OED*.

123–4 **strangling a snake** Hercules wasted
no time in showing his strength. When
Juno sent two large snakes to attack him
in his cradle, he took one in each hand
and strangled them.

124 **apology** explanatory justification

134 **fadge not** does not turn out well, is a
flop (*OED, v.* 4). Compare *Twelfth Night*
2.2.33: 'How will this fadge?'

186

HOLOFERNES *Via,* Goodman Dull! Thou hast spoken no
    word all this while.
DULL Nor understood none neither, sir.
HOLOFERNES *Allons!* We will employ thee.
DULL I'll make one in a dance, or so; or I will play on the   140
    tabor to the Worthies, and let them dance the hay.
HOLOFERNES Most dull Dull, honest Dull! To our sport,
    away!   *Exeunt*

5.2   *Enter the Princess, Maria, Katherine, and Rosaline*
PRINCESS
    Sweethearts, we shall be rich ere we depart,
    If fairings come thus plentifully in.
    A lady walled about with diamonds!
    Look you what I have from the loving King.
ROSALINE
    Madam, came nothing else along with that?
PRINCESS
    Nothing but this? Yes, as much love in rhyme
    As would be crammed up in a sheet of paper,
    Writ o' both sides the leaf, margin and all,
    That he was fain to seal on Cupid's name.

1 39 *Allons!*] ROWE; *Alone* QF   1 42 dull Dull] This edition; *Dull* QF   1 43 *Exeunt*] Q; *Exit* F
5.2.0.1 *Enter ... Rosaline*] CAPELL (*subs.*); *Enter the Ladyes.* Q; *Enter Ladies.* F   1–709
PRINCESS] ROWE; *Quee⟨n⟩.* QF   6 this?] ROWE; ~ : QF   8 o'] Q (a); *on* F

1 36 *Via* come on, show a bit of life
1 40 **make one** join, take part
1 41 **tabor** small drum used by clowns and
    jesters, and much in demand on festive
    occasions
    the hay a country dance having a wind-
    ing or serpentine movement (*OED, sb.⁴*)
1 42 **Most dull Dull** Q and F both read 'Most
    Dull', showing that the personal name is
    intended. It seems likely, therefore, that
    the word 'dull' was either deliberately,
    since the line is a very tight one, or
    accidentally omitted.
5.2.2 **fairings** gifts (originally 'a present
    given or bought from a fair')
3 **A lady ... diamonds** During Elizabeth's
    reign English taste and fashion came
    under the influence of France and Italy

and, as a result, 'the earlier geometrical
arrangements of stones in heavy gothic
settings gradually gave way to the use of
minute nude figures, realistically
modelled with exquisite taste and precision and set amongst enamelled
strapwork or arabesques, accentuated at
important points with precious stones;
this flat treatment was particularly suitable for the pendants so much sought
after and worn by both men and women'
(*Shakespeare's England,* ii. 1 14). Compare
Contention 3.2.106–7: 'I took a costly
jewel from my neck— | A heart it was,
bound in with diamonds'.

9 **That ... name** so that he was compelled
    to put his seal on the name of Cupid

ROSALINE

That was the way to make his godhead wax,   10

For he hath been five thousand year a boy.

KATHERINE

Ay, and a shrewd unhappy gallows too.

ROSALINE

You'll ne'er be friends with him; a killed your sister.

KATHERINE

He made her melancholy, sad, and heavy,

And so she died. Had she been light, like you,

Of such a merry, nimble, stirring spirit,

She might ha' been a grandam ere she died.

And so may you, for a light heart lives long.

ROSALINE

What's your dark meaning, mouse, of this light word?

KATHERINE

A light condition in a beauty dark.   20

ROSALINE

We need more light to find your meaning out.

KATHERINE

You'll mar the light by taking it in snuff,

Therefore I'll darkly end the argument.

ROSALINE

Look what you do, you do it still i'th' dark.

KATHERINE

So do not you, for you are a light wench.

ROSALINE

Indeed I weigh not you, and therefore light.

11 year] Q (yeere); yeeres F   17 been a] F (bin a); bin Q   22 You'll] F; Yole Q

10 **wax** (a) grow up, spread (b) sealing-wax
11 **five thousand year** The world was thought to be five thousand years old.
12 **shrewd** ill-disposed, wicked
    unhappy trouble-making (*OED, a.* 5)
    gallows gallows-bird, one deserving to be hanged (*OED*, 3; earliest example)
15 **light** lively, cheerful
18 **a light heart lives long** proverbial (Tilley H320a)
19 **dark** hidden
    mouse a term of endearment. Compare *Hamlet* 3.4.166–7: 'Let the bloat King ... call you his mouse'.

19 **light** frivolous
20 **light condition** wanton nature
22 **taking it in snuff** taking offence at it— proverbial (Tilley S598). The *snuff* is that portion of a candle-wick which is only partly burnt and, if not removed, gives off an unpleasant smell, as well as spoiling the *light*.
24 **Look what** whatever
    do it (almost certainly bawdy)
26 **weigh not** am not as heavy as. Katherine, however, takes *weigh* to mean 'value', 'think much of' (*OED, v.*¹ 13).

KATHERINE

You weigh me not? O, that's you care not for me.

ROSALINE

Great reason, for past cure is still past care.

PRINCESS

Well bandied both, a set of wit well played.

But, Rosaline, you have a favour too.   30

Who sent it, and what is it?

ROSALINE   I would you knew.

An if my face were but as fair as yours,

My favour were as great: be witness this.

Nay, I have verses too, I thank Biron;

The numbers true, and, were the numb'ring too,

I were the fairest goddess on the ground.

I am compared to twenty thousand fairs.

O, he hath drawn my picture in his letter!

PRINCESS Anything like?

ROSALINE

Much in the letters, nothing in the praise.   40

PRINCESS

Beauteous as ink—a good conclusion.

KATHERINE

Fair as a text B in a copy-book.

ROSALINE

'Ware pencils, ho! Let me not die your debtor,

My red dominical, my golden letter.

O that your face were not so full of O's!

28 cure ... care] THEOBALD (*conj.* Thirlby); care ... cure QF   43 ho!] HANMER; How? QF
45 not so] Q; *not in* F

28 **past cure is still past care** proverbial
(Tilley C921)
29 **Well ... played** The Princess sees the
stichomythic exchanges between the two
girls as a game of tennis or 'bandy'.
30 **favour** love-token (*OED, sb.* 7), twisted by
Rosaline at line 33 to mean 'looks',
'appearance' (*OED*, 9)
35 **numbers true** metre sound
numb'ring reckoning of, value set on (my
beauty) (*OED, v.* 1c)
37 **fairs** beautiful women (*OED, sb.*² 2).
Compare *Dream* 1.1.182: 'O happy fair!'
40 **Much ... praise** i.e. Biron's black letters
on the white page correspond to Rosaline's black hair and eyebrows set against
her pale cheeks, but there is no such

correspondence between the praise he
gives her and what she is.
42 **text B** capital B (Onions), possibly meant
to suggest *black*
43 **'Ware** beware
pencils paint-brushes, especially of a fine
pointed kind, used by artists, and also by
ladies when applying cosmetics
Let ... debtor i.e. I mean to get my own
back—proverbial (Tilley D165)
44 **red dominical** Almanacs used a red S for
Sundays. Rosaline refers to Katherine's
ruddy complexion.
golden letter Used, like the *red dominical*,
to mark Sundays, this term glances at
Katherine's 'amber hairs' (4.3.85).
45 **O's** i.e. small round scars caused by

PRINCESS

A pox of that jest; I beshrew all shrews.

But, Katherine, what was sent to you from fair
　　Dumaine?

KATHERINE

Madam, this glove.

PRINCESS　　　　　　　Did he not send you twain?

KATHERINE Yes, madam, and moreover

Some thousand verses of a faithful lover:　　　　　　　　50

A huge translation of hypocrisy,

Vilely compiled, profound simplicity.

MARIA

This and these pearls to me sent Longueville.

The letter is too long by half a mile.

PRINCESS

I think no less. Dost thou not wish in heart

The chain were longer and the letter short?

MARIA

Ay, or I would these hands might never part.

PRINCESS

We are wise girls to mock our lovers so.

ROSALINE

They are worse fools to purchase mocking so.

That same Biron I'll torture ere I go.　　　　　　　　60

O that I knew he were but in by th' week!

How I would make him fawn, and beg, and seek,

And wait the season, and observe the times,

46 jest; I] OXFORD; iest, and I QF; jest, and CAPELL　　47 Katherine] QF; *omitted* THEOBALD
53, 57 MARIA] F (*Mar.*); *Marg.* Q　　53 pearls] F; Pearle Q　　55 not] Q; *not in* F

smallpox and requiring the use of the
cosmetic *pencil*

46 **A pox ... jest** By using this strong imprecation the Princess makes it clear not only
that she sees what Rosaline is getting at
but also that she strongly disapproves.
I ... shrews I say the devil take all shrews
(pronounced to rhyme with *shows*)

51 **huge translation of hypocrisy** monstrous
transformation of hypocrisy into words,
i.e. great pack of lies (*OED, translation*,
2b; earliest example of this sense)

52 **compiled** thrown together (*OED*, 5)
profound simplicity (a) learned silliness
(b) extreme folly

54 **too long by half a mile** possibly proverbial
(Dent M924.1)

57 **Ay ... part** Capell's note seems worth
printing for its period flavour: 'Maria's
words spring from having her "chain" in
both hands, or twisted (perhaps) about
them in a womanish wantonness'.

59 **purchase mocking so** i.e. pay such a high
price for the privilege of being mocked

61 **in by th' week** caught for good and all—a
well-used phrase (Tilley W244), especially with reference to being in love

63 **wait the season** wait expectantly for the
right time
observe the times keep to the recognized
rules

And spend his prodigal wits in bootless rhymes,
And shape his service wholly to my hests,
And make him proud to make me proud that jests!
So fortune-like would I o'ersway his state
That he should be my fool, and I his fate.

PRINCESS

None are so surely caught, when they are catched,
As wit turned fool. Folly, in wisdom hatched,   70
Hath wisdom's warrant and the help of school,
And wit's own grace to grace a learnèd fool.

ROSALINE

The blood of youth burns not with such excess
As gravity's revolt to wantonness.

MARIA

Folly in fools bears not so strong a note
As fool'ry in the wise when wit doth dote,
Since all the power thereof it doth apply
To prove, by wit, worth in simplicity.

                    Enter Boyet

PRINCESS

Here comes Boyet, and mirth is in his face.

BOYET

O, I am stabbed with laughter! Where's her grace?   80

65 hests] DYCE (*conj.* Knight); deuice QF   67 fortune-like] This edition; perttaunt like Q;
pertaunt like F; Pair-Taunt like DAVID (*conj.* Simpson); planet-like WILSON (*conj.* Moore Smith);
pursuivant-like OXFORD   70 fool.] F2 (~ :); ~ , QF   hatched,] F2; ~ : QF   74 wanton-
ness] F2 (wantonesse); wantons be QF   79 is] Q; *not in* F   80 stabbed] F (stab'd); stable Q

64 **bootless** ineffectual
65 **hests** orders. Q and F read 'deuice' to the
   detriment of both metre and rhyme.
   Knight's happy conjecture satisfies the
   demands of both.
66 **And … jests** i.e. Rosaline would like to
   bring Biron into such a state of subjection
   that he would take pride in being the
   object of her proud mockeries
   jests jest. For examples of Shakespeare's
   use of a verb in the third person after a
   relative that now requires the first, see
   Abbott 247.
67 **fortune-like** Q reads 'perttaunt like'; F
   'pertaunt like'. The crux that results,
   together with the more important solutions proposed, is discussed in detail by
   Stanley Wells (*Re-Editing*, pp. 34–5). I
   share his misgivings about them, but I

am not convinced by his own solution—
'pursuivant-like'. It sounds 'too peregrinate', whereas 'fortune-like' has the support of *Romeo* 3.1.136: 'O, I am fortune's
fool!' and of *Tragedy of Lear* 4.5.186–7: 'I
am even | The natural fool of fortune.'
'Fortune' is, of course, capricious, and
that is exactly what Rosaline wants to be.
69 **catched** captivated, charmed (*OED*, *v.*
   37)
74 **revolt to** falling into, going over to
75 **note** stigma
77–8 **Since … simplicity** i.e. since the wise
   man turned fool will avail himself of all
   the intelligence he has to show that folly
   is true wisdom
80 **I … laughter** I have laughed so much
   that I have the stitch

PRINCESS

  Thy news, Boyet?

BOYET   Prepare, madam, prepare!

  Arm, wenches, arm! Encounters mounted are

  Against your peace. Love doth approach disguised,

  Armèd in arguments. You'll be surprised.

  Muster your wits, stand in your own defence,

  Or hide your heads like cowards and fly hence.

PRINCESS

  Saint Denis to Saint Cupid! What are they

  That charge their breath against us? Say, scout, say.

BOYET

  Under the cool shade of a sycamore

  I thought to close mine eyes some half an hour,   90

  When, lo, to interrupt my purposed rest,

  Toward that shade I might behold addressed

  The King and his companions. Warily

  I stole into a neighbour thicket by,

  And overheard what you shall overhear:

  That, by and by, disguised they will be here.

  Their herald is a pretty knavish page,

  That well by heart hath conned his embassage.

  Action and accent did they teach him there:

  'Thus must thou speak', and 'thus thy body bear'.   100

  And ever and anon they made a doubt

  Presence majestical would put him out;

  'For', quoth the King, 'an angel shalt thou see;

  Yet fear not thou, but speak audaciously.'

  The boy replied, 'An angel is not evil;

83 peace.] THEOBALD (*subs.*); Peace ∧ Q; ∼, F   89 sycamore] Q (Siccamore), F   93 companions. Warily ∧] F (*subs.*); companions, warely, Q   96 they] F; thy Q   97 page,] Page: QF   101 doubt ∧] COLLIER; ∼, QF

82 **Encounters mounted are** an attack has been organized

84 **surprised** (a) taken unawares (b) taken prisoners (*OED, v.* 2b)

87 **Saint Denis** patron saint of France

88 **charge** Two different senses of *charge* are equally appropriate: (a) load (as with a gun: *OED, v.* 5) (b) level (as with a lance: *OED, v.* 21). Compare *K. John* 2.1.382: 'Their battering cannon, chargèd to the mouths', and *Much Ado* 5.1.135–6: 'I shall meet your wit in the career an you

charge it against me.'

88 **scout** spy, reconnoitrer

92 **might behold** beheld

    addressed making their way (*OED, v.* 5)

95 **overhear** hear told over again, hear at second hand (*OED, v.* 4; nonce-use)

96 **by and by** very soon

98 **conned his embassage** learned his message

101 **made a doubt** voiced their apprehension

102 **put him out** make him forget his part

I should have feared her had she been a devil.'
With that all laughed and clapped him on the
        shoulder,
Making the bold wag by their praises bolder.
One rubbed his elbow thus, and fleered, and swore
A better speech was never spoke before.   110
Another, with his finger and his thumb,
Cried '*Via*, we will do't, come what will come!'
The third he capered and cried 'All goes well.'
The fourth turned on the toe, and down he fell.
With that they all did tumble on the ground,
With such a zealous laughter, so profound,
That in this spleen ridiculous appears,
To check their folly, passion's solemn tears.
PRINCESS
But what, but what? Come they to visit us?
BOYET
They do, they do, and are apparelled thus,   120
Like Muscovites or Russians, as I guess.
Their purpose is to parley, court, and dance,
And every one his love-suit will advance
Unto his several mistress, which they'll know
By favours several which they did bestow.

111 thumb] Q (thume), F   118 folly,] THEOBALD; ∼ ∧ QF   solemn] Q (solembe), F
120] *Omission marked after this line* OXFORD   122 parley, court] POPE; parlee, to court QF;
parle, to court CAPELL   123 love-suit] DYCE (*conj.* Collier); Loue-feat QF

109 **rubbed his elbow** a sign of satisfaction. Compare *1 Henry IV* 5.1.76–8: 'fickle changelings and poor discontents, | Which gape and rub the elbow at the news | Of hurly-burly innovation'. The phrase, first recorded here, seems to have caught on (Tilley E100).
fleered grinned (*OED*, *v.* 1)

111 **with ... thumb** i.e. snapping finger and thumb together

112 **come ... come** proverbial (Tilley C529)

114 **turned on the toe** made a pirouette

117–18 **That ... tears** i.e. they laughed until they cried. It is no wonder that the Princess becomes impatient with such circumlocution as this.

120 Oxford, following Keightley's example, marks an omission after this line because

there is no rhyme word to correspond with 'guess' (l. 121), and nothing to correspond with 'thus'.

121 **Like ... Russians** It seems highly likely (see Introduction, pp. 45–7) that Shakespeare in devising this disguise was thinking of the elaborate shows staged at Gray's Inn to celebrate Twelfth Night in 1595. An account of these revels, in which an Ambassador 'from the mighty Emperor of Russia and Muscovy', together with two companions, took part, was published in 1688 under the title *Gesta Grayorum*. The relevant passages from it are most easily accessible in Bullough i. 438–41.

124 **several** respective
mistress lady-love, sweetheart

PRINCESS

And will they so? The gallants shall be tasked;
For, ladies, we will every one be masked,
And not a man of them shall have the grace,
Despite of suit, to see a lady's face.
Hold, Rosaline, this favour thou shalt wear,   130
And then the King will court thee for his dear.
Hold, take thou this, my sweet, and give me thine,
So shall Biron take me for Rosaline.
        She changes favours with Rosaline
(*To Maria and Katherine*) And change you favours too.
        So shall your loves
Woo contrary, deceived by these removes.
        Maria and Katherine change favours

ROSALINE

Come on, then, wear the favours most in sight.

KATHERINE

But in this changing what is your intent?

PRINCESS

The effect of my intent is to cross theirs.
They do it but in mockery merriment,
And mock for mock is only my intent.   140
Their several counsels they unbosom shall
To loves mistook, and so be mocked withal
Upon the next occasion that we meet,
With visages displayed, to talk and greet.

ROSALINE

But shall we dance if they desire us to't?

---

127 ladies,] F4; ~; QF   130–1 Hold ... dear.] QF; *relegated to 'Additional Passages'* OXFORD
(*conj.* Riverside)   133.1 *She ... Rosaline*] *not in* QF   134 you] Q; your F   too] F; two Q
135.1 *Maria ... favours*] *not in* QF   139 mockery] Q (mockerie); mocking F   141 Their] Q
(*text*), F; The Q (*c.w.*)   142 withal ∧] DYCE; ~. QF

---

126 **tasked** put to the proof, tested
128 **grace** privilege
129 **suit** his pleading
130–1 **Hold ... dear** Oxford (following Riverside's suggestion) omits these lines on the assumption that they are a 'first shot' at 132–3. They are retained in this edition because, taken in conjunction with 132–3, they make it crystal clear what the Princess's plan is.

134 **change** exchange
135 **removes** exchanges
136 **most in sight** very conspicuously
139 **mockery** Shakespeare also uses this word as an adjective at *Richard II* 4.1.250: 'a mockery king of snow'.
140 **mock ... intent** Compare 'He who mocks shall be mocked' (Tilley M1031).
141 **counsels** secret purposes, confidences (*OED, sb.* 5)

PRINCESS

No, to the death we will not move a foot,
Nor to their penned speech render we no grace,
But while 'tis spoke each turn away her face.

BOYET

Why, that contempt will kill the speaker's heart,
And quite divorce his memory from his part.   150

PRINCESS

Therefore I do it, and I make no doubt
The rest will ne'er come in, if he be out.
There's no such sport as sport by sport o'erthrown,
To make theirs ours, and ours none but our own.
So shall we stay, mocking intended game,
And they, well mocked, depart away with shame.

A trumpet sounds

BOYET

The trumpet sounds. Be masked; the masquers come.

The ladies mask.
Enter blackamoors with music, Moth with a speech,
and the King and his lords disguised as Russians

MOTH

'All hail, the richest beauties on the earth!'

⌈BOYET⌉

Beauties no richer than rich taffeta.

MOTH

'A holy parcel of the fairest dames   160

The ladies turn their backs to him

That ever turned their—backs—to mortal views.'

148 her] F2; his QF   149 speaker's] Q (speakers); keepers F   151 doubt ∧] ROWE
1714; ~, QF   152 ne'er] F2; ere QF   155 stay,] THEOBALD; ~ ∧ QF   156.1 *A trumpet
sounds*] Q (*Sound Trom.*); *Sound.* F   157.1–2 *Enter ... Russians*] Q (*Enter Black-moores with
musicke, the Boy with a speach, and the rest of the Lordes disguysed.*), F (*subs.*)   158–73 MOTH]
ROWE; *Page.* QF   159 BOYET] THEOBALD; *Berow⟨ne⟩.* QF   160.1 *The ... him*] Q (*in roman and
after l. 161*), F   161 their—backs—to] CAPELL; *their backes to* QF

146 **to the death** i.e. though we should die
for it

147 **penned speech** speech specially composed and written out for the occasion

149 **kill ... heart** completely dishearten the
speaker. Compare *Winter's Tale*
4.3.82–3: 'Offer me no money, I pray
you. That kills my heart.'

152 **out** i.e. put out of his part (so that he
'dries up')

157.2 **blackamoors** i.e. attendants got up as

African negroes

159 BOYET Theobald's emendation of Q's
'*Berow.*' is adopted here because the King
says explicitly and angrily that it was
Boyet who 'put Armado's page out of his
part' (5.2.336).
taffeta i.e. the material of which the
ladies' masks are made

160 **parcel** group, company (*OED, sb.* 6).
Compare *All's Well* 2.3.53–4: 'This
youthful parcel | Of noble bachelors'.

BIRON

'Their eyes', villain, 'their eyes!'

MOTH

'That ever turned their eyes to mortal views!
Out'—

BOYET   True, out indeed!

MOTH

'Out of your favours, heavenly spirits, vouchsafe
Not to behold'—

BIRON

'Once to behold', rogue.

MOTH

'Once to behold with your sun-beamèd eyes—
With your sun-beamèd eyes'—   170

BOYET

They will not answer to that epithet.
You were best call it 'daughter-beamèd eyes'.

MOTH

They do not mark me, and that brings me out.

BIRON

Is this your perfectness? Be gone, you rogue!   *Exit Moth*

ROSALINE (*as the Princess*)

What would these strangers? Know their minds, Boyet.
If they do speak our language, 'tis our will
That some plain man recount their purposes.
Know what they would.

BOYET   What would you with the Princess?

BIRON

Nothing but peace and gentle visitation.

ROSALINE   What would they, say they?   180

BOYET

Nothing but peace and gentle visitation.

ROSALINE

Why, that they have; and bid them so be gone.

163 ever] F (*euer*); *euen* Q   174 *Exit Moth*] CAPELL (*subs.*); *not in* QF   175 strangers] Q (*stranges*), F   178 Princess] F4; *Princes* QF

172 **daughter-beamèd** Boyet quibbles, not
very happily, on *sun* | *son*.
173 **brings** puts
174 **perfectness** being word-perfect
175 **strangers** foreigners

177 **plain** plain-spoken
179, 181 **gentle visitation** a courtesy call.
OED cites no instance of *visit* as a noun
prior to 1621.

BOYET

She says you have it, and you may be gone.

KING

Say to her we have measured many miles
To tread a measure with her on this grass.

BOYET

They say that they have measured many a mile
To tread a measure with you on this grass.

ROSALINE

It is not so. Ask them how many inches
Is in one mile. If they have measured many,
The measure then of one is easily told.   190

BOYET

If to come hither you have measured miles,
And many miles, the Princess bids you tell
How many inches doth fill up one mile.

BIRON

Tell her we measure them by weary steps.

BOYET

She hears herself.

ROSALINE   How many weary steps,
Of many weary miles you have o'ergone,
Are numbered in the travel of one mile?

BIRON

We number nothing that we spend for you.
Our duty is so rich, so infinite,
That we may do it still without account.   200
Vouchsafe to show the sunshine of your face,
That we, like savages, may worship it.

ROSALINE

My face is but a moon, and clouded too.

KING

Blessèd are clouds, to do as such clouds do.

---

185 her on this] Q; you on the F

184 **measured** traversed
185 **tread a measure** dance a courtly dance
203 **but a moon** Rosaline gives the men a
hint, which they fail to notice, that she is
not the sun and that her light is merely
borrowed.
203 **clouded** i.e. masked

Vouchsafe, bright moon, and these thy stars, to
    shine—
Those clouds removed—upon our watery eyne.

ROSALINE

O vain petitioner, beg a greater matter!
Thou now requests but moonshine in the water.

KING

Then in our measure do but vouchsafe one change.
Thou bid'st me beg; this begging is not strange.   210

ROSALINE

Play, music, then! ⌈*Music plays*⌉ Nay, you must do it
    soon.
Not yet? No dance. Thus change I like the moon.

KING

Will you not dance? How come you thus estranged?

ROSALINE

You took the moon at full, but now she's changed.

KING

Yet still she is the moon, and I the man.
The music plays, vouchsafe some motion to it.

ROSALINE

Our ears vouchsafe it.

KING   But your legs should do it.

ROSALINE

Since you are strangers, and come here by chance,
We'll not be nice. Take hands. We will not dance.

---

209 do but vouchsafe] Q; vouchsafe but F   212 yet?] HANMER; ~ ∧ QF   214 changed.] F4;
~ ? QF   215] *Omission marked after this line* OXFORD   217 ROSALINE] THEOBALD; *before
previous line* QF   219 nice.] COLLIER 1858; ~, QF

---

205 **moon ... stars** 'To be like stars to the
    moon' was proverbial (Dent S826.2).
208 **requests** For verbs ending in *t* Shake-
    speare often uses *ts* in the second person
    singular (Abbott 340).
    moonshine in the water nothing at all,
    the essence of insubstantiality—pro-
    verbial (Tilley M1128)
209 **change** (a) round (of a dance) (b)
    change of the moon
210 **strange** outlandish, odd
211 **Music plays** Some such direction seems
    to be called for by Rosaline's 'Not yet?' in
    the following line, suggesting that the

men are slow to start dancing.
212 **Thus ... moon** proverbial (Tilley
    M1111)
215 **she ... man** i.e. we belong together like
    the moon and the man in the moon
216 **motion** (a) movement (the King's
    meaning) (b) sympathetic response (Ro-
    saline's perversion of the King's mean-
    ing). Compare Sonnets 128.1–3: 'How
    oft, when thou, my music, music
    play'st | Upon that blessèd wood whose
    motion sounds | With thy sweet fingers'.
219 **nice** pernickety, punctilious

KING

Why take we hands then?

ROSALINE   Only to part friends.   220

Curtsy, sweethearts—and so the measure ends.

    ⌈*Music stops*⌉

KING

More measure of this measure. Be not nice.

ROSALINE

We can afford no more at such a price.

KING

Price you yourselves. What buys your company?

ROSALINE

Your absence only.

KING   That can never be.

ROSALINE

Then cannot we be bought. And so adieu—

Twice to your visor, and half once to you.

KING

If you deny to dance, let's hold more chat.

ROSALINE

In private then.

KING   I am best pleased with that.

    They converse apart

BIRON (*to the Princess, taking her for Rosaline*)

White-handed mistress, one sweet word with thee.   230

PRINCESS

Honey, and milk, and sugar: there is three.

BIRON

Nay then, two treys, an if you grow so nice,

220 we] Q; you F   222 this measure] Q (this measue), F   224 you] Q; *not in* F   226 cannot] Q (cennot), F   229.1, 237.1, 241.1 *They converse apart*] CAPELL (*subs.*); *not in* QF

220–1 **Why ... ends** The form a courtly dance should take is set out in *Tempest* 1.2.378–82: 'Come unto these yellow sands, | And then take hands; | Curtsied when you have and kissed— | The wild waves whist— | Foot it featly here and there'. Rosaline refuses to let the formalities go beyond the *curtsy*.

222 **More measure** i.e. a fuller amount

224 **Price you** set your own price on

227 **Twice ... you** 'Unless this means that she bids his visor a double adieu, as wishing never to see it again, and only half an adieu to himself in the hope that it is not a full complete farewell, I do not understand it' (Furness).

228 **deny** refuse. Compare *Shrew* 2.1.179: 'If she deny to wed'.

231 **Honey, and milk, and sugar** All three were proverbially sweet (Dent H544, M930.1, S957.1).

232 **treys** threes—a *trey* being a throw of three with the dice

Metheglin, wort, and malmsey. Well run, dice!
There's half a dozen sweets.

PRINCESS   Seventh sweet, adieu.

Since you can cog, I'll play no more with you.

BIRON

One word in secret.

PRINCESS   Let it not be sweet.

BIRON

Thou griev'st my gall.

PRINCESS   Gall—bitter!

BIRON   Therefore meet.

        They converse apart

DUMAINE (*to Maria, taking her for Katherine*)

Will you vouchsafe with me to change a word?

MARIA

Name it.

DUMAINE   Fair lady—

MARIA   Say you so? Fair lord!

Take that for your 'fair lady'.

DUMAINE   Please it you,   240

As much in private, and I'll bid adieu.

        They converse apart

KATHERINE

What, was your visor made without a tongue?

LONGUEVILLE (*taking Katherine for Maria*)

I know the reason, lady, why you ask.

---

237 griev'st] F (greeu'st); greeuest Q   240 Take that] Q; Take you that F   242–55
KATHERINE] ROWE; *Mar⟨ia⟩*. QF

233 **Metheglin, wort, and malmsey** All three
    were strong sweet drinks but not
    proverbially so. *Metheglin*, Welsh in ori-
    gin, was made from honey and spices;
    wort was sweet unfermented beer; and
    malmsey a potent sweet wine.
235 **cog** cheat
237 **Thou ... bitter** Biron accuses the Prin-
    cess of causing him pain by rubbing on
    his *gall*, i.e. sore place. She retorts by
    giving *gall* its other meaning *bile*,
    proverbial for its bitterness (Tilley G11).
    meet fitting, appropriate
238 **change** interchange. Compare *Tempest*
    1.2.444–5: 'At the first sight | They have
    changed eyes.'

239 **Fair lord** The term is evidently used in
    mockery.
242–6 **What ... half** 'The old vizard was
    what the youngster of today calls "a false
    face". Made of black velvet on a leather
    base, it covered the entire features and
    was kept in place by a *tongue*, or interior
    projection, held in the mouth' (W. J.
    Lawrence, *TLS*, 7 June 1923). Longue-
    ville's point is that Katherine has two
    tongues, and so is being deceptive and
    ambiguous. She would do well to give
    him one of them, that which holds the
    mask in place, thus revealing the truth
    about herself.

KATHERINE

O, for your reason! Quickly, sir; I long.

LONGUEVILLE

You have a double tongue within your mask,

And would afford my speechless visor half.

KATHERINE

'Veal', quoth the Dutchman. Is not 'veal' a calf?

LONGUEVILLE

A calf, fair lady?

KATHERINE   No, a fair lord calf.

LONGUEVILLE

Let's part the word.

KATHERINE   No, I'll not be your half.

Take all, and wean it, it may prove an ox.   250

LONGUEVILLE

Look how you butt yourself in these sharp mocks.

Will you give horns, chaste lady? Do not so.

KATHERINE

 Then die a calf, before your horns do grow.

LONGUEVILLE

One word in private with you ere I die.

KATHERINE

Bleat softly then; the butcher hears you cry.

They converse apart

BOYET

The tongues of mocking wenches are as keen

As is the razor's edge invisible,

---

247 **'Veal', quoth the Dutchman** 'The Dutchman is trying to say "well", which represents Katherine's sarcastic judgement on Longaville's *reason*. At the same time, *Veal* puns on | "veil" (often spelled "veal"), this being Katherine's substitution for the *speechless visor* of the preceding line. Further, *Veal*, when tacked on to Katherine's last spoken word, *long* (line 244), makes up her wooer's name. By adopting Longaville's *half* (uttering *half* his name to make up the whole), Katherine demonstrates her ability to see through the *Veal* on her suitor's face' (Kerrigan).

Is not 'veal' a calf? In French *le veau* is both 'veal' and 'calf'; and in Shake-

speare's time a *calf* was the emblem of physical and mental imbecility. Compare Hamlet's calling Polonius 'so capital a calf' (*Hamlet* 3.2.101).

249 **part** share, divide. Longueville means 'let us both admit we are *calves*, and have done with it', but Katherine takes him literally and refuses to be his 'better half' i.e. wife. Compare *Caesar* 2.1.273, where Portia, speaking to Brutus, calls herself 'your self, your half', and also Dent H49.

250 **prove an ox** grow up to be a numskull (*OED*, *ox*, 4)

251 **butt** strike (as an ox does with its horns)

252 **give horns** (a) equip with horns (b) cuckold your husband

Cutting a smaller hair than may be seen;
    Above the sense of sense, so sensible
Seemeth their conference; their conceits have wings   260
Fleeter than arrows, bullets, wind, thought, swifter
    things.

ROSALINE

Not one word more, my maids. Break off, break off!

BIRON

By heaven, all dry-beaten with pure scoff!

KING

Farewell, mad wenches, you have simple wits.

        Exeunt the King, his lords, and the blackamoors
    ⌜*The ladies unmask*⌝

PRINCESS

Twenty adieus, my frozen Muscovites.
Are these the breed of wits so wondered at?

BOYET

    Tapers they are, with your sweet breaths puffed out.

ROSALINE

Well-liking wits they have; gross, gross; fat, fat.

PRINCESS

O poverty in wit, kingly-poor flout!
Will they not, think you, hang themselves tonight?   270
    Or ever but in visors show their faces?
This pert Biron was out of count'nance quite.

---

259 sense, so sensible] POPE; sence so sensible QF (subs.); *Exe.* Q; *Exeunt.* F; *after l.* 265 CAPELL 266 wondered] F (wondred); wondered Q

264.1 *Exeunt ... blackamoors*] THEOBALD 264.2 *The ladies unmask*] *not in* QF

259–60 **Above ... conference** i.e. their conversation is so pointed and piercing that it outgoes the power of the senses to perceive it

259 **sensible** acutely felt by the hearer (*OED*, *a.* 6)

260 **conceits** witty sallies (*OED*, *sb.* 8)

261 **arrows, bullets, wind, thought** four time-honoured examples of speed (Dent A322, B719.1, W411, T240)

263 **dry-beaten** thoroughly beaten without blood being drawn
scoff contemptuous ridicule

264 **mad wenches** a common saying (Dent

W274.1)

266 **breed** species, kind (*OED*, *sb.* 2c; earliest example of this sense)

268 **Well-liking** plump, obese—*OED*'s first citation of the word in a figurative sense

269 **O ... flout** The Princess refers to the King's supercilious dismissal of her and her ladies as 'mad wenches' who have but 'simple wits' at line 264, characterizing it as a poverty-stricken jeer for a king to indulge in.

272 **out of count'nance quite** completely disconcerted

ROSALINE

Ah, they were all in lamentable cases.

The King was weeping-ripe for a good word.

PRINCESS

Biron did swear himself out of all suit.

MARIA

Dumaine was at my service, and his sword.

'*Non point*,' quoth I. My servant straight was mute.

KATHERINE

Lord Longueville said I came o'er his heart,

And trow you what he called me?

PRINCESS   'Qualm', perhaps.

KATHERINE

Yes, in good faith.

PRINCESS   Go, sickness as thou art.   280

ROSALINE

Well, better wits have worn plain statute-caps.

But will you hear? The King is my love sworn.

PRINCESS

And quick Biron hath plighted faith to me.

KATHERINE

And Longueville was for my service born.

MARIA

            Dumaine is mine as sure as bark on tree.

BOYET

Madam, and pretty mistresses, give ear:

Immediately they will again be here

273 Ah, they] OXFORD; They QF; O they F2   277 *Non point*] QF (No poynt)   servant ∧]
F; ∼ , Q   279 perhaps] Q (perhapt), F

273 **cases** (a) states (b) outfits, costumes (including their masks)

274 **weeping-ripe** ready to weep. According to *OED* the word first appears in 1548 as the English equivalent of the Latin *Lachrymabundus*.

275 **out of all suit** i.e. in an utterly incongruous manner, entirely out of keeping with his *love-suit*

277 *Non point* not at all (with a quibble on the *point* of Dumaine's sword). See 2.1.188 and note.

278 **came o'er** took possession of (*OED*, *v.* 43c). This instance antedates *OED*'s earliest.

279 **trow you** do you know

279 **Qualm** sudden feeling of illness that 'comes over' one unexpectedly

281 **plain statute-caps** caps of the simple kind required by the law. Attempts to regulate dress were so common in the latter half of the 16th century that it is not clear as to precisely which statute Rosaline is thinking of. The likeliest would seem to be a regulation passed by the Common Council of the City of London in 1582 ordering that apprentices should wear one sort of headgear only: 'a woollen cap, without any silk in or about the same'.

285 **as sure as bark on tree** proverbial simile for close union (Dent B83 and H88)

In their own shapes, for it can never be
They will digest this harsh indignity.

PRINCESS

Will they return?

BOYET   They will, they will, God knows,   290
And leap for joy, though they are lame with blows.
Therefore change favours, and when they repair,
Blow like sweet roses in this summer air.

PRINCESS

How 'blow'? How 'blow'? Speak to be understood.

BOYET

Fair ladies masked are roses in their bud;
Dismasked, their damask sweet commixture shown,
Are angels vailing clouds, or roses blown.

PRINCESS

Avaunt, perplexity! What shall we do,
If they return in their own shapes to woo?

ROSALINE

Good madam, if by me you'll be advised,   300
Let's mock them still, as well known as disguised.
Let us complain to them what fools were here,
Disguised like Muscovites in shapeless gear;
And wonder what they were, and to what end
Their shallow shows, and prologue vilely penned,
And their rough carriage so ridiculous,
Should be presented at our tent to us.

BOYET

Ladies, withdraw. The gallants are at hand.

297 vailing] F; varling Q

288 **In their own shapes** i.e. without their disguises
289 **digest** swallow, put up with
292 **repair** return (*OED, v.* 2)
293 **Blow** bloom. There may be a punning reference back to 'blows' (line 291). If so, we have the reason for the Princess's demand for clarification in the next line.
296 **Dismasked** unmasked—earliest citation in *OED*
    damask red and white, blush-coloured—earliest citation of this sense in *OED*
    commixture 'complexion', bodily habit or constitution (a sense peculiar to Shakespeare—*OED*, 3)

297 **vailing clouds** i.e. letting fall the clouds that have hidden them. Compare *1 Henry VI* 5.3.24–6: 'Now the time is come | That France must vail her lofty-plumèd crest | And let her head fall into England's lap.'
    blown in full bloom
298 **Avaunt, perplexity** i.e. away, you speaker of riddles
301 **as well ... disguised** i.e. as much when they appear as themselves as when they were disguised
303 **shapeless gear** uncouth dress, badly cut clothes
306 **carriage** behaviour

PRINCESS

Whip to our tents as roes runs o'er land!

> *Exeunt the Princess and her ladies*
> *Enter the King and his lords in their proper habits*

KING

Fair sir, God save you! Where's the Princess?   310

BOYET

Gone to her tent. Please it your majesty

Command me any service to her thither?

KING

That she vouchsafe me audience for one word.

BOYET

I will, and so will she, I know, my lord.   *Exit*

BIRON

This fellow pecks up wit as pigeons peas,

And utters it again when God doth please.

He is wit's pedlar, and retails his wares

At wakes and wassails, meetings, markets, fairs;

And we that sell by gross, the Lord doth know,

Have not the grace to grace it with such show.   320

This gallant pins the wenches on his sleeve.

Had he been Adam, he had tempted Eve.

A can carve too, and lisp. Why, this is he

That kissed his hand away in courtesy.

---

309 runs] Q, F (runnes); run F4   o'er] QF (ore); over STEEVENS; o're the F3   309.1 *Exeunt*
... ladies] CAPELL (*subs.*); *Exeunt.* QF   309.2 *Enter ... habits*] ROWE (*subs.*); *Enter the King and*
the rest QF   312 thither?] Q (∼ ,); *not in* F   315 pecks] Q (peckes); pickes F   316 God] Q;
loue F   323 A] Q; He F   324 his hand away] Q (his hand, a way); away his hand F

309 **Whip** move quickly, dash
   as ... land proverbial (Tilley R158)
   runs run. The third person plural in -s is
   quite common in Shakespeare (Abbott
   333).
309.2 *proper* own, usual
315–16 **This ... please** This simile appears
   to have become proverbial (Dent C333).
316 **utters** (a) speaks (b) puts up for sale
318 **wakes** festivals (held in each parish
   annually to celebrate the patron saint of
   the church)
   wassails revels, carousals. Compare
   Hamlet 1.4.9–10: 'The King doth wake
   tonight and takes his rouse, | Keeps was-
   sail ...', cited by *OED* as its earliest
   example of this sense.

319 **by gross** wholesale
321 **pins ... sleeve** i.e. flaunts his power over
   the girls, makes a show of their complete
   dependence on him (*OED*, *pin*, *v.*[1] 4)—
   proverbial (Dent S534).
322 **had** would have
323 **carve** The precise meaning of this word,
   which Shakespeare uses again in *Merry*
   Wives 1.3.39–40, where Falstaff says of
   Mistress Ford: 'I spy entertainment in
   her. She discourses, she carves, she gives
   the leer of invitation', is not known. It
   appears to have something to do with
   table manners of a rather affected kind,
   but whether it refers to 'come hither'
   looks or mincing speech is by no means
   clear.

This is the ape of form, Monsieur the Nice,
That when he plays at tables chides the dice
In honourable terms. Nay, he can sing
A mean most meanly; and in ushering
Mend him who can. The ladies call him sweet.
The stairs, as he treads on them, kiss his feet.   330
This is the flower that smiles on everyone,
To show his teeth as white as whale's bone;
And consciences that will not die in debt
Pay him the due of 'honey-tongued Boyet'.

KING

A blister on his sweet tongue, with my heart,
That put Armado's page out of his part!
> *Enter the Princess, Maria, Katherine, and Rosaline,*
> *ushered by Boyet*

BIRON

See where it comes! Behaviour, what wert thou
Till this map o' man showed thee, and what art thou
    now?

---

328 ushering ∧] F; hushering. Q   331 everyone,] F (euerie one,); euery one. Q   332
whale's] QF (Whales); whalës SINGER   334 due] Q; dutie F   336.1–2 *Enter ... Boyet*] ROWE
(*subs.*); *Enter the Ladies.* QF   338 map o' man] This edition; mad man Q; madman F; man
THEOBALD

325 **ape of form** i.e. slave of what he regards
    as 'good form'
    Nice punctilious
326 **tables** backgammon
327 **honourable** polite (dice games were
    accompanied by strong language)
328 **mean** the middle part (tenor or alto)
    between bass and treble
    most meanly i.e. quite respectably
    ushering carrying out the duties of a
    gentleman-usher
329 **Mend him who can** let anyone who
    thinks he can improve on his perfor-
    mance try, i.e. no one can touch him
331–3 **This ... debt** This passage is a string
    of commonplaces (Dent T430.1, W279,
    D165).
332 **whale's bone** ivory from the walrus
    (*OED*, *whalebone*, 1). The word *whale's* is
    disyllabic in pronunciation to emphasize,
    perhaps, the antiquity of the simile.
333 **consciences** conscientious people (ab-
    stract for concrete)
334 **honey-tongued** 'It is interesting to note
    here that Meres, who gives us the earliest

reference to *Love's Labour's Lost* by name,
and also the earliest tribute of praise to
Shakespeare by name, applies this term
to Shakespeare himself' (David). See Introduction, p. 81. *OED* cites no other use
of this typically Shakespearian compound until 1861.
337 **Behaviour** good manners, politeness
338 **map o' man** Q reads 'mad man' and F
    'madman'. The result is a metrically
    irregular line that also lacks bite and
    cogency. The reading of this edition dis-
    poses of both difficulties, and can be
    justified on three grounds. Shakespeare
    probably wrote 'map a man'; but the Q
    compositor dropped the 'a' just as he had
    done at 4.1.147. He also used a turned
    letter in setting 'map' (compare 'pader'
    for 'paper' at 4.3.40). Finally, Shake-
    speare often uses 'map' as a synonym for
    'model' or 'ideal form'. Particularly rele-
    vant in this case is the conclusion of
    Sonnets 68: 'And him as for a map doth
    nature store, | To show false art what
    beauty was of yore.'

KING

  All hail, sweet madam, and fair time of day.

PRINCESS

    'Fair' in 'all hail' is foul, as I conceive.   340

KING

  Construe my speeches better, if you may.

PRINCESS

    Then wish me better; I will give you leave.

KING

  We came to visit you, and purpose now

    To lead you to our court; vouchsafe it then.

PRINCESS

  This field shall hold me, and so hold your vow.

    Nor God nor I delights in perjured men.

KING

  Rebuke me not for that which you provoke.

    The virtue of your eye must break my oath.

PRINCESS

  You nickname virtue; 'vice' you should have spoke;

    For virtue's office never breaks men's troth.   350

  Now, by my maiden honour, yet as pure

    As the unsullied lily, I protest,

  A world of torments though I should endure,

    I would not yield to be your house's guest.

  So much I hate a breaking cause to be

  Of heavenly oaths, vowed with integrity.

KING

  O, you have lived in desolation here,

    Unseen, unvisited, much to our shame.

---

341 Construe] Q (Consture), F   speeches] Q (spaches), F   350 men's] Q (mens); men F
352 unsullied] F2; vnsallied QF   356 vowed] F (vow'd); vowed Q

340 **'Fair' ... foul** The Princess deliberately misinterprets the King's greeting, *hail*, as 'hailstorm'.

346 **Nor** neither

348 **virtue** power. In the next line the Princess gives the word its alternative sense 'goodness'.

349 **nickname** miscall, misname (*OED, v.* 1). Compare *Hamlet* 3.1.147–8: 'You jig,

you amble, and you lisp, and nickname God's creatures'.

350 **office** operation, proper functioning

351–2 **pure ... lily** proverbial (Dent L295.3)

355 **breaking cause** reason for breaking. See Abbott 419a.

357 **in desolation** i.e. forsaken, without companions (*OED*, 3)

PRINCESS

  Not so, my lord. It is not so, I swear.

    We have had pastimes here and pleasant game.   360

  A mess of Russians left us but of late.

KING

  How, madam? Russians?

PRINCESS   Ay, in truth, my lord;

  Trim gallants, full of courtship and of state.

ROSALINE

  Madam, speak true.—It is not so, my lord.

  My lady, to the manner of the days,

  In courtesy gives undeserving praise.

  We four indeed confronted were with four

  In Russian habit. Here they stayed an hour,

  And talked apace; and in that hour, my lord,

  They did not bless us with one happy word.   370

  I dare not call them fools, but this I think,

  When they are thirsty, fools would fain have drink.

BIRON

  This jest is dry to me. My gentle sweet,

  Your wits makes wise things foolish. When we greet,

  With eyes' best seeing, heaven's fiery eye,

  By light we lose light. Your capacity

  Is of that nature that to your huge store

  Wise things seem foolish, and rich things but poor.

ROSALINE

  This proves you wise and rich, for in my eye—

BIRON

  I am a fool, and full of poverty.   380

ROSALINE

  But that you take what doth to you belong,

  It were a fault to snatch words from my tongue.

---

368 Russian] Q (*Russian*); Russia F   373 My] MALONE; *not in* QF   374 foolish.] ROWE
(*subs.*); ~ ∧ QF   375 With] Q (Wtih), F   379 eye—] F (eie ∧); ~ . Q

361 **mess** group of four. See 4.3.204 and
    note.
363 **courtship** courtliness of manners (*OED*,
    1)
365 **to … days** in keeping with the present
    fashion. For this use of 'to', see Abbott
    187.
369 **talked apace** rattled on, chattered

370 **happy** felicitous
371 **dare not** hesitate to, would not go so far
    as to
373 **dry** stale, dull (quibbling on 'thirsty')
374–6 **When … lose light** i.e. when we look
    directly at the sun, we become blind.
    Compare Dent S971.1.
377 **to** compared to

BIRON

O, I am yours, and all that I possess.

ROSALINE

All the fool mine?

BIRON   I cannot give you less.

ROSALINE

Which of the visors was it that you wore?

BIRON

Where? When? What visor? Why demand you this?

ROSALINE

There, then, that visor, that superfluous case,

That hid the worse, and showed the better face.

KING (*aside to his lords*)

We were descried. They'll mock us now downright.

DUMAINE (*aside to the King*)

Let us confess, and turn it to a jest.   390

PRINCESS

Amazed, my lord? Why looks your highness sad?

ROSALINE

Help! Hold his brows! He'll swoon. Why look you
        pale?

Seasick, I think, coming from Muscovy.

BIRON

Thus pour the stars down plagues for perjury.

   Can any face of brass hold longer out?

Here stand I, lady, dart thy skill at me,

   Bruise me with scorn, confound me with a flout,

Thrust thy sharp wit quite through my ignorance,

   Cut me to pieces with thy keen conceit;

And I will wish thee never more to dance,   400

   Nor never more in Russian habit wait.

O, never will I trust to speeches penned,

   Nor to the motion of a schoolboy's tongue,

384 mine?] POPE; ~ . QF   389 were] Q; are F

387–8 **that visor ... face** Proverbial in the
   form 'A well-favoured visor will hide her
   ill-favoured face' (Dent V92).
387 **case** covering, mask. Compare *Romeo*
   1.4.29: 'Give me a case to put my visage
   in'.
391 **Amazed** bewildered, confounded

395 **face of brass** brazen-faced effrontery—
   proverbial (Dent F8)
397 **confound** destroy
399 **keen conceit** capacity for bitter repartee
400 **wish** invite, entreat (*OED*, *v.* 5)
401 **wait** attend upon you

Nor never come in visor to my friend,
　Nor woo in rhyme, like a blind harper's song.
Taffeta phrases, silken terms precise,
　Three-piled hyperboles, spruce affectation,
Figures pedantical—these summer flies
　Have blown me full of maggot ostentation.
I do forswear them, and I here protest   410
　By this white glove—how white the hand, God
　　knows—
Henceforth my wooing mind shall be expressed
　In russet yeas and honest kersey noes.
And to begin, wench, so God help me, law!
My love to thee is sound, sans crack or flaw.

ROSALINE

Sans 'sans', I pray you.

407 hyperboles] Q (Hiberboles), F　　affectation] ROWE; affection QF　　414 begin,] THEOBALD;
~ ∧ QF; ~ : DAVID

404 **friend** sweetheart, mistress. Compare
Measure 1.4.29: 'He hath got his friend
with child.'

405 **a blind harper's song** Harpers were
proverbially blind (Dent H175 and 176),
and made their living by singing traditional ballads.

407 **Three-piled hyperboles** i.e. hyperboles
that are splendidly excessive. *Three-piled*
(*OED*, *a.*¹ 2) is a term, first used in
writing, if not invented, by Shakespeare here, to describe the richest and
finest kind of velvet. Compare *Measure*
1.2.31–2: 'Thou art good velvet, thou'rt
a three-piled piece, I warrant thee.'
　affectation Q and F read 'affection',
which could mean (*OED*, *sb.* 13) 'affectation', as it does at 5.1.4 in the speech of
Nathaniel and in *Hamlet* 2.2.445 in Q2
only. F significantly reads 'affectation'.
With these two exceptions, of which the
second has only a doubtful validity,
Shakespeare distinguishes between the
words, as we do today. It is true that the
rhyme 'affection' | 'ostentation' would
have presented no difficulty for an Elizabethan, since *-ion* at the end of a word
was disyllabic, but the triple rhyme offered by *-ation* is both more pronounced
and funnier.

408 **Figures** rhetorical figures
　pedantical *OED* cites this as its first exam-

ple of the word, but, as David points out,
Shakespeare had been anticipated by
Gabriel Harvey in 1589.

408–9 **these ... ostentation** Through an
associative process that leads from textile
materials to the source of one of them,
Shakespeare is now thinking of *sheep*,
whose wool and flesh can become the
breeding ground for 'summer flies',
which lay their eggs, that soon turn to
maggots, in them.

409 **blown me** deposited their eggs on
me (*OED*, *v.*¹ 28c). Compare *Othello*
4.2.68–9: 'as summer flies ... | That
quicken even with blowing'.
　ostentation pretentious showing off
(*OED*, 3)

411 **By ... knows** probably ironical

413 **russet** homely, simple. 'Russet' was 'a
coarse homespun woollen cloth' worn by
countryfolk, and also the name of the
colour of that cloth, a reddish-brown.
　kersey plain, unpretentious. 'Kersey',
like 'russet', was a rough woollen cloth.
This is the only example (4b) that *OED*
offers of the word in a figurative sense.

414 **law** An interjection of an asseverative
kind equivalent to 'Yes, indeed'.

416 **Sans 'sans'** without 'sans', i.e. drop this
affectation of using French words instead
of plain English

BIRON   Yet I have a trick
  Of the old rage. Bear with me, I am sick.
  I'll leave it by degrees. Soft, let us see:
  Write 'Lord have mercy on us' on those three.
  They are infected, in their hearts it lies,   420
  They have the plague, and caught it of your eyes.
  These lords are visited; you are not free,
  For the Lord's tokens on you do I see.
PRINCESS
  No, they are free that gave these tokens to us.
BIRON
  Our states are forfeit. Seek not to undo us.
ROSALINE
  It is not so; for how can this be true,
  That you stand forfeit, being those that sue?
BIRON
  Peace, for I will not have to do with you.
ROSALINE
  Nor shall not, if I do as I intend.
BIRON (*to the lords*)
  Speak for yourselves. My wit is at an end.   430
KING
  Teach us, sweet madam, for our rude transgression
  Some fair excuse.
PRINCESS   The fairest is confession.
  Were not you here but even now disguised?
KING
  Madam, I was.

433 not you] Q; you not F

416–17 **Yet ... rage** I still have a touch
  (Onions) of my former madness (*OED*,
  rage, sb. 1)
419 **Lord have mercy on us** These words had
  to be written on the door of every house
  affected by the plague to serve as a
  warning to all who might wish to enter.
  They were also, of course, a genuine
  prayer, since an outbreak of plague was
  regarded as God's punishment of the
  wicked.
420 **it** i.e. the plague (of love)
422 **visited** afflicted (by the plague)
423 **the Lord's tokens** (a) plague-spots

which appeared on the patient's body in
the final stages of the disease (b) the lords'
tokens i.e. the favours they gave to their
ladies
424 **free** unfettered by love, fancy-free
425 **Our states are forfeit** i.e. we have for-
  feited our status (as honourable men)
  (*OED, state, sb.* 15)
  undo us bring us to utter ruin
426–7 **how ... sue** Rosaline plays on two
  senses of *sue*: (a) prosecute a law suit (b)
  prosecute a love suit.
428 **have to do with** (a) have dealings with
  (b) have sexual intercourse with

PRINCESS　　　　　　And were you well advised?

KING

　I was, fair madam.

PRINCESS　　　　　　　　When you then were here,

　What did you whisper in your lady's ear?

KING

　That more than all the world I did respect her.

PRINCESS

　When she shall challenge this, you will reject her.

KING

　Upon mine honour, no.

PRINCESS　　　　　　　　Peace, peace, forbear!

　Your oath once broke, you force not to forswear.　　　　　440

KING

　Despise me when I break this oath of mine.

PRINCESS

　I will, and therefore keep it. Rosaline,

　What did the Russian whisper in your ear?

ROSALINE

　Madam, he swore that he did hold me dear

　As precious eyesight, and did value me

　Above this world: adding thereto, moreover,

　That he would wed me, or else die my lover.

PRINCESS

　God give thee joy of him! The noble lord

　Most honourably doth uphold his word.

KING

　What mean you, madam? By my life, my troth,　　　　　450

　I never swore this lady such an oath.

ROSALINE

　By heaven, you did! And to confirm it plain,

　You gave me this; but take it, sir, again.

KING

　My faith and this the Princess I did give.

　I knew her by this jewel on her sleeve.

434 **well advised** in your right senses. Compare *Errors* 2.2.215–16: 'Am I . . . | Sleeping or waking? Mad or well advised?'

437 **respect** value, esteem (*OED*, *v.* 4b)

438 **challenge this** i.e. demand that you keep your word (*OED*, *challenge*, *v.* 5)

440 **Your ... forswear** i.e. now you have broken your oath once, you will make no bones about breaking your word again (*OED*, *force*, *v.* 14). Compare *Lucrece* 1021: 'I force not argument a straw'.

444–5 **dear | As precious eyesight** proverbial (Dent E249.1)

453 **again** back again

PRINCESS

Pardon me, sir, this jewel did she wear,
And Lord Biron, I thank him, is my dear.
What, will you have me, or your pearl again?

BIRON

Neither of either; I remit both twain.
I see the trick on't. Here was a consent,   460
Knowing aforehand of our merriment,
To dash it like a Christmas comedy.
Some carry-tale, some please-man, some slight zany,
Some mumble-news, some trencher-knight, some Dick
That smiles his cheek in years, and knows the trick
To make my lady laugh when she's disposed,
Told our intents before; which once disclosed,
The ladies did change favours; and then we,
Following the signs, wooed but the sign of she.
Now, to our perjury to add more terror,   470
We are again forsworn, in will and error.
Much upon this 'tis. (*To Boyet*) And might not you
Forestall our sport, to make us thus untrue?
Do not you know my lady's foot by th' squier,

463 zany] F (Zanie); saine Q   465 smiles ∧] F; ∼, Q   472 'tis] QF (tis); it is F2

459 **Neither of either** neither of the two
(*OED, neither*, B 2b)
remit give up, surrender (*OED, v.* 2)
both twain both the one and the other
460 **consent** agreement, compact, plot
461 **Knowing** i.e. since they knew (Abbott
378)
462 **dash** wreck, spoil (*OED, v.* 6)
like a Christmas comedy 'it would seem
that the "dashing" (by the spectators)
was a recognized part of the fun at
impromptu festival plays and masques;
compare the treatment of Quince's company in *Dream*, of Holofernes' company
in this play, and the story of the "Night of
Errors" at Gray's Inn, Dec. 28, 1594'
(Wilson).
463 **carry-tale** tale-bearer. Compare *Venus*
655–7: 'This sour informer, this bate-
breeding spy ... | This carry-tale, dissen-
tious jealousy'.
please-man toady, sycophant. *OED* can
cite no other example.
zany the rustic servant of the pantaloon
in the *commedia dell' arte*, buffoon, clown.
The word seems to have been introduced

into English, as David says, by Nashe in
his *Pierce Penniless* of 1592 (Nashe i. 215.
10).
464 **mumble-news** gossip, prattler. *OED*
cites no other example.
trencher-knight parasite with a noble
appetite—*OED*'s only example
Dick common fellow, base companion
465 **in years** i.e. into wrinkles (like those on
an old man's face)
466 **my lady** i.e. the lady he serves or
addresses
469 **she** i.e. each respective mistress. Compare *As You Like It* 3.2.10: 'The fair, the
chaste, and unexpressive she'.
472 **Much ... 'tis** this is pretty much what
has happened
474 **know ... squier** i.e. know exactly how
to flatter the Princess. A *squier* is a
carpenter's set-square (*OED, square, sb.*
1b), and is indeed the older but now
obsolete form of *square*. It is preserved
here for the sake of the rhyme. The
phrase 'To know the length of one's foot'
(Tilley L202) was a proverbial synonym
for 'to measure with great accuracy'.

And laugh upon the apple of her eye?
And stand between her back, sir, and the fire,
    Holding a trencher, jesting merrily?
You put our page out. Go, you are allowed;
Die when you will, a smock shall be your shroud.
You leer upon me, do you? There's an eye   480
Wounds like a leaden sword.
BOYET   Full merrily
Hath this brave manège, this career, been run.
BIRON
Lo, he is tilting straight. Peace, I have done.
        Enter Costard
Welcome, pure wit. Thou partest a fair fray.
COSTARD
O Lord, sir, they would know
Whether the three Worthies shall come in or no.
BIRON
What, are there but three?
COSTARD   No, sir, but it is vara fine,
For every one pursents three.
BIRON   And three times thrice is nine.
COSTARD
Not so, sir—under correction, sir—I hope it is not so.
You cannot beg us, sir, I can assure you, sir, we know
    what we know.   490
I hope, sir, three times thrice, sir—

482 manège] THEOBALD (manage); nuage Q; manager F   483.1 *Enter Costard*] ROWE; *Enter Clowne.* QF   484 partest] POPE; partst Q; part'st F   485 *(and for the rest of the scene)* COSTARD] ROWE; *Clo⟨wne⟩.* QF   491 sir—] ROWE; ~. QF

475 **laugh ... eye** i.e. jest with her in a very
    intimate way. 'As dear as the apple
    (pupil) of my eye' was proverbial (Tilley
    A290).
476 **stand ... fire** i.e. act as a fire-screen for
    her
477 **Holding a trencher** i.e. obsequiously
    ready to perform any service
478 **allowed** licensed. Compare *Twelfth
    Night* 1.5.89–91: 'There is no slander in
    an allowed fool, though he do nothing
    but rail'.
479 **a smock ... shroud** you'll die like the
    woman you are, covered by a smock
    (Kerrigan)
481 **Wounds like a leaden sword** proverbial

(Tilley S1054). Leaden or wooden swords
were, of course, common stage
properties.
482 **this brave manège, this career** this fine
    gallop at full speed (*OED, manage, sb.* 2),
    this charge (*OED, career, sb.* 2). Boyet is
    using the language of the riding school
    and the tournament.
483 **is tilting straight** has gone straight back
    to his verbal jousting
485 **would** want to
487 **vara** very (of which it is a dialectal
    pronunciation)
488 **pursents** Costard's version of *presents*
    i.e. represents, personates
490 **You cannot beg us** i.e. we are not fools.

214

BIRON   Is not nine?

COSTARD Under correction, sir, we know whereuntil it
doth amount.

BIRON

By Jove, I always took three threes for nine.

COSTARD O Lord, sir, it were pity you should get your
living by reckoning, sir.

BIRON How much is it?

COSTARD O Lord, sir, the parties themselves, the actors, sir,
will show whereuntil it doth amount. For mine own
part, I am, as they say, but to parfect one man in one   500
poor man, Pompion the Great, sir.

BIRON Art thou one of the Worthies?

COSTARD It pleased them to think me worthy of Pompey
the Great. For mine own part, I know not the degree of
the Worthy, but I am to stand for him.

BIRON Go, bid them prepare.

COSTARD

We will turn it finely off, sir; we will take some care.

Exit

KING

Biron, they will shame us. Let them not approach.

BIRON

We are shame-proof, my lord; and 'tis some policy
To have one show worse than the King's and his
company.   510

KING I say they shall not come.

---

500 they] F; thy Q   parfect] Q; perfect F   507 *Exit*] QF (*after l.* 506)

'Let him be begged for a fool' (Dent F496)
was a well known saying alluding to a
form of abuse practised by the Crown
through its Court of Wards. If the heir to
an estate was mentally deficient, the
Court took over the guardianship of his
property, and then transferred it to a
petitioner, either as a reward for services
rendered to the Crown or for a monetary
consideration. The successful petitioner
then enjoyed the full use of the estate he
had *begged*. See Joel Hurstfield, *The
Queen's Wards* (1958), *passim*.

492 **whereuntil** (dialectal) to what, to how

much
495 **were ... get** would be a sad thing for you
if you had to earn
500 **parfect** Costard's old-fashioned pronunciation of *perfect* which, in his mouth,
seems to be a constructive muddle of his
pursent and of a verb of his own meaning
'to be word-perfect in the role of'. See
l. 553.
501 **Pompion** pumpkin (a nice bit of folk-
etymology)
504 **degree** rank
509 **some policy** i.e. a wise move, a sound
stratagem

PRINCESS

  Nay, my good lord, let me o'errule you now.

  That sport best pleases that doth least know how:

  Where zeal strives to content, and the contents

  Dies in the zeal of that which it presents,

  There form confounded makes most form in mirth,

  When great things labouring perish in their birth.

BIRON

  A right description of our sport, my lord.

    Enter Armado

ARMADO Anointed, I implore so much expense of thy royal

  sweet breath as will utter a brace of words.   520

    He converses apart with the King, to whom he gives a
    paper

PRINCESS Doth this man serve God?

BIRON Why ask you?

PRINCESS

  A speaks not like a man of God his making.

ARMADO That is all one, my fair, sweet, honey monarch;

  for, I protest, the schoolmaster is exceeding fantastical,

  too too vain, too too vain. But we will put it, as they say,

  to *fortuna de la guerra.* I wish you the peace of mind,

  most royal couplement.   *Exit*

KING (*studying the paper*) Here is like to be a good presence

  of Worthies. He presents Hector of Troy; the swain,   530

513 least] F; best Q   516 There] CAPELL; Their QF   518.1 *Enter Armado*] ROWE; *Enter Bragart.* QF   519 (*and for the rest of the scene*) ARMADO] ROWE; *Brag⟨gart⟩.* QF   520.1–2 *He . . . paper*] CAPELL (*subs.*); *not in* QF   523 A] Q; He F   God his] Q; God's F   524 That is] Q; That's F   527 *fortuna de la guerra*] THEOBALD; *Fortuna delaguar* QF   528 *Exit*] Q; *not in* F   529 *studying . . . paper*] *not in* QF

514 **zeal** i.e. eager performers
    content give pleasure
514–15 **the contents . . . presents** i.e. the
    substance of the show is murdered by the
    excessive enthusiasm and earnestness of
    the company that puts it on
516 **There . . . mirth** i.e. the collapse of
    ambitious enterprises is a prime source of
    mirth
517 **When . . . birth** Probably an allusion to
    Horace's '*Parturiunt montes, nascetur ridi-*
    culus mus' (*Ars Poetica*, 139), proverbial
    in English as 'The mountain was in
    labour and brought forth a mouse' (Tilley
    M1215).
518 **right** accurate

518 **our sport** i.e. the masque of Muscovites
    (in which the King and his companions
    'laboured' to little effect)
519 **Anointed** i.e. your majesty (a king being
    'the Lord's anointed')
523 **A . . . making** proverbial (Dent M162)
    God his God's
524 **That is all one** it is all the same to me.
    Compare *Twelfth Night* 5.1.403: 'But
    that's all one, our play is done'.
    honey (a term of endearment)
527 *fortuna de la guerra* the chance of
    war—proverbial (Dent C223)
528 **couplement** couple, pair
529 **presence** company, assembly (*OED*, 3)

Pompey the Great; the parish curate, Alexander; Arma-
do's page, Hercules; the pedant, Judas Maccabeus.
And if these four Worthies in their first show thrive,
These four will change habits, and present the other
    five.

BIRON
There is five in the first show.

KING
You are deceived, 'tis not so.

BIRON
The pedant, the braggart, the hedge-priest, the fool,
    and the boy.
Abate throw at novum, and the whole world again
Cannot pick out five such, take each one in his vein.

KING
The ship is under sail, and here she comes amain.   540
    Enter Costard as Pompey

COSTARD
  'I Pompey am'—

BIRON   You lie, you are not he.

COSTARD
  'I Pompey am'—

BOYET   With leopard's head on knee.

BIRON
Well said, old mocker. I must needs be friends with
    thee.

539 pick] Q (picke); pricke F   in his] Q; in's F   540.1 *Enter ... Pompey*] ROWE (*subs.*);
Enter Pompey. QF   541, 542 am—] THEOBALD; ~. QF

537 **hedge-priest** illiterate or uneducated
    priest of inferior status, priest like Sir
    Oliver Martext in 3.3 of *As You Like It*
538–9 **Abate ... vein** *Novum* was a dice-
    game also known as *novem quinque*, in
    which the winning throws appear to
    have been nine and five. Beyond that
    nothing is now known about it. Kerrigan
    glosses the passage thus: 'set aside a
    throw of five or nine ... and there is
    nothing in the whole world good enough
    to be compared with these splendid char-
    acters, taken for what they are'. Biron's
    arithmetic tells him 'five into nine won't
    go'.
540 **amain** at full speed ahead
541 **You lie** There may well be a quibble here

pointing to some stage business which
has Costard running in 'amain', stopping
suddenly to bow to the stage audience,
and falling flat on his face.
542 **With ... knee** As David points out,
Pompey's arms were traditionally supposed to have been a leopard or a lion
'with a sword clasped in his claw'.
Painted on Pompey's shield, these arms
would, if he has fallen down, be covering
his *knee* rather than the main part of his
body as he scrambles clumsily to his feet.
Alternatively, the words may allude to
what the French called *masquine*, the
representation of a leopard's or a lion's
head on the knees or elbows of some old-
fashioned garments.

COSTARD

'I Pompey am, Pompey surnamed the Big'—

DUMAINE 'The Great'.

COSTARD

It is 'Great', sir. 'Pompey surnamed the Great,

That oft in field, with targe and shield, did make my
     foe to sweat,

And travelling along this coast, I here am come by
     chance,

And lay my arms before the legs of this sweet lass of
     France.'

If your ladyship would say, 'Thanks, Pompey', I had   550
done.

⌈PRINCESS⌉ Great thanks, great Pompey.

COSTARD 'Tis not so much worth, but I hope I was perfect.
I made a little fault in 'Great'.

BIRON My hat to a halfpenny, Pompey proves the best
Worthy.

> *Costard stands aside.*
> *Enter Nathaniel as Alexander*

NATHANIEL

'When in the world I lived, I was the world's
     commander.

By east, west, north, and south, I spread my
     conquering might.

My scutcheon plain declares that I am Alisander'—

BOYET

Your nose says no, you are not, for it stands too right.   560

BIRON (*to Boyet*)

Your nose smells 'no' in this, most tender-smelling
     knight.

---

552 PRINCESS] F2 ; *Lady.* QF   556.1 *Costard … aside*] CAPELL (*subs.*); *not in* QF   556.2 *Enter
… Alexander*] ROWE (*subs.*); *Enter Curate for Alexander.* QF   557–63 NATHANIEL] ROWE;
Cura⟨te⟩. QF   561 this] F; his Q

547 **targe** (pronounced like 'large') buckler,
     light shield
552 PRINCESS Q reads '*Lady.*' and F '*La.*'; but
     both the tone and the content of the line
     point to the Princess as its speaker.
553 **perfect** word-perfect
555 **My hat to a halfpenny** i.e. I'll bet
     anything—proverbial (Dent C63.1)

559 **scutcheon** coat of arms
560 **Your nose … right** According to some
     authorities,   including   Plutarch,
     Alexander had a wry neck.
561 **Your nose … knight** Alexander was
     supposed, according to Plutarch, to have
     had a sweet-smelling skin, something,
     says Biron, that Nathaniel certainly has

PRINCESS

The conqueror is dismayed. Proceed, good Alexander.

NATHANIEL

'When in the world I lived, I was the world's
     commander'—

BOYET

Most true, 'tis right. You were so, Alisander.

BIRON (*to Costard*) Pompey the Great—

COSTARD Your servant, and Costard.

BIRON Take away the conqueror, take away Alisander.

COSTARD (*to Nathaniel*) O, sir, you have overthrown Alisander the conqueror. You will be scraped out of the
painted cloth for this. Your lion, that holds his pole-axe   570
sitting on a close-stool, will be given to Ajax. He will be
the ninth Worthy. A conqueror, and afeard to speak?
Run away for shame, Alisander.

    ⌈*Nathaniel retires*⌉

There, an't shall please you, a foolish mild man, an
honest man, look you, and soon dashed. He is a
marvellous good neighbour, faith, and a very good
bowler. But for Alisander, alas, you see how 'tis, a little
o'erparted. But there are Worthies a-coming will speak
their mind in some other sort.

PRINCESS Stand aside, good Pompey.   580

   Enter Holofernes as Judas Maccabeus, and Moth as
   Hercules

562–80 PRINCESS] ROWE; *Qu⟨een⟩*. QF   567 conqueror] Q (Conqueronr), F   572 afeard] Q
(a feard); affraid F   573.1 *Nathaniel retires*] CAPELL; *Exit Cu⟨rate⟩.* QF (*after l. 579*)
574 you,] F (∼ :); ∼ ∧ Q   576 faith] Q (fayth); insooth F   580.1–2 *Enter ... Hercules*]
ROWE (*subs.*); *Enter Pedant for Iudas, and the Boy for Hercules.* QF

not, as Boyet's sensitive nose must have
informed him. Compare Andrew Mar-
vell's 'Upon Appleton House', ll. 427–8.

569–70 **the painted cloth** The Nine Worthies were one of the subjects painted in oil
on the cloth or canvas hangings that
were draped over the walls of rooms in an
Elizabethan house.

570–1 **Your lion ... Ajax** The coat of arms
the Middle Ages gave Alexander was a
lion sitting on a chair or throne and
holding a battle-axe. Costard turns the

chair into a 'close-stool' (a chamber-pot
enclosed in a stool or box) and awards
this coat of arms to Ajax whose name was
jestingly transformed into 'a jakes', i.e. 'a
privy'.

574–7 **an honest man ... and a very good
bowler** Shakespeare takes an old saying
'To lack but a bowl and a besom of being
an honest man' (Dent B568.1), and
makes a new saying, which in its turn
became proverbial (Dent M183), out of it.

577–8 **a little o'erparted** i.e. not quite up to
the part—earliest instance cited by *OED*

HOLOFERNES

  'Great Hercules is presented by this imp,

    Whose club killed Cerberus, that three-headed *canus*,

  And when he was a babe, a child, a shrimp,

    Thus did he strangle serpents in his *manus*.

  Quoniam he seemeth in minority,

  Ergo I come with this apology.'

  (To Moth) Keep some state in thy exit, and vanish.

      Moth retires

  'Judas I am'—

DUMAINE A Judas!

HOLOFERNES Not Iscariot, sir.   590

  'Judas I am, yclipèd Maccabeus'—

DUMAINE Judas Maccabeus clipped is plain Judas.

BIRON A kissing traitor. How art thou proved Judas?

HOLOFERNES

  'Judas I am'—

DUMAINE The more shame for you, Judas.

HOLOFERNES What mean you, sir?

BOYET To make Judas hang himself.

HOLOFERNES Begin, sir, you are my elder.

BIRON Well followed: Judas was hanged on an elder.

HOLOFERNES I will not be put out of countenance.   600

BIRON Because thou hast no face.

587.1 *Moth retires*] CAPELL *(subs.)*; *Exit Boy.* QF   588 'Judas] MALONE; *Peda.* Iudas QF
590 Not Iscariot, sir] QF *(in italics)*   591 yclipèd] Q *(ecliped)*, F   593 proved] F *(prou'd)*;
proud Q   599 elder] Q *(Flder)*, F

581 **imp** child
582 **Cerberus** The three-headed dog that
    guarded the entrance to Hades.
    canus This should be *canis*, but Holo-
    fernes makes grammar and orthography
    subservient to rhyme.
584 *manus* hands
585 *Quoniam* since
586 *Ergo* therefore
587 **state** dignity
589–622 **A Judas ... stumble** What Shake-
    speare gives us here is something that
    John Webster would have called 'the
    well with four buckets' as the three
    courtiers and Boyet vie with one another
    in pouring insult after insult on the head
    of the wretched Holofernes. See *The White
    Devil* 1.1.9–30.
592 **clipped** cut short, abbreviated *(OED, v.²*

5) with a quibble on *yclipèd*. The word
    can, however, also mean 'embraced'
    (OED, v.¹ 1), the sense Biron has given it
    when he speaks the next line.
593 **A kissing traitor** Alluding, of course, to
    the kiss with which Judas betrayed
    Christ.
    How ... Judas doesn't this prove you are
    Judas
596 **mean you** (a) is your meaning (b) is
    your purpose (the sense in which Boyet
    takes it)
598 **Begin ... elder** i.e. hang yourself first,
    since you are older than I am (and so
    entitled to take precedence of me)
599 **Judas ... elder** Alluding to the medieval
    legend that Judas hanged himself on a
    branch of an elder tree.

HOLOFERNES What is this?

BOYET A cittern-head.

DUMAINE The head of a bodkin.

BIRON A death's face in a ring.

LONGUEVILLE The face of an old Roman coin, scarce seen.

BOYET The pommel of Caesar's falchion.

DUMAINE The carved-bone face on a flask.

BIRON Saint George's half-cheek in a brooch.

DUMAINE Ay, and in a brooch of lead.   610

BIRON Ay, and worn in the cap of a tooth-drawer. And
     now, forward, for we have put thee in countenance.

HOLOFERNES You have put me out of countenance.

BIRON False! We have given thee faces.

HOLOFERNES But you have outfaced them all.

BIRON

An thou wert a lion, we would do so.

BOYET

Therefore, as he is an ass, let him go.

And so adieu, sweet Jude. Nay, why dost thou stay?

DUMAINE For the latter end of his name.

BIRON

For the ass to the Jude? Give it him. Jud-as, away!   620

HOLOFERNES

This is not generous, not gentle, not humble.

617 is ∧ an ass,] Q2 ; is, an Asse, QF   620 Jud-as] F ; *Judas* Q

602 **this** Holofernes points to his face and
thus unwittingly opens the way for
the barrage of insults that follows,
all of them referring to grotesquely
carved heads and faces on various objects.

603 **cittern-head** The *cittern* or *cithern* was a
musical instrument of the same family as
the guitar, and often had a carved head.
OED cites this as its earliest example of
cittern-head.

604 **bodkin** large pin used to keep ladies'
hair in place. The more expensive ones,
made of gold or silver, had elaborately
decorated heads.

605 **death's face in a ring** Rings engraved
with a death's head and the words
memento mori were common in
Shakespeare's time.

606 **scarce seen** i.e. almost obliterated

607 **pommel** 'knob terminating the hilt of a
sword' (*OED, sb.* 3)

607 **falchion** Originally and properly 'a broad
sword more or less curved with the edge
on the convex side' (*OED, sb.* 1), *falchion*
in Shakespeare is simply a convenient
synonym for *sword*.

608 **flask** gunpowder flask (made of horn or
bone)

609 **half-cheek** profile—only instance of this
sense given by *OED*

610–11 **brooch ... tooth-drawer** Trades-
men appear to have worn leaden
brooches in their caps to show the nature
of their business.

612 **put ... countenance** utterly disconcerted me

615 **outfaced them all** put them all to shame
(with your mockery)

616–17 **lion ... ass** Referring to Aesop's
fable of the ass in the lion's skin, where
the ass succeeded in his imposture until
his ears betrayed him.

621 **generous** noble-minded, magnanimous

BOYET

A light for Monsieur Judas! It grows dark, he may
    stumble.

    Holofernes retires

PRINCESS

Alas, poor Maccabeus, how hath he been baited!

    Enter Armado as Hector

BIRON

Hide thy head, Achilles, here comes Hector in arms.

DUMAINE Though my mocks come home by me, I will now
    be merry.

KING Hector was but a Trojan in respect of this.

BOYET But is this Hector?

KING I think Hector was not so clean-timbered.

LONGUEVILLE His leg is too big for Hector's.   630

DUMAINE More calf, certain.

BOYET No, he is best endowed in the small.

BIRON This cannot be Hector.

DUMAINE He's a god or a painter, for he makes faces.

ARMADO

'The armipotent Mars, of lances the almighty,

    Gave Hector a gift' —

DUMAINE A gilt nutmeg.

BIRON A lemon.

622.1 *Holofernes retires*] CAPELL; *not in* QF   623.1 *Enter ... Hector*] ROWE; *Eeter Braggart.* Q;
Enter Braggart F   630 Hector's] Q (*Hectors*); *Hector* F   637 gilt] F; gift Q

621 **gentle** courteous, befitting well-born
    people (*OED, a.* 3c)
    humble kind

622 **A light ... stumble** Boyet probably refers
    to the *Judas candlestick* once used in parish
    churches at Easter. Made of brass, this
    candlestick had seven branches, from the
    seventh or middle one of which a tall
    thick piece of wood, painted like a candle,
    and called *the Judas of the Paschal*, rose
    nearly to the roof, and on the top of this
    was placed at Eastertide the paschal
    candle of wax (*OED, Judas*, 2). Boyet thus
    completes the list of carved or painted
    objects with which the courtiers identify
    Holofernes.

625 **come home by me** may recoil on my
    own head (the Princess has already ex-
    pressed her disapproval of the baiting)

626 **merry** facetious (*OED, a.* 3c)

627 **Trojan** (a) inhabitant of Troy (b) an
    ordinary bloke (*OED, sb.* 2; earliest cita-
    tion in this sense)

629 **clean-timbered** well-built—only cita-
    tion in *OED*

631 **calf** (a) part of the leg (b) naïve fool

632 **small** part of the leg below the calf

634 **makes** (a) creates (b) pulls

635 **armipotent** mighty in arms. Chaucer
    uses this word of Mars in *The Knight's
    Tale*, l. 1982: 'Ther stood the temple of
    Mars armypotente'.

637 **A gilt nutmeg** a nutmeg glazed with the
    yolk of an egg. Used for spicing wine or
    ale, gilt nutmegs were a common lover's
    gift.

638–40 **A lemon ... cloven** Lemons and
    oranges 'stuck with cloves' were em-
    ployed, like nutmegs, to flavour and

LONGUEVILLE Stuck with cloves.

DUMAINE No, cloven.   640

ARMADO Peace!

> 'The armipotent Mars, of lances the almighty,
>   Gave Hector a gift, the heir of Ilion;
> A man so breathed that certain he would fight, yea,
>   From morn till night, out of his pavilion.
> I am that flower'—

DUMAINE   That mint.

LONGUEVILLE   That columbine.

ARMADO Sweet Lord Longueville, rein thy tongue.

LONGUEVILLE I must rather give it the rein, for it runs
    against Hector.

DUMAINE Ay, and Hector's a greyhound.   650

ARMADO The sweet war-man is dead and rotten. Sweet
    chucks, beat not the bones of the buried. When he
    breathed, he was a man. But I will forward with my
    device. (*To the Princess*) Sweet royalty, bestow on me the
    sense of hearing.

> *Biron steps forth ⌈and whispers to Costard⌉*

PRINCESS Speak, brave Hector, we are much delighted.

ARMADO I do adore thy sweet grace's slipper.

BOYET Loves her by the foot.

DUMAINE He may not by the yard.

---

640 No,] ROWE; ～ ∧ QF   641 Peace!] Q (*Peace.*); *not in* F   646 I … flower] QF (*in roman*)
flower—] CAPELL; ～. QF   652–3 When … man] Q; *not in* F   655.1 Biron … forth] QF
and whispers to Costard] CAPELL (*subs.*); *not in* QF   657 I … slipper] F; Q (*in italics*)

---

preserve drinks. Dumaine, however, determined to be 'merry', i.e. 'bawdy', takes
'lemon' as 'leman' ('sweetheart'), and,
referring to the female genitals, replaces
'cloves' with 'cloven'.

643 **Ilion** Troy
644 **breathed** fit, in training
645 **pavilion** ceremonial tent for the use of
    combatants in a medieval tournament
648 **give it the rein** proverbial (Dent B671)
650 **Hector's a greyhound** Hector was
    famous as a runner.
651 **dead and rotten** proverbial (Dent
    D126.1)
652 **beat not … buried** A characteristically

Shakespearian variant on the very old
saying 'Speak well of the dead' (Dent
D124).
654 **device** dramatic representation (*OED*,
    11; earliest example of this meaning)
655.1 *Biron … Costard* Both Q and F say
    only that Biron *steps forth*; but he must
    step forth, i.e. leave the stage audience, for
    some reason, and his likeliest motive
    would seem to be to put Costard up to
    making the spectacular intervention that
    he does at 662. TC suggests that Biron
    may be trying to prevent Armado from
    continuing.
659 **yard** (a) measurement of three feet (b)
    penis (*OED, sb.²* 11)

223

ARMADO

    'This Hector far surmounted Hannibal.   660

      The party is gone'—

COSTARD Fellow Hector, she is gone. She is two months on

    her way.

ARMADO What meanest thou?

COSTARD Faith, unless you play the honest Trojan, the

    poor wench is cast away. She's quick; the child brags in

    her belly already. 'Tis yours.

ARMADO Dost thou infamonize me among potentates?

    Thou shalt die.

COSTARD Then shall Hector be whipped for Jaquenetta that   670

    is quick by him, and hanged for Pompey that is dead by

    him.

DUMAINE Most rare Pompey!

BOYET Renowned Pompey!

BIRON Greater than 'Great'! Great, great, great Pompey!

    Pompey the Huge!

DUMAINE Hector trembles.

BIRON Pompey is moved. More Ates, more Ates! Stir them

    on, stir them on!

DUMAINE Hector will challenge him.   680

BIRON Ay, if a have no more man's blood in his belly than

    will sup a flea.

ARMADO By the North Pole, I do challenge thee.

660] *Omission marked after this line* OXFORD   661 The party is gone.] *spoken by Armado,*
POPE; *centred and italicized* QF; *given to Costard* THEOBALD   678–9 them on, stir] ROWE; them,
or stir Q; them, or stirre F   681 in his] Q; in's F

661 **The party is gone** Centred and printed in
italics in both Q and F, these words
appear at first sight to be a stage direction. As such, however, they make no
sense, and since the line preceding them
is also in italics, apart from the two
personal names 'Hector' and 'Hanniball',
it seems reasonable to take them as a
continuation of Armado's speech, meaning much the same thing as 'The sweet
warman is dead and rotten'.

662 **gone** pregnant, gone with child

666 **quick** pregnant

    brags swaggers, shows off (*OED*, *v.* 2b)
(thus proving itself Armado's). Compare
Nashe i. 176. 12–14: 'properly Pride is
the disease of the Spaniard, who is borne
a Bragart in his mothers wombe' (*Pierce*

Penniless).

668 **infamonize** defame, infamize (of which
it is a perverted form peculiar to Armado)

670 **whipped** Whipping was the punishment for fornication. Compare *Measure*
5.1.506, where the Duke tells Lucio he is
to be 'Whipped first, sir, and hanged
after.'

671 **quick** (a) pregnant (b) living

671–2 **Pompey ... him** i.e. killing Pompey

678 **Ates** i.e. provocative remarks. Ate (disyllabic) was the Greek goddess of strife.
Compare *K. John* 2.1.63, where John's
mother is described as 'An Ate stirring
him to blood and strife.'

682 **sup** make a supper for (*OED*, *v.*³3b)

683 **By the North Pole** The fashionable
practice of coining 'strange oaths', which

COSTARD I will not fight with a pole like a northern man.
   I'll slash, I'll do it by the sword. I bepray you, let me
   borrow my arms again.

DUMAINE Room for the incensed Worthies.

COSTARD I'll do it in my shirt.

DUMAINE Most resolute Pompey!

MOTH Master, let me take you a buttonhole lower. Do you   690
   not see Pompey is uncasing for the combat? What mean
   you? You will lose your reputation.

ARMADO Gentlemen and soldiers, pardon me, I will not
   combat in my shirt.

DUMAINE You may not deny it. Pompey hath made the
   challenge.

ARMADO Sweet bloods, I both may and will.

BIRON What reason have you for't?

ARMADO The naked truth of it is I have no shirt. I go
   woolward for penance.   700

⌈MOTH⌉ True, and it was enjoined him in Rome for want
   of linen. Since when, I'll be sworn, he wore none but a
   dishclout of Jaquenetta's, and that a wears next his
   heart for a favour.

   Enter a Messenger, Monsieur Marcadé

685 bepray] Q; pray F   699 have] Q (hane), F   701 MOTH] CAPELL; *Boy.* QF   703 a
wears] Q; hee wears F

Shakespeare tilts at here, is ridiculed at
length by Ben Jonson through the
speeches of Bobadill in *Every Man in his
Humour* (1598).

684–5 **I … sword** Costard, the party challenged, asserts his rights to the choice of
weapons.

684 **with … man** Hart is probably right in
his suggestion that Costard has in mind
the cattle-thieves, or reavers, as they
were called, of the northern borders who
fought with very long poles tipped with
steel.

685 **bepray** pray. Appearing in F as 'pray'
and not to be found anywhere else, this
word is of doubtful authenticity. It is
retained in this edition because it could
well be a 'Costardism', combining 'beseech' and 'pray' in a single word.

686 **my arms** i.e. the arms and armour I
wore as Pompey

690 **take … lower** (a) help you off with your
doublet (b) take you down a peg or two—

proverbial (Tilley P181)

691 **uncasing** undressing, taking off his
outer garments

695 **deny it** refuse

697 **bloods** men of mettle, fiery spirits

699 **The naked truth** proverbial (Dent
T589)

700 **woolward** i.e. with no linen between my
skin and my outer wear—proverbial
(Dent W757.1); not elsewhere in
Shakespeare

701 MOTH The two substantive texts head
this speech '*Boy.*' which could signify
either '*Boyet*' or '*Moth*'. Moth seems the
likelier candidate, since he can be expected to know something about the state
of Armado's wardrobe.

701–2 **for want of linen** Moth's point is that
Armado's shirtless state is a consequence
of penury not penance.

703 **dishclout** dishcloth

704.1 *Enter … Marcadé* See Introduction
p. 10. He could leave after 709.

MARCADÉ

God save you, madam.

PRINCESS   Welcome, Marcadé,

But that thou interrupt'st our merriment.

MARCADÉ

I am sorry, madam, for the news I bring

Is heavy in my tongue. The King your father—

PRINCESS

Dead, for my life!

MARCADÉ   Even so. My tale is told.

BIRON

Worthies, away! The scene begins to cloud.   710

ARMADO For mine own part, I breathe free breath. I have
    seen the day of wrong through the little hole of discre-
    tion, and I will right myself like a soldier.

Exeunt Worthies

KING How fares your majesty?

QUEEN

Boyet, prepare. I will away tonight.

KING

Madam, not so. I do beseech you, stay.

QUEEN

Prepare, I say. I thank you, gracious lords,

For all your fair endeavours, and entreat,

Out of a new-sad soul, that you vouchsafe

In your rich wisdom to excuse, or hide,   720

The liberal opposition of our spirits.

If over-boldly we have borne ourselves

In the converse of breath, your gentleness

Was guilty of it. Farewell, worthy lord!

706 interrupt'st] CAPELL; interrnpptest Q; interruptest F   708 father—] QF (~ ∧)
709 Dead,] THEOBALD; ~ ∧ QF   718 entreat,] ROWE 1714; intreat: Q; entreats: F
719 new-sad soul] THEOBALD; new sad-soule QF   721–4 spirits. | If ... ourselves | In ...
breath, your ... it.] ROWE; spirites, | If ... our selues, | In ... breath (your ... it.) QF

711–13 **I breathe ... soldier** i.e. I have a
    wonderful sense of relief (at having es-
    caped from a tight corner). I have real-
    ized and avoided, through the little loophole
    discretion gave me, the full nature of the
    disgrace I was in danger of incurring, and
    I will now vindicate myself as a soldier
    should. Armado brings two common
    sayings together: 'One may see day at a

little hole' and 'Discretion is the better
part of valour' (Dent D99 and D354).
720 **hide** disregard, overlook
721 **liberal** unrestrained
723 **the converse of breath** i.e. our conversa-
    tions with you
    gentleness courtesy, gentlemanly for-
    bearance
724 **guilty of** to blame for, responsible for

A heavy heart bears not a nimble tongue.
Excuse me so, coming too short of thanks
For my great suit so easily obtained.

KING

The extreme parts of time extremely forms
All causes to the purpose of his speed,
And often at his very loose decides   730
That which long process could not arbitrate.
And though the mourning brow of progeny
Forbid the smiling courtesy of love
The holy suit which fain it would convince,
Yet, since love's argument was first on foot,
Let not the cloud of sorrow jostle it
From what it purposed; since to wail friends lost
Is not by much so wholesome-profitable
As to rejoice at friends but newly found.

QUEEN

I understand you not: my griefs are double.   740

BIRON

Honest plain words best pierce the ear of grief,
And by these badges understand the King.
For your fair sakes have we neglected time,
Played foul play with our oaths. Your beauty, ladies,
Hath much deformed us, fashioning our humours

725 nimble] THEOBALD; humble QF   726 too] Q; SO F   733 love ∧] HANMER; ~, Q; ~ : F
738 wholesome-profitable] WALKER; holdsome profitable Q; wholsome profitable F   740
double] QF; dull COLLIER 1858   743 time,] F; ~. Q

725 **nimble** Theobald's emendation of
'humble', found in Q and F, is adopted
here for two reasons. First, 'nimble
tongue' provides the right antithesis to
'heavy heart'; and, secondly, as Oxford
points out, 'in all nine cases where
Shakespeare uses "humble" preceded by
the indefinite article, the form is "an",
not—as here—"a"' (*TC*, p. 275).

727 **my ... obtained** The dispute over Aquitaine has evidently been settled in a way
favourable to the Princess. Shakespeare
characteristically does not—supposing
he ever knew—tell us how, since the
matter is no longer of any consequence.

728–31 **The extreme ... arbitrate** i.e. when
the time for making important decisions
is extremely short, its extreme pressure
subjects all issues to its demand for speed,

and often at the critical moment settles
matters that could never be decided by
protracted negotiation

730 **loose** the decisive moment in which an
arrow is loosed from the bow

734 **convince** give proof of (*OED*, *v*. 8).

735 **on foot** in action, begun. Shakespeare's—or is it the King's?—awareness
of the literal meaning of the phrase leads
him on to the rather ludicrous image
of love's cause being 'jostled' by a 'cloud
of sorrow'.

738 **wholesome-profitable** good for the spirits

740 **double** (because I'm sorry for my inability to understand you as well as for my
father's death)

742 **badges** signs, tokens; i.e. the words I am
about to speak (*OED*, *sb*. 2b)

745 **deformed us** made us look ugly

Even to the opposèd end of our intents;
And what in us hath seemed ridiculous—
As love is full of unbefitting strains,
All wanton as a child, skipping and vain,
Formed by the eye and therefore like the eye,   750
Full of strange shapes, of habits, and of forms,
Varying in subjects as the eye doth roll
To every varied object in his glance;
Which parti-coated presence of loose love
Put on by us, if, in your heavenly eyes,
Have misbecomed our oaths and gravities,
Those heavenly eyes, that look into these faults,
Suggested us to make. Therefore, ladies,
Our love being yours, the error that love makes
Is likewise yours. We to ourselves prove false   760
By being once false for ever to be true
To those that make us both—fair ladies, you.
And even that falsehood, in itself a sin,
Thus purifies itself and turns to grace.

QUEEN

We have received your letters, full of love;
Your favours, the ambassadors of love;

751 strange] CAPELL; straying QF   756 misbecomed] Q (misbecombd), misbecom'd F
gravities,] CAPELL; ~ . QF   758 make] QF; make them POPE   762 both—] F (~ ,); ~ ∧ Q
766 the] F; *not in* Q

746 **Even ... intents** into the exact opposite
    of what we intended
748 **strains** impulses, tendencies (including,
    perhaps, a tendency to break into song)
751 **strange** The 'straying' of Q and F is
    probably due to the Q compositor's misin-
    terpreting the 'straing' or 'straynge' of
    the manuscript, both being recognized
    spellings of *strange* at the time the play
    was written. In *Sir Thomas More* D, at line
    11, Lincoln speaks of 'straing rootes',
    meaning 'parsnips'.
    habits (a) modes of behaviour (b) clothes
    forms ideal forms, figures created by the
    imagination
752 **the eye doth roll** Compare *Dream*
    5.1.12: 'The poet's eye, in a fine frenzy
    rolling'.
754–8 **Which ... make** i.e. and if the
    motley appearance and behaviour of
    casual lovers that we adopted have ac-
    corded ill (*misbecomed*), in your heavenly

eyes, with the grave oaths we took, don't
forget that it was those same heavenly
eyes of yours, which now see our faults
with such clarity, that tempted us into
committing those faults in the first place
754 **Which** and this (see Abbott 418)
    parti-coated parti-coloured, part of one
    colour and part of another like the garb of
    a licensed fool—only instance cited by
    OED
    presence appearance (Schimdt)
758 **Suggested** tempted (*OED*, *v.* 2). Com-
    pare *Henry V* 2.2.111: 'other devils that
    suggest by treasons', and *LLL* 1.1.157.
759 **Our love being yours** i.e. since you are
    the cause of our being in love
761 **once** (when we broke our academic
    oaths)
763 **falsehood** i.e. failure to keep the initial
    oath
764 **grace** virtue (*OED*, *sb.* 13b)

And in our maiden counsel rated them
At courtship, pleasant jest, and courtesy,
As bombast and as lining to the time.
But more devout than this in our respects   770
Have we not been, and therefore met your loves
In their own fashion, like a merriment.

DUMAINE

Our letters, madam, showed much more than jest.

LONGUEVILLE

So did our looks.

ROSALINE   We did not quote them so.

KING

Now, at the latest minute of the hour,
Grant us your loves.

QUEEN   A time, methinks, too short
To make a world-without-end bargain in.
No, no, my lord, your grace is perjured much,
Full of dear guiltiness, and therefore this:
If for my love—as there is no such cause—   780
You will do aught, this shall you do for me:
Your oath I will not trust; but go with speed
To some forlorn and naked hermitage,
Remote from all the pleasures of the world.
There stay until the twelve celestial signs
Have brought about the annual reckoning.
If this austere insociable life
Change not your offer made in heat of blood;

770 this in] HANMER; this Q; these are F   779 therefore] Q (rherefore), F   786 the] Q, their F
788 blood;] F (~ :); ~ . Q

767 **rated** assessed, estimated their value
768 **At** i.e. as amounting to no more than
   courtship an exercise in courtly manners
769 **As ... time** i.e. as a way of filling in the
   time. *Bombast* was cotton wool used for
   stuffing and *lining* garments, and so became a synonym for words employed as
   mere 'padding'.
770–1 **more devout ... been** i.e. we have
   paid no more serious attention to the
   matter than this
772 **merriment** bit of fun
774 **quote** regard, think (*OED, v.* 6a)
777 **world-without-end** everlasting. Taken
   from *The Book of Common Prayer*, where it

appears as a phrase at the end of Matins,
this evocative compound adjective recurs
at Sonnets 57.5.
779 **dear** grievous, dire (*OED, a.²* 2). Compare Sonnets 37.3: 'I, made lame by
   fortune's dearest spite'. The Princess also
   has in mind, however, the normal sense
   of *dear*, since the King's *guiltiness* has
   made him *dear* to her.
780 **as ... cause** i.e. I can't see that as a good
   reason for your doing anything
783 **forlorn** desolate
   naked unfurnished (*OED, a.* 10b)
785 **signs** signs of the zodiac (each account-
   ing for a month)

If frosts and fasts, hard lodging and thin weeds
Nip not the gaudy blossoms of your love,   790
But that it bear this trial, and last love;
Then, at the expiration of the year,
Come challenge me, challenge me by these deserts,
And, by this virgin palm now kissing thine,
I will be thine; and till that instance shut
My woeful self up in a mourning house,
Raining the tears of lamentation
For the remembrance of my father's death.
If this thou do deny, let our hands part,
Neither entitled in the other's heart.   800

KING

If this, or more than this, I would deny,
    To flatter up these powers of mine with rest,
The sudden hand of death close up mine eye!
    Hence, hermit, then—my heart is in thy breast.
        The King and the Queen converse apart

DUMAINE (*to Katherine*)

But what to me, my love? But what to me?
A wife?

KATHERINE   A beard, fair health, and honesty;
With threefold love I wish you all these three.

DUMAINE

O, shall I say, 'I thank you, gentle wife'?

KATHERINE

Not so, my lord. A twelvemonth and a day
I'll mark no words that smooth-faced wooers say.   810

793 challenge me, challenge me] QF; challenge me, challenge HANMER; challenge, challenge
me MALONE   795 instance] Q; instant F   800 entitled] F (intitled); intiled Q   804
hermit] WILSON (*conj.* Pollard); herrite Q; euer F   then—my heart ∧] F (then, my heart);
then my hart, Q   804.1 *The . . . apart*] *not in* QF.   *At this point* Q, *followed by* F, *prints the lines
given in Appendix A (ii).*   806 A wife?] *continued to Dumaine,* DYCE; *part of Katherine's next
line,* QF

789 **weeds,** clothes
790 **Nip . . . blossoms** proverbial (Dent B702)
791 **last love** endure as love
793 **challenge** lay claim to (*OED, v.* 5)
    deserts deservings, fulfilment of my re-
    quirements
795 **instance** instant (*OED, sb.* 4)
800 **entitled in** having a claim to
802 **flatter up** indulge, pamper (*OED, v.*¹ 10)
804 **my heart is in thy breast** A version of the

common saying 'The lover is not where
he lives but where he loves' (Dent L565).
After this line Q and F print six lines of
dialogue between Biron and Rosaline
which are evidently the first draft of lines
819 to 853. They are to be found in
Appendix A.
810 **smooth-faced** plausibly seductive. Compare *K. John* 2.1.574: 'That smooth-
faced gentleman, tickling commodity'.

Come when the King doth to my lady come;
Then, if I have much love, I'll give you some.

DUMAINE

I'll serve thee true and faithfully till then.

KATHERINE

Yet swear not, lest ye be forsworn again.

    They converse apart

LONGUEVILLE

What says Maria?

MARIA   At the twelvemonth's end
I'll change my black gown for a faithful friend.

LONGUEVILLE

I'll stay with patience; but the time is long.

MARIA

The liker you; few taller are so young.

    They converse apart

BIRON (*to Rosaline*)

Studies my lady? Mistress, look on me,
Behold the window of my heart, mine eye,   820
What humble suit attends thy answer there.
Impose some service on me for thy love.

ROSALINE

Oft have I heard of you, my lord Biron,
Before I saw you; and the world's large tongue
Proclaims you for a man replete with mocks,
Full of comparisons and wounding flouts,
Which you on all estates will execute
That lie within the mercy of your wit.
To weed this wormwood from your fruitful brain,
And therewithal to win me, if you please,   830
Without the which I am not to be won,
You shall this twelvemonth term from day to day

814.1 *They ... apart*] *not in* QF   818.1 *They ... apart*] *not in* QF   822 thy] Q; my F
827 estates] Q (estetes), F   828 wit.] F; wi: Q

816 **change** exchange
   friend lover (*OED, sb.* 4)
817 **stay** wait
819 **Studies my lady?** Is my lady lost in thought?
820 **Behold ... eye** proverbial (Dent E231)
821 **attends** waits for
826 **comparisons** scoffing similes (*OED, sb.*

3b; earliest example of this sense)
826 **flouts** jeers
827 **estates** 'sorts and conditions of men'
   execute inflict. Compare *Richard III* Add.
   Pass. C.3 (1.4.68 + 3): 'execute thy wrath in me alone'.
829 **wormwood** (the emblem of bitterness)

Visit the speechless sick, and still converse
With groaning wretches; and your task shall be
With all the fierce endeavour of your wit
To enforce the painèd impotent to smile.

BIRON

To move wild laughter in the throat of death?
It cannot be, it is impossible.
Mirth cannot move a soul in agony.

ROSALINE

Why, that's the way to choke a gibing spirit,   840
Whose influence is begot of that loose grace
Which shallow laughing hearers give to fools.
A jest's prosperity lies in the ear
Of him that hears it, never in the tongue
Of him that makes it. Then if sickly ears,
Deafed with the clamours of their own dear groans,
Will hear your idle scorns, continue then,
And I will have you and that fault withal.
But if they will not, throw away that spirit,
And I shall find you empty of that fault,   850
Right joyful of your reformation.

BIRON

A twelvemonth? Well, befall what will befall,
I'll jest a twelvemonth in an hospital.

QUEEN (*to the King*)

Ay, sweet my lord, and so I take my leave.

KING

No, madam, we will bring you on your way.

BIRON

Our wooing doth not end like an old play:
Jack hath not Jill. These ladies' courtesy
Might well have made our sport a comedy.

---

833 **still converse** i.e. spend all your time associating

835 **fierce** ardent, strenuous. Compare *Tragedy of Lear* 2.1.33–4: 'Some blood drawn on me would beget opinion | Of my more fierce endeavour.'

836 **the painèd impotent** those who are in pain and incapable of helping themselves

839 **agony** the throes of death (*OED*, 3)

841 **Whose ... grace** i.e. which draws its inspiration from that easy-going indulgence

846 **dear** heartfelt, grievous. See line 779.

852 **befall what will befall** proverbial (Dent C529)

855 **bring** accompany, escort

857 **Jack hath not Jill** (contrary to the proverb Tilley A164). Contrast *Dream* 3.3.45–8: 'Jack shall have Jill, | Naught shall go ill, | the man shall have his mare again, and all shall be well.'

These ladies' courtesy i.e. a kind reception (of our efforts) by these ladies

KING

    Come, sir, it wants a twelvemonth an' a day,

    And then 'twill end.

BIRON   That's too long for a play.   860

    Enter Armado

ARMADO (*to the King*) Sweet majesty, vouchsafe me—

QUEEN Was not that Hector?

DUMAINE The worthy knight of Troy.

ARMADO I will kiss thy royal finger, and take leave. I am a
    votary, I have vowed to Jaquenetta to hold the plough
    for her sweet love three year. But, most esteemed
    greatness, will you hear the dialogue that the two
    learned men have compiled in praise of the owl and the
    cuckoo? It should have followed in the end of our show.

KING Call them forth quickly, we will do so.   870

ARMADO Holla! Approach.

    Enter all ⌈those not yet on stage⌉

    This side is Hiems, Winter; this Ver, the Spring: the
    one maintained by the owl, th'other by the cuckoo.
    Ver, begin.

THE SONG

SPRING (*sings*)

        When daisies pied, and violets blue,

          And lady-smocks all silver-white,

        And cuckoo-buds of yellow hue

          Do paint the meadows with delight,

        The cuckoo then, on every tree,

        Mocks married men, for thus sings he: 880

          'Cuckoo!

---

859 an' a day] Q (an'aday); and a day F   860.1 *Enter Armado*] ROWE; *Enter Braggart.* QF
861 me—] THEOBALD; ~. QF   866 year] Q (yeere); yeares F   871.1 *Enter ... stage*] QF
(*Enter all.*)   872 This] F; *Brag.* This Q   873 th'other] Q; Th'other F; The other ROWE
874 Ver, begin] *as part of Armado's speech*, F; *separated from the previous words by a space, and
preceded by 'B.',* Q   874.1 SPRING *(sings)*] *not in* QF   876, 877] *as here,* THEOBALD;
in reverse order, QF

867 **dialogue** disputation, debate
872 Since no entry is provided for either
    Spring or Winter, these parts may have
    been represented by Sir Nathaniel and
    Holofernes.
873 **maintained** supported, upheld (*OED, v.*
    14). The tentative suggestion that *main-*

tained here means *represented* (*OED, v.* 16)
    seems unnecessary.
876 **lady-smocks** cuckoo flowers
877 **cuckoo-buds** *OED* circumspectly glosses
    cuckoo-bud as 'a name of some plant'.
880 **Mocks married men** (since its cry is so
    reminiscent of *cuckold*, and its habit of

Cuckoo, cuckoo!' O word of fear,
Unpleasing to a married ear.

When shepherds pipe on oaten straws,
    And merry larks are ploughmen's clocks,
When turtles tread, and rooks, and daws,
    And maidens bleach their summer smocks,
The cuckoo then, on every tree,
Mocks married men, for thus sings he:
        'Cuckoo!   890
Cuckoo, cuckoo!' O word of fear,
Unpleasing to a married ear.

WINTER (*sings*)

When icicles hang by the wall,
    And Dick the shepherd blows his nail,
And Tom bears logs into the hall,
    And milk comes frozen home in pail,
When blood is nipped, and ways be foul,
Then nightly sings the staring owl:
'Tu-whit, Tu-whoo!'—
A merry note,   900
While greasy Joan doth keel the pot.

When all aloud the wind doth blow,
    And coughing drowns the parson's saw,
And birds sit brooding in the snow,
    And Marian's nose looks red and raw,
When roasted crabs hiss in the bowl,
Then nightly sings the staring owl:
'Tu-whit, tu-whoo!'—
A merry note,
While greasy Joan doth keel the pot.   910

893 *(sings)] not in* QF   897 foul] F (fowle); full Q

laying its eggs in another bird's nest
resembles the behaviour of a man who
seduces another man's wife or of a married woman who couples with a man
other than her husband)

886 **turtles tread** turtle-doves mate
    daws jackdaws
894 **blows his nail** blows on his finger-nails

(to warm his hands)
901 **keel** 'cool (a hot or boiling liquid) by
    stirring, skimming, or pouring in some-
    thing cold, in order to prevent it from
    boiling over' (*OED, v.*¹ 1b)
902 **all aloud** extremely loudly
903 **saw** sermon, discourse
906 **crabs** crab-apples
    bowl i.e. bowl filled with ale

⌈ARMADO⌉ The words of Mercury are harsh after the
songs of Apollo. You that way. We this way.   *Exeunt*

911 ARMADO] F (*Brag.*); *not in* Q   912 You that way. We this way.] F; *not in* Q   *Exeunt*] F
(*Exeunt omnes.*); *not in* Q

911-12 **The ... Apollo** In Q these words, not
assigned to any character, conclude the
play. 'The words' in question are almost
certainly those of Marcadé, the messenger of death, and therefore the play's
Mercury, while 'the songs of Apollo' are
probably the courtiers' sonnets and Biron's praise of love in 4.3.

912 **You ... this way** Found only in F, where
it is given, as is the previous speech, to
Armado, this line could be addressed to
the audience about to leave the theatre,
or to the Princess and her entourage
about to return to France. In either case it
marks the end of the revels.

TWO 'FALSE STARTS'

(i) After 4.3.292, the following lines appear in Q and F:

And where that you have vowed to study, lords,
In that each of you have forsworn his book,
Can you still dream and pore and thereon look?
For when would you, my lord, or you, or you,
Have found the ground of study's excellence
Without the beauty of a woman's face?
From women's eyes this doctrine I derive:
They are the ground, the books, the academes,
From whence doth spring the true Promethean fire.
Why, universal plodding poisons up   10
The nimble spirits in the arteries,
As motion and long-during action tires
The sinewy vigour of the traveller.
Now, for not looking on a woman's face,
You have in that forsworn the use of eyes,
And study too, the causer of your vow;
For where is any author in the world
Teaches such beauty as a woman's eye?
Learning is but an adjunct to ourself,
And where we are our learning likewise is.   20
Then when ourselves we see in ladies' eyes,
With ourselves,
Do we not likewise see our learning there?

(ii) After 5.2.804, the two substantive texts read:

BIRON
And what to me, my love? And what to me?

10 poisons] QF (poysons); prisons THEOBALD   18 woman's] Q (womas), F

i.1 **where that** whereas (Abbott 134)
 2 **In that** i.e. seeing that
    have has (Abbott 412)
 5 **ground** basis, foundation
 9 **Promethean fire** i.e. divine inspiration.
    Prometheus stole fire from heaven and
    brought it to men. Shakespeare probably
    took the word, as David suggests, from
    George Chapman's *The Shadow of Night*

(1594), where Chapman writes: 'There-
fore Promethean poets with the coals | Of
their most genial, more than human
souls, | In living verse created men like
these' (lines 131–3).
10 **up** totally, absolutely
11 **The ... arteries** It was thought that the
    arteries contained an etherial fluid, called
    'spiritual blood' or 'vital spirits'. Quite

237

ROSALINE

> You must be purgèd till your sins are racked.
> You are attaint with faults and perjury.
> Therefore, if you my favour mean to get,
> A twelvemonth shall you spend and never rest
> But seek the weary beds of people sick.

2 till] This edition (*conj.* Wilson); to Q; too F   racked] Q (rackt), F; rank ROWE

distinct from the blood in the veins, it was regarded as the source of motion and sensation.

ii.2 **till** Q reads 'to,' and F 'too,', a mere difference in spelling. But 'too, your sins are racked' yields no ready sense. The emendation adopted here rests on Wilson's suggestion 'that the compositor printed "to" for "till" (a common type of error) ... The word "attaint" in the next line seems to make the connexion between "rack" and torture certain. Rosaline has "purgatory" in mind.' She is also, it may be added, carrying out her vindictive threat at 5.2.60 to 'torture' Biron. **racked** tormented (as though on the rack)

3 **attaint with** (a) disgraced by (Onions) (b) found guilty of (*OED*, *v.* 3)

ALTERATIONS TO LINEATION

THE principles governing what follows have been set out by Gary Taylor in his edition of *Henry V*. He writes:

> Since this list records only changes of verse to prose, of prose to verse, or of line-arrangement within verse, it differs from the textual collations in a few details of presentation. Both within the lemma and in the quotation of a rejected line-arrangement, punctuation at the end of the line is ignored, and spelling modernized. Attribution of an emendation or variant reading indicates only that the text or editor cited *arranges* the lines in a certain way; sometimes ... not all the words of the text are identical with those printed in this edition. (p. 303)

In what follows the word *line* means 'line of verse'.

1.1.140   What ... forgot] Q; *as two lines divided after* 'lords' F
2.1.37–8   Who ... Duke] ROWE 1714; *as prose* QF
   105–6   And ... bold] F; *as one line* Q
   115–16 How ... question] CAPELL; *as one line* QF
   179–80 Pray ... it] Q; *as two lines divided after* 'commendations' F
   198   She ... shame] Q; *as two lines divided after* 'self' F
   202–5   Good ... lady] F; *as two lines divided after* 'Falconbridge' Q
3.1.30   But ... love] Q; *as separate line* F
   55–6   Thy ... slow] POPE; *as prose* QF
   101–6   Come ... market] Q; *as eight lines divided after* 'hither', 'begin', 'shin', '*l'envoi*', 'plantain', 'in', *and* 'bought' F
   110–11 Thou ... *l'envoi*] Q; *as two lines divided after* 'Moth' F
   130   Like ... adieu] Q; *as two lines divided after* 'I' F
   131   My ... Jew] Q; *as prose* F
   156–7   It ... this] QF; *as one line* CAPELL; *as two lines divided after* 'slave' OXFORD
   167   And ... whip] Q; *as two lines divided after* 'love' F
   168–71 A ... magnificent] POPE; *as two lines divided after* 'constable' Q; *as four lines divided after* 'critic', 'constable', *and* 'boy' F
4.1.53   I ... Rosaline] Q; *as two lines divided after* 'Biron' F
   56   Stand ... carve] Q; *as two lines divided after* 'bearer' F
   93–4   What ... better] Q; *as prose* F
   108–9   Why ... off] CAPELL; *as one line* QF
   114–15 If ... indeed] F3; *as prose* QF
   117   But ... now] Q; *as two lines divided after* 'lower' F

126–7	An ... can] F; *as one line* Q
4.2.22–3	Twice-sod ... look] DYCE; *as prose* QF
25	He ... ink] Q; *as two lines divided after* 'were' F
27–8	And ... he] HANMER; *as prose* QF
33–4	You ... yet] Q; *as prose* F
56–61	The ... more 'L'] CAPELL; *as twelve lines divided after* 'pricked', 'pricket', 'not a sore', 'shooting', 'sore', 'thicket', 'sorel', 'a-hooting', 'to sore', 'sore "L"', *and* 'make' QF
95–6	*Venetia ... pretia*] CAPELL; *as prose* QF
141–2	Good ... life] Q; *as two lines divided after* 'me' F
160–2	Sir ... recreation] POPE; *as two lines divided after* 'verba' QF
4.3.1–2	The ... myself] POPE; *as two lines divided after* 'deer' QF
87–8	As ... child] THEOBALD; *as two lines divided after* 'cedar' QF
181–4	In ... limb] ROWE; *as prose* QF
208–9	True ... gone] ROWE 1714; *as one line* QF
5.2.3–4	A ... King] POPE; *as prose* QF
14	He ... heavy] Q; *as prose* F
15–18	And ... long] F2; *as prose* QF
47	But ... Dumaine] THEOBALD; *as two lines divided after* 'you' QF
160–1	A ... views] THEOBALD; *as prose* QF
175	What ... Boyet] POPE; *as two lines divided after* 'strangers' QF
216–17	The ... it] Q; *as prose* F
234–5	Seventh ... you] ROWE 1714; *as two lines divided after* 'cog' QF
239–40	Say ... lady] F; *as one line* Q
240–1	Please ... adieu] F; *as one line* Q
311–2	Gone ... thither] CAPELL; *as prose* Q; *as two lines divided after* 'tent' F
386	Where ... this] Q; *as two lines divided after* 'visor' F
389	We ... downright] Q; *as two lines divided after* 'descried' F
431–2	Teach ... excuse] Q; *as prose* F
439–40	Peace ... forswear] F; *as prose* Q
450	What ... troth] *as two lines divided after* 'madam' F
481–2	Full ... run] ROWE 1714; *as prose* QF
508	Biron ... approach] Q; *as two lines divided after* 'us' F
509–10	We ... company] Q; *as prose* F
533–4	And ... five] ROWE 1714; *as prose* QF
543	Well ... thee] Q; *as two lines divided after* 'mocker' F
550–1	If ... done] *as one line* QF
560	Your ... right] Q; *as two lines divided after* 'not' F
562	The ... Alexander] Q; *as two lines divided after* 'dismayed' F
611–12	Ay ... countenance] CAPELL; *as two lines divided after* 'tooth-drawer' QF

635–6 The ... gift] *as prose* QF

651–3 The ... man] CAPELL; *as three lines divided after* 'rotten' *and*
'buried', Q; F *omits* 'When ... man' *and divides after* 'rotten'

653–5 But ... hearing] Q; *as two lines divided after* 'device' F

668–9 Dost ... die] POPE; *as two lines divided after* 'potentates' QF

699–700 The ... penance] POPE; *as two lines divided after* 'shirt' QF

705–6 Welcome ... merriment] CAPELL; *as prose* QF

707–8 I ... father] ROWE 1714; *as prose* QF

864–6 I ... year] F; *as three lines divided after* 'leave' *and* 'Jaquenetta' Q

876–7 And ... hue] THEOBALD; *lines in reversed order* QF

911–12 The ... Apollo] Q; *as two lines divided after* 'Mercury' F

A NOTE ON THE MUSIC

By John Caldwell

THE original production of *Love's Labour's Lost* would have included a considerable amount of incidental music. Apart from the usual introductory music while the audience was arriving and getting settled, the two masques in Act 5 both call for it. The first of these is announced with the sound of a trumpet (5.2.156.1); the instrumentalists enter in the guise of blackamoors (5.2.157.2); and their playing of dance-music is stated or implied by the text from 5.2.211. The punning on the word 'measure' begins at 5.2.184; the dance music that begins at 5.2.211 ends at line 221, but possibly begins again; some may well have ensued before the various tête-à-têtes are roughly broken off at line 264.[1]

The Masque of the Worthies does not specifically require music, though the individual masquers could well have been introduced by a trumpet call; but its delayed conclusion, the Dialogue between Spring and Winter, certainly does. The context implies a degree of formality—the actors concerned were probably accomplished musicians—but unfortunately no contemporary setting of the two poems survives. One possibility would be to sing the verses to a popular tune of the day, 'The leaves be green' (known as *Browning*: see Ex. 1). In itself this would be wearisomely repetitive, but the tune was often used as the basis of

Ex. 1

[1] On the 'measure' as a term of dance-music see J. M. Ward, 'The English Measure', *Early Music*, xiv (1986), 15–21. Suitable music for dancing and for incidental purposes may be found in *Elizabethan Consort Music*, ed. Paul Doe, 2 vols. (London: Stainer and Bell, 1979–88, = *Musica Britannica*, xliv–xlv) and in Anthony Holborne's *Pavans, Galliards, Almains*, 1599, ed. B. Thomas (London, 1980; score and five parts).

instrumental compositions, the melody being transferred from one part to another at each variation. Not all settings would be suitable, but there are two quite straightforward Elizabethan five-part versions, by Stoning and Woodcock respectively,[1] either of which could easily be adapted for the purpose. Ideally, each actor would play an instrumental part, singing the tune with its pre-arranged pair of lines whenever appropriate. But if this is impracticable, the actors can simply join in with the tune in turn while the piece is played independently. If the 'Cuckoo' and 'Tu-who' refrains are each extended to make a complete pair of lines the five variations of Stoning's piece and the ten of Woodcock's will be exactly the right length for the performance of one and two stanzas respectively.

Of the other musical references, the song given as 'Concolinel' (3.1.3) cannot be identified; any straightforward lute-song of the period may be used.[2] The musical notes 'Ut re sol la mi fa' (4.2.98), whatever their significance in the context, would presumably have been sung as shown (Ex. 2, at any pitch). The only song for which a contemporary musical setting appears to have existed is 'Thou canst not hit it' (4.1.124–7). A tune labelled simply 'hit' is found in the so-called Ballet Lute-Book, Dublin, Trinity College, MS D.1.21, p. 84.[3] Another version, labelled 'Altra canson englesa', is to be found in Emanuel Adriaenssen's *Pratum musicum* (Antwerp, 1584; second edn. 1600); and this was copied, with Adriaenssen's title, into the 'Dallis' Lute Book (Dublin, Trinity College, MS D.3.30/I) on p. 171. Adriaenssen's version suits the words of the play less well, though its regular structure offers some encouragement to

Ex. 2

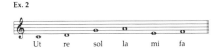

Ut   re   sol   la   mi   fa

---

[1] *Musica Britannica*, xliv, nos. 40, 41. The settings by Baldwin (ibid., xlv, no. 124) and Byrd are unduly complex for the purpose. William Cobbold's consort song *New Fashions* (*Musica Britannica*, xxii, no. 71), though not itself suitable, offers a parallel to the suggested method of performance and to the adaptation of new text to the 'Browning' tune.

[2] Volumes of songs by Dowland, Morley, Campion, and others are included in the series *The English Lute-Songs*, published by Stainer and Bell.

[3] See J. M. Ward in *The Lute Society Journal*, x (1968), 15–32. The Alman 'Hit it and take it', by Robert Johnson, is unconnected and cannot be fitted to Shakespeare's words. A manuscript dated 1620, supposedly given to the Oxford Music School by Dr Fell, Bishop of Oxford (W. Chappell, *Popular Music of the Olden Time* (London, 1855–9, vol. i, p. 239)‡) cannot now be traced. In Wooldridge's revision of Chappell (London and New York, 1893, vol. i, p. 249), the 'Ballet' version is adapted and re-harmonized.

adapt the clearly corrupt Ballet copy to the rhythm of the words. We give
both the Ballet version and an adaptation of the tune for use in the play
(Ex. 3).

Ex. 3
(a)

(b)

Ros. Thou canst not hit it, hit it, hit it, thou canst not hit it my good man.

Boy. An I can - not, can - not, can - not, An I can-not, an - o - ther can.

THE NAME OF ARMADO'S PAGE

It is not easy to be sure what the name of Armado's page should be in a modernized edition. John Kerrigan, in his New Penguin *Love's Labour's Lost* (1982), calls him 'Mote', a procedure which he justifies thus:

> The argument for modernizing the Q and F 'Moth' (which other editors have preserved) to *Mote* goes as follows. As a result of changes in pronunciation, that form of the word 'moth' which derived from Old English *mohðe* developed a hard final 't' and became indistinguishable in Elizabethan and Jacobean English from the word 'mote', derived from Old English *mot*. This led to the spellings 'moth' and 'mote' where we should have 'mote' and 'moth'. Setting aside references to Armado's page and Titania's fairy (with whom similar difficulties arise), of the sixteen appearances of 'mo(a)th(e)(s)' in the Quartos and F, five mean 'insect(s)' and eleven (including four at IV.3.159 of Q and F *Love's Labour's Lost*) 'particle(s)'. 'Moats' occurs once, in the Shakespearian part of *Pericles* (1609 Q). In view of the ambiguity of 'moth' in these texts (including several set from Shakespeare's manuscripts and therefore likely to reflect his own spelling), the modernizing editor must decide which sense is dominant in the case of Armado's page. Since there are no references to his being insect-like but several to his being tiny ... and like a word (V.1.39–40)—a joke which relies on a pun with the French word for 'word', *mot*, which had a sounded final 't' in the sixteenth century—the primary sense is undoubtedly 'particle'. So, despite the spelling of Q and F, *Mote* must be the page's name in a modern-spelling text. (pp. 160–1)

This notion is strongly endorsed by Stanley Wells (*Re-Editing*, pp. 23–4), and adopted by him and Gary Taylor in their edition of *The Complete Works*, where the name of the page is *Mote*. Yet there are several objections to it. In the first place it is not true to say, as Kerrigan does, that 'there are no references to his being insect-like'. There is one such reference, and it is a significant one. At 4.1.147 Costard, who is much taken with the boy, his polar opposite in so many respects, describes him admiringly as a 'most pathetical nit'; and a 'nit', says *OED*, is 'an insect parasitic on man or animals ... in a young state.' It then goes on to list two obsolete uses of the word, 'gnat, or small fly' (1b), and its figurative application 'to persons in contempt or jest' (2). Its first two examples of this last meaning are both from Shakespeare: the eulogistic phrase under discussion and Petruchio's railing assault on the Tailor, whom he addresses as 'Thou flea, thou nit, thou winter-cricket, thou' (*The Taming of the Shrew*, 4.3.109). As for 'pathetical', it obviously means 'appealing', as it does again at 1.2.93, where Armado uses it in his praise of the page's 'invocation'—'My father's wit and my mother's tongue assist me!' In fact, Shakespeare employs the adjective on one other occasion only, when Rosalind tells Orlando 'if you break one jot of your promise ... I will think you the most pathetical break-promise ... that may be chosen out of the gross band of the unfaithful' (*As You Like It* 4.1.180–5). There the meaning is, of course, different, though Rosalind's mockingly ambiguous idiom leaves room for just a touch of the sense the word has when applied to Armado's page and to that page's felicity of phrasing.

A 'most pathetical nit' sums up the essence of the boy. Praised and admired by Costard, praised and loved by Armado to whom he is 'dear', he is attractive, as many an insect can be. But he also has an insect-like capacity for making a nuisance of himself by pricking and deflating the pretentious, especially in his exchanges with the pompous schoolmaster Holofernes. Moreover, it is not true to say with Kerrigan that because there are several references 'to his being tiny ... the primary sense [of his name] is undoubtedly "particle"'. What the play insists on most is not his diminutive stature but his youth. And youth is a quality of living, growing things not of inanimate objects such as specks of dust in a sunbeam. *Moth*, therefore, seems a far more appropriate name for this very lively boy than does *Mote*.

INDEX

THIS is a guide to points made and names mentioned in the Introduction and Commentary. Citations from other texts are not listed. An asterisk signifies that the note supplements information given in *OED*. A = Appendix A.

247